WHAT THE CIVILIAN MANAGER ISN'T TAUGHT

What the Civilian Manager isn't Taught

From the Battlefield to the Boardroom and Back again

by Colin Lyle

"Management is constant in concept, whether one is running a business, a hospital or an aircraft carrier. Only the terminology differs".
A H Cartmell

"Wars, conflict, it's all business. . ."
Charles Chaplin

The Book Guild Ltd

Sussex, England.

WHAT THE CIVILIAN MANAGER ISN'T TAUGHT

by

Colin Lyle

© Copyright: Colin Lyle, 1987

The Book Guild Ltd.
25 High Street,
Lewes, Sussex

First published 1989

Typeset by Triste Ltd. Croydon
Printed in Great Britain by
Antony Rowe Ltd.
Chippenham, Wiltshire

ISBN 0 86332 380 4

CONTENTS

"My argument is that War makes rattling good history, but Peace is poor reading."

— Thomas Hardy

"When the Duke of Wellington learnt that his great flank attack at Toulouse had completely broken down he merely shrugged his shoulders and remarked: 'Well, I suppose I must try something else', which he did, with complete success."

— Colonel A H Burne

AN INTRODUCTION: MANAGERIAL INSPIRATION

Military History as a Source of Managerial Example — Book Aims and Methods.

SECTION A: GENERAL CASE HISTORIES

"How can you remember which paintings are yours?"
"If I like it, I say it's mine. If I don't I say it's a fake."

— Pablo Picasso, quoted by the
Sunday Times

Page

ACKNOWLEDGEMENTS

The author and publisher wish to express their thanks to the following publishers and authors for their kind permission to reproduce extracts from their copyright material:

A D Peters & Co. Ltd. *Hornblower and the Hotspur* by C S Forester [published by Michael Joseph Ltd., 1962], *The Western Front* by John Terraine, and *War in the Air* edited by Gavin Lyall; Blandford Press Ltd. *The Russian Front* edited by James F Dunnigan; Allen & Unwin *Wellington's Masterpiece* by Col. J P Lawford and Brig. Peter Young; Batsford Ltd. *The Making of the Roman Army* by Dr L Keppie, *Marlborough as Military Commander* by David Chandler, and *Trafalgar* by Oliver Warner; Buchan & Enright *A Drop Too Many* by Maj-Gen J D Frost; Cassell Ltd. [publishers] and David Higham Associates *History of the Second World War* (1970) by Sir Basil Liddell Hart; *A History of the English Speaking Peoples* (1956) by Sir Winston Churchill; Col. Albert Seaton *The Battle for Moscow* by Col. A Seaton [published by Rupert Hart-Davis, 1971]; Col. Albert Seaton and Batsford Ltd. *The Fall of Fortress Europe* by Col. A Seaton [published by B T Batsford Ltd., 1981]; David Higham Associates Ltd. *Britain and her Army* by Corelli Barnett [published by Penguin Books Ltd., 1974]; David Higham Associates Ltd. and MacMillan Publishing Co. *The Other Side of the Hill* by Sir Basil Liddell Hart [published by Cedric Chivers Ltd., 1970; originally published by Cassell Ltd.] Eyre & Spottiswoode *The Decisive Battles of the Western World* and *The Generalship of Alexander the Great* by Maj-Gen J F C Fuller; *The Financial Times Ltd.* for the article on Dr Schein in the Financial Times [4 October 1985], by Michael Dixon; Faber and Faber Ltd. *The Strategy of Indirect Approach* by Sir Basil Liddell Hart; Goodall Publications Ltd. *Lancaster to Berlin* by Walter R Thompson; Hamlyn Publishing Group Ltd. *Great Contemporaries* by Sir Winston Churchill [published by Collins, 1937]; Harvard University Press *Command in War* by Dr Martin van Creveld; Hodder & Stoughton Ltd. and David Higham

Associates Ltd. *Operation Victory* by Maj-Gen Sir Francis de Guingand; Ian Allan Ltd. *The Battle of the Phillipine Sea* by W D Dickson; J M Dent & Sons Ltd. *The History of Rome* by T Mommsen (Everyman edition); Little, Brown & Co. *Grant takes Command* by Bruce Catton [published by J M Dent & Sons Ltd., 1970]; Macdonald *Morale in War and Work* by Dr T T Paterson; Jane's Publishers Co. and Col. T N Dupuy *A Genius for War* by Col. T N Dupuy; Methuen & Co. *The Art of War on Land* by Col. A H Burne; Muller, Blond & White Ltd. *Imperial Defence* by Maj-Gen H Rowan-Robinson; Oxford University Press *Fisher of Kilverstone* (1974) by R F Mackay, and *A History of the Great War* (1936) by C R M F Cruttwell; Curtis Brown and Penguin Books Ltd. *The Nature of Alexander* by Mary Renault (London, 1983); Prentice-Hall Inc. *Triumph in the Pacific* edited by E B Potter and Admiral C W Nimitz (copyright 1963); Sir Alistair Frame, speech to the Engineering Project Management Forum, November 1985; Tate & Lyle PLC for the photograph on the rear of the dust jacket from *The Plaistow Story* by Sir Oliver Lyle; Thames and Hudson Ltd. *Hannibal* by Sir Gavin de Beer; The Rainbird Publishing Group Ltd. *A History of Warfare* by Field-Marshal Viscount Montgomery; Thorsons Publishing Group Ltd. *Hannibal's Campaigns* by Tony Bath; Times Books Ltd. *The Times Atlas of World History* edited by Prof. Geoffrey Barraclough; Victor Gollancz Ltd. [publisher] and Doubleday & Co. Inc. *The Centennial History of the Civil War* (a trilogy comprising *The Coming Fury*, *Terrible Swift Sword* and *Never Call Retreat)* by Bruce Catton; Weidenfeld (Publishers) Ltd. [publisher] and Curtis Brown *Wellington* by Elizabeth Longford; William Heinemann Ltd. [publisher] and Harper & Row *Management* by Peter F Drucker (copyright 1973, 1974 by Peter F Drucker. Reprinted by permission of William Heinemann Ltd.); The Hamlyn Publishing Group Ltd. *History of the World* edited by W N Weech.

FOREWORD

by

William E Engbretson, Ph.D.
Chancellor, California University for
Advanced Studies

Colin Lyle's work is a striking example of what one might entitle, "Management Left Out Of The Textbooks". A directory or bibliography of the works published purporting to teach the essentials of management would rival a respectable dictionary in size and complexity. These works are useful; serving as texts in universities, as "bibles" in corporate organizations, and as planning guides in governments, they find their place and purpose.

Too often, these texts, one by one, are replaced by others, thought to be new in ideals and approach to the magic key that somehow or another will solve the "ills" that beset the managers at all levels of control.

Mr Lyle approaches the problems of management from outside management. The intent in his work is not to serve the corporate structure, or to fulfil the requirements of a university in need of a "new" textbook; but to examine or re-examine the basic identity of management and perhaps proceed from there to integrate the lessons learned long before the first modern-day corporate president put pen to paper.

Textbooks sum up management abstractions in planning, organizing, and controlling. Many books on management examine the minutiae of abstract organisation and control, attempting to define the nuts and bolts of a management machine. Broadly, like a bikini, they too often reveal only the interesting and conceal the vital. Consulting managers like mechanical systems that can be graded by check lists and testing schemes. All too often, the management schemes produce reams of neat data listed in rows upon sheet after sheet and prove little toward the efficiency of the systems.

His comments on controls point out that for the most part they are unproductive, costly, and restrictive. Management's controls signal distrust — an audit is to search out cheating and deceitful behaviour. Management skills are deemed transferable. But, how can the newly imported senior, just appointed to run a complex operation, compete?

Top management's horizons are surprisingly limited. This quarter's profit, next year's budget, a five-year-plan, seems to be the limit of today's management in top level corporations as well as in most governments. Today's top level companies differ greatly from those of the past decade, the sustenance of performance being more difficult than the initial creation. The textbooks have little comfort here, despite history's warnings. At the battle of Waterloo, the three chief actors — Blücher, Napoleon, Wellington, all world famous, all near the peak of their powers — *all* muffed their lines. People do not operate consistently.

Like good generals, managers in their role must think of how to win tomorrow's battles. Recruitment policy, leadership type, management development, a sense of purpose, the Board of Director's balance of power — these are not just today's concerns but tomorrow's critical areas.

Mr. Lyle's thrust is, "Conquer these and you can dictate to posterity".

As too few companies manage well, the conclusion is it must not be easy. The selection, training, development and promotion of personnel presupposes intuitive assessment and imagination nicely combined with inferential judgement and calculated foresight. It may not be scholar's work, but it fails without abstract thought and a great deal of study.

Management in commerce as a recognized code or subject has been around for something over a century as a codified, recognized profession. The military men have been at it a bit longer. From the time of Alexander the Great (c. 356 BC) and even before, we have good accounts of Caesar's and Hannibal's efforts. What then causes the civilian in commerce and in government to turn away from the lessons learned in over 2,000 years' of experience?

Mr Lyle's work in this volume brings to the management world, be it faculty, corporate management, or government, a thought-provoking study useful to the student or the master.

William E Engbretson, Ph.D.
Novato, California
14 November, 1986

AUTHOR'S PREFACE

In this book I write military history — mostly, but think about Management — mostly. Nothing of the former is original; the references at the end of each chapter show some of the sources. The latter is based on thirty-eight years' experience as a manager. Some impartial comments on the outcome have been kindly provided by Dr. William Engbretson in his Foreword; for these I am indebted to him as I am to his University for its encouragement and help in my academic work for it. I am equally grateful to the family business, Tate & Lyle, for the opportunity it gave me over many years to see so much Management in action in such diverse circumstances — varied as to industry and country and seniority and style.

I must acknowledge help from numerous people, most prominently from Austin Cartmell, who has read, criticised and made profitable suggestions to improve the whole manuscript; his experience, unusually combining military and civilian management, fills gaps in my own. I wish also to thank my brother, Robin Lyle, for his forthright advice and exhilarating example, and my daughter, Catherine Wardlow, for her professional work on the diagrams in Chapters III and X. I have had advice from my son and daughter-in-law, Andrew and Hilary Lyle (completing the book's being a family affair) and also from Charles Runge, Ian Debenham, Paul Phelps and Ronald Richards. Finally, I owe a debt to Dr. Forrest L Edwards, of the faculty of the California University for Advanced Studies, for his contribution — which he will recognise in its place.

In conclusion, my love to 'Maggs' for her enduring wifely support.

Colin Lyle
Limpsfield Chart
November, 1986

AN INTRODUCTION

MANAGERIAL INSPIRATION

"Every schoolboy knows who imprisoned Montezuma and who strangled Atahualpa."

— Lord Macaulay

Perhaps we forget the history we learned or perhaps we never learned much anyway. I read that Alfred, King of Wessex, burned his cakes but I preferred to discover (years later) that some of his great battles occurred near my home. I was taught that Admiral Nelson destroyed the French fleet at Trafalgar but nothing of the sophisticated strategy that positioned him there. Lord Olivier's admirable film, Henry V, showed a version of the battle of Agincourt; actually the English archers were probably trouserless as they all had dysentery and they chose to take two hours off in the middle of the fray to plunder the dead knights piled up in front of them.

Military History as a Source of Managerial Example
Businessmen have been studying management for about a century but two institutions have been practising it since history began — government and the military. The speedy organisation and the dramatic success of the British Task Force in the far distant Falkland Islands showed many people that the services know a thing or two about organisation and management as well as about fighting. They thus obtained an insight into a military operation's support, as well as feeling the alarming situation of the combatants and observing the technology of their business.

25

The first military action of which history has a reliable account is the battle of Kadesh (near modern Beirut) in 1288 BC, in which Ramses II, Pharoah of Egypt, defeated the Hittites, a powerful people from Asia Minor. We thus have thirty-two centuries of experience from which to learn how to organise and lead people, make plans, delegate authority, manage our work-load, and invent and apply new tactics and equipment. These activities are shared by military men with managers in industry, commerce, service institutions and government. This book looks at some soldiers' experience, but through the eyes of a manager, and one who is as interested in military dramas and its characters as in their methods for achieving success.

My thesis is that Alexander the Great would have made an excellent chairman of British Leyland — or of General Motors. Of course he would have had to learn about cars and their markets, about production methods and — lucky man — about government regulations and about the media, but no one could have taught him much about planning and decision-making or anything at all about leadership. Other great captains could have been as usefully transplanted. (Which company would benefit most from Genghis Khan's management style?) They knew a lot about management and some of the most successful ones studied their predecessors' campaigns as a natural part of their professional education. Maybe we should too.

Management, people, technology, are the strands that weave military history but its context differs from its civilian counterpart. The stakes are very high and concern life and death issues; individuals' influence can often be great and they usually work in the glare of wide publicity and high emotion. Costs may not matter at all, but resources may still be short; many a general has lacked both cannon and cannon fodder. Most seriously, soldiers have to fight with unproved equipment using conscripted labour and untried tactics at a moment's notice.

Suppose industry were in the services' situation. Suppose a sweet manufacturer, the Flavoured Flannel Company, with 100,000 employees paid by a changing short-sighted and reluctant state, spent its time *not* making sweets but preparing to do so sometime, no one knows when, and in competition with no one knows whom. It practices imitation sweet-making; it develops new machinery but can only test it artificially. Once a year it conducts 'manoeuvres' and goes through the motions of making dummy sweets; umpires rule on their tasting of fruit or flannel and on whether they can be sold. Some real sweets are bought in "for realism", making some people sick. Every twenty or thirty years a national emergency is declared and sweet-making is to be the country's salvation. A million randomly selected half-hearted 'civilians', who are patriotic in moderation and totally ignorant about sweets, are conscripted and required, guided by FF's own staff, to make real sweets — all experimental and of unpredictable appeal — in unprecedented quantities. No wonder the services have to study training. And other things. How much can civilians learn from them?

In May 1940 the German army attacked France. In twenty-five days the British troops there had been swept out to sea at Dunkirk and ten days later Paris fell. For this *blitzkrieg* much of the technique had been developed by British theorists between the wars. Germany adopted it, polished it and used it — for Britain's defeat. The Japanese imported western technology, adopted it, polished it and invaded western markets . . . a neat 'me-too' strategy.

The Japanese humbled the USA in 1941 at Pearl Harbour. They also missed all the American aircraft carriers, which they themselves had deemed the important targets, and effectively bounced the US into the war, thus ensuring their own destruction. Sir Freddie Laker's attack on the high volume segment of the airline market sank his company; commanding your special market niche is of the essence but you fight outside your class at your peril.

The Allies dropped their élite airborne forces at Arnhem in 1944 in a bid to end the war. They dropped them almost on top of the 2nd Panzer Corps, ". . . whose presence north of Arnhem . . . was known to HQ's Army Group, Army and Airborne Corps".[1] To compound the error: "Failure by both the Army and the Air Force to make full use of the Dutch underground meant that a most effective means of producing and confirming information was discarded".[1] So can industry neglect its market research and believe only what it wants to believe. We all break the most basic rules.

One can draw innumerable analogies of this sort. More illuminating are complete battles or campaigns where one perceives a leader in action and his entire situation, where one can get inside the skin of the general and live with his problems and decisions. He usually has his difficulties. We manage our companies through a recession, he through government retrenchment, perhaps exacerbated by political manoeuvres. He survives that, then war comes. All engines are reversed : bad becomes good — except that the enemy now has more weapons. Improvisation, tactics and courage are expected to compensate. One week he trains to defeat a Russian invasion, the next he has to send a task force at two weeks' notice — prepared, equipped, loaded, competent — 8000 miles to the South Atlantic. Could we in industry do as well? Of course, there are contrasts between our methods, as Churchill felicitously describes :

> "Much is gained in Peace by ignoring or putting off disagreeable or awkward questions ... There is no place for compromise in War. In War the clouds never blow over, they gather unceasingly and fall in thunderbolts. Things do not get better by being left alone ... The State cannot afford division or hesitation at the executive centre. To humour a distinguished man, to avoid a fierce dispute ... cannot, except as an alternative to sheer anarchy, be held to justify half-measures. The peace of the Council may for the moment be won, but the price is paid on the battlefield by brave men ... in the belief that conviction and coherence have animated their orders."[2]

Book Aims and Methods

The historical examples have been chosen here *primarily to entertain while being thought-provoking*, with each chapter self-contained, but the common threads binding them are an emphasis on people and an interest in the 'how' as well as the 'what' — in short, notable soldiering by notable people and means, and requiring (but not always getting) clever management. They all offer us lessons or guides and in some variety; some are left implicit when readers can recognise analogies and applications for themselves, others are commented on but briefly. In some cases, we shall be tempted to reverse roles : could we have bettered Hitler's performance in Russia? How would we have fought the Philippine Sea battle? Should Hooker have defeated Lee at Chancellorsville? Managers and soldiers have much in common!

I grew up believing soldiers are stupid. They were described in World War I as "lions led by donkeys". My father, a wartime one, used gleefully to remind military friends that "Intelligence" in the Encylopaedia Britannica was discussed under three headings: "Human", "Animal" and "Military". After reading about Scipio at Ilipa *(Chapter II)* or Marlborough at Arleux *(Chapter III)*, readers can judge for themselves. For this they do not need a prior reading of world history but it is easily forgotten that — while Britain was sleeping under Roman occupation, before being invaded by the Saxons around 400 AD, who in turn were harried by the Vikings in 800 to 950 and followed by the Normans in 1066 — the Mediterranean and the Middle East were passing through vastly longer histories. Some we shall see in a little detail but *Appendix A*, in the simplest of sketches, hints at their scope. After all, by 1066 their history was already two-thirds written.

In this book are many maps, to assist orientation and comprehension; these have been simplified to favour clarity over precision where this seemed helpful. Some contemporaneous events anywhere in the world are noted at the end of some chapters, to identify interesting or merely entertaining simultaneities. For example, it intrigues me to realise that Ivan the Terrible and Queen Elizabeth I were contemporaries; indeed, he proposed marriage to her! A sense of chronology imparts structure to the human story.

Certain elaborations of a specialised or technical nature are cast into (short) appendices, to be skipped by those uninterested. Not much history outside the military field is covered and then only when very relevant. Some technical information, for example on weapons, is provided to put more flesh on the narrative bones; readers may wish to visualise actual soldiering, to which this summary — offered in a piece of graffiti — does not perhaps do full justice:

> "Join the army, meet interesting people,
> And kill them."[3]

If the reader distils but two or three ideas to apply in his or her own work or business, this book will have fulfilled its purpose and the defence for its particular context lies in Carlyle's reassurance: "In a certain sense all men are historians"![4]

*　　　*　　　*　　　*

References

[1] Major-General J D Frost, A Drop too Many.

[2] Sir Winston Churchill, The World Crisis.

[3] Nigel Rees, Graffiti Lives OK.

[4] Thomas Carlyle, Essays. On History.

SECTION A:

GENERAL CASE HISTORIES

"This case bristles with simplicity."
— Mr Justice Comyn

"The development of management and managers has become a necessity because the modern business enterprise has become a basic institution of our society. In any major institution — the Church, for instance, or the Army — finding, developing and proving out the leaders of tomorrow is an essential job to which the best men give fully of their time and attention."

— P F Drucker

CHAPTER I

MILITARY WEAPONS, PRINCIPLES AND MANAGEMENT

"Military History is about people, about how they react to the stresses and strains of war . . . Dr Johnson once said: 'Every man thinks meanly of himself for not having been a soldier, or not having been at sea'. To which Boswell replied: 'Lord Mansfield does not.' Johnson: 'Sir, if Lord Mansfield were in a company of admirals and generals who'd seen service he'd wish to creep under the table!'"

— Brigadier Peter Young

The Art of Warfare

War is an extension of politics, the use of force to acquire or keep resources or power. It aims, or should aim, to win these economically, not to make war for its own sake; the purpose is a better peace, not just being victorious. (A company's equivalent is making a profit, which it uses to survive, not to make for its own sake.) Grand strategy is the overall direction of the war effort; strategy is the contrivance of battle on advantageous terms while tactics is its local conduct. The means is military force — ground, sea, air: that is, people and weapons organised, armed and skilfully led. (In commerce the Board of Directors determines, or should determine, strategy and it appoints 'generals'; the resources are people and equipment organised, equipped and skilfully led.)

Throughout history the basic elements of warfare have been constant — mobility, firepower, security. In the distant past mobility was enhanced by the chariot and by cavalry; both were mobile firing platforms and shock weapons. The horse was widely used, chariots only by states with skills and resources. A manoeuvrable and stable chariot was not easily made; it required an axle set to the rear, light spoked wheels and a light body. Its crew was a driver, a spearman or archer and sometimes a shield bearer. Horsemen had to wait for the invention of the stirrup before they

could wield a bow or sword to full effect and Europe only had
this in AD times.

Personal weapons were either close-quarter or missile ones;
the former were sword, spear, mace and axe, and the latter sling,
bow and javelin. The sling threw a stone of 1 to 2 ounces up to
350 yards; it could inflict a very nasty wound but needed much
skill and practice — a limitation it shared with the Welsh long-bow.
The simple bow was used in pre-historic times. Much later some
genius invented the compound bow made of ". . . two or more
strips of wood partially over-lapping, glued together or bound
with tendons and cord".[1] Supreme was the composite bow,
made of several woods, animal horn and tendons and sinews,
and glue. It had an effective range of 300 to 400 yards and an
absolute one of twice that. Being only 3 feet long, it very well
suited the mounted archer and its fearsome penetrating power
hastened the development of body armour. It can be recognised
in ancient friezes by its double curvature when in repose. All
missiles kill at a distance and thus they introduced an increasing
impersonality into fighting. (Modern communications do the
same to management; hence the saying, 'the managing director
is the Board member who knows where the factory is'.)

Security involves armour, shields and fortifications. A few
practical points may interest. There is a trade-off between protection and mobility; a high shield hampers movement but helps
morale. The ancients fortified with skill, sometimes on a huge
scale. For example, the outer walls of ancient Babylon were
ten miles in circumference and fifty feet high. The approach
ramp to a fort's main gate — always a weak point in the defence
— was from the left (looking out), to expose the attackers' un-
shielded sides.

The deployment of armies in the field, which looks so rigid
and amateurish in films, had very practical limitations. On the
march, probably on a narrow track, an army's 'order of march'
might be a vanguard, the main body with the supply train, and
a rear guard, all extending over several miles. To fight it had
to deploy into 'order of battle' and even the most skilful could
take several hours to accomplish this. Each infantry unit had
to be arranged many ranks deep and in close order as its effectiveness depended on its integration. Light and heavy infantry, missile
troops, skirmishers, would complement each other if suitably
positioned. Masses of horsemen, impetuous and wild, were placed

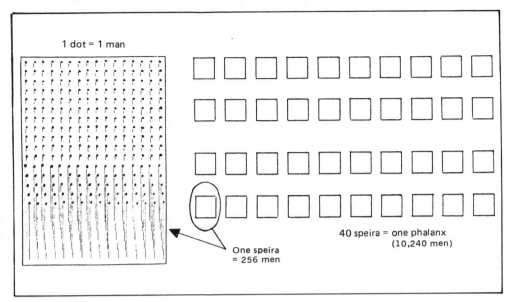

Fig.I. 1 The Macedonian Phalanx

Fig.I. 2 A Roman Legion in Battle Formation

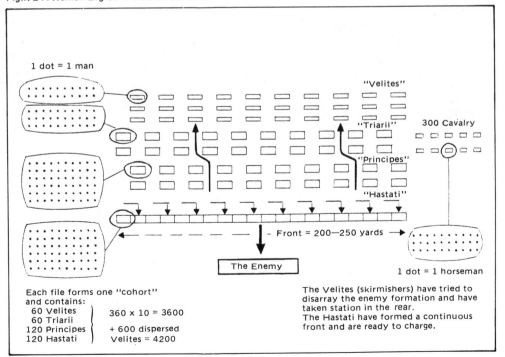

on the flanks where they could move freely. The baggage camp
with its guards was sited in the rear. The general had to arrange
all this, having scouted the enemy's position, divined his intentions, made a plan, and perhaps beaten off a harassing attack.
The generals of old took trouble over these procedures; they were
not all stupid though mostly they practised the thinking of the
times. Every now and then a genius among them re-wrote the
rules.

Tactics followed the principle of concentration, to mass superior
force at the decisive point. This has a mathematical basis. [2] If two
armies of equal strength confront each other exactly man to man,
the average outcome will be $1 : 1$, or a 50% chance of either
winning. But if you can first concentrate all your army against
half the enemy's, then you have a $2 : 1$ arrangement and in unit
time one of your force receives half a hit while one enemy receives
2 hits, a ratio of $2 : 0.5$ or $4 : 1$; so the advantage varies as the
square of the relative strengths. Having thus wiped out half the
foe you can repeat the process on the other half — if it has not
run away. Of course, in practice there are other factors — surprise,
weapons, movement, morale — and the good general uses all of
these.

Military Formations

A dominant Greek state was Macedon *(see Chapter XII);* its basic
infantry formation was the phalanx and a description may assist
visualising an ancient battlefield. Lined up on it were the lines
of battle, say 2 to 3 miles long but only a few hundred yards
deep, made up of many formations, including the heavy infantry
of Macedon in phalanx*. There would be skirmishers in front,
slingers and spearmen alongside the phalanx, cavalry on the wings.
The phalanx was a dense grouping of armoured spearmen, equipped with a round shield and an 18 foot spear. This extraordinary
weapon is not unique; the Swiss medieval infantry, in their time
the terror of Europe, had a similar one. The basic unit *(Fig. I . 1)*
was the *speira* [3], 16 rows of 16 columns of men; the front 5 rows
couched their spears forward to present a sharp array to the foe
while the rows behind carried them erect to help ward off missiles.
In close order a trained phalanx could propel a daunting and
immensely powerful thrust so it is little wonder that, if its
cohesion were preserved, it was virtually irresistible but rough
ground or casualties could spoil that bristling facade and an agile

*The splendid drawings in books by Peter Connolly, e.g. "Greece and Rome
at War", give one a firm idea of what it all looked like.*

enemy exploit the resulting gap. The more flexible Roman legion (originally a Samnite invention which Rome adopted when it conquered that Latin tribe) did just that.

The early legion contained 4200 infantry and 300 horsemen; the Romans were never great horsemen and used allies. *Figure 1.2* shows a legion in battle formation. The front was first covered by agile skirmishers, the 'velites', which after initial sparring would retire through open files to the rear. There were three main lines, in order of age with the youngest men at the front; the first two were armed with two throwing spears and a short sword (invented in Spain), the third with spears. All were partly armoured and carried large rectangular shields. Having let the 'velites' pass the young men would form a continuous front, advance, throw their spears and charge. Each man needed about six feet to swing his sword freely, whose slashing action opened hideous wounds. With the enemy softened up by the barrage of spears, each legionary's weight pushing on his big shield, a close-quarter fight ensued. If this were not won, the second line would replace the first, both moving so as always to present a solid front. The third line, the veterans, was the last resort; they were seldom needed. The cohesive line of aggressive armoured swordsmen, the disciplined movements, the flexible organisation — all controlled by tough professional warrant officers, the 'centurions' — made a superb military instrument which usually more than offset the often indifferent Roman generalship.

The supremacy of the legion lasted until the 4th century AD when Asiatic tribesmen, increasingly well mounted and armoured, introduced the west to heavy cavalry. At Adrianople (in modern Bulgaria) a Roman army was annihilated in AD 378. For a thousand years the mailed horsemen ruled the battlefield until archers at Crécy in 1346 informed Europe that his reign was over. Their long-bow had been a Welsh weapon, over six feet long and requiring a 100 lb. pull to draw. Its accurate range was 250 yards but it could only be used by a tall and strong man and after constant practice, which was compulsory in England. Inevitably its popularity declined.

Increasing firepower, first muskets and cannon and later the magazine rifle and heavy artillery, swept cavalry off the field and made infantry attacks hideously costly. New tactics and weapons have in turn created a fresh balance of forces. To accommodate these and the specialised services and arms, organisation has become more sophisticated. The basic army component in World War II — and this book's examples go no later — was the division, the smallest self-contained unit with all the staff functions and a balanced array of weapons. Here is the structure of a 1939 German infantry division, the sort much used in Russia:

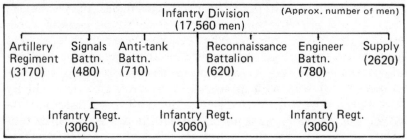

It will be seen that little more than half the strength is in the 'line' regiments.[4] Specialist units can be readily included in the structure, to be deployed by its commander (in the British Army a Major-General) to support the regiments.

Armoured divisions sound powerful affairs, composed, one imagines, wholly of tanks — say a thousand of them. Here is a 1944 German Panzer division:[4]

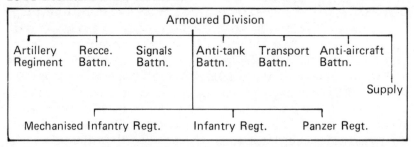

The tank regiment had 170 tanks when at full strength, which it rarely was. The mix of forces in the division provided complementary strengths. Above the division is the corps, typically with three or more divisions according to need. The corps also has staff and HQ functions. The British Army could concentrate all 'corps artillery' on one or more targets with ease and in a matter of minutes. Armies have now superimposed on this structure the battlegroup system, the unit for this being the German 'Kampfgruppe', the US 'Regimental Combat Team' or the British 'Brigade Group', each a regiment in size, for specific tasks. The result is great flexibility with clarity of command.

The Principles of War

Why principles? Generals have often been good learners, reading about their predecessors' methods, thinking hard, training hard, exercising in war games. Napoleon at his zenith was not above reading text-books, for example, one by a young Swiss who had been a Paris bank clerk, the 26-year-old Jomini. Said the great man: "Why here is a young major . . . who teaches you what my professors never taught me, and what very few generals understand!" He felt fortunate: "The old generals who command against me will never read [the book], and young men who will read it do not command."[5] When much is at stake — survival, power, wealth — there is a motive to learn. Another one is to keep pace with an accelerated promotion: Wolfe captured Quebec at 32; Gustavus Adolphus, King of Sweden, reorganised his army and led it to war at 36; Alexander the Great was dead at 33. To improve their performance soldiers have codified methods and guides, to distil the essence of military wisdom accumulated over generations, and adduce practical precepts. Hence the 'principles of war', which are —

> ". . . modes of action which have normally proved successful. They are in no sense rules . . . A close study of history will assist the embryo commander in judging the rare occasions on which they may be ignored with impunity."[6]

No one list is agreed by all (Appendix B gives one alternative). This is a widely accepted one:

1. Maintenance of the objective.
2. Offensive action.
3. Surprise.
4. Concentration.
5. Economy of force.
6. Security.
7. Mobility.
8. Co-operation.

Each is explained briefly here; several would appear to guide civilian life too.

Hitler's disastrous war with Russia was the outcome of confused and variable aims. As it is easy to confuse means and ends, deciding one's ultimate objective may be hard (but necessary) work. Having found it, the *Maintenance of the Objective* says one needs a good reason not to pursue it consistently.

The principle of *Offensive Action* reminds one that defence wins no wars though an active one leading on to a counter-attack can be very effective, as Wellington *(Chapter V)* will show us. However, defending relinquishes the initiative so the enemy can surprise one. The defender also finds it difficult to apply the other principles; he is both constrained and losing morale. Acting rather than reacting is often preached; here one is reminded always to practise it.

The Great Captains have invariably sought *Surprise.* They choose the difficult route like Hannibal, or practise deception like Marlborough, or novelty like Wellington. Military discipline and such originality need not be antipathetic. Consider the sergeant shouting to the French recruit: "If I march you march. If I run you run. If I fall wounded what do you do?" The recruit mumbles something about helping . . . "No, you run right over me and keep going!"[7] Surprise capitalises on the initiative and reinforces it, but usually managers in industry are not schooled constantly to seek it. (A short memorable list of guides helps keep better ways in the mind. There are writings on management rules running to hundreds of pages; most of us need readier reminding of the basic virtues).

All our examples will show generals following the *Concentration* principle to apply leverage at the decisive point. Dividing one's resources is often beguiling and usually regrettable though great men, like Robert E Lee, *(see Chapter VI)* could get away with it. Deciding on what to concentrate limited amounts of time or energy confronts us in work or play. What is critical? Get that right and the rest can follow.

In military terms *Economy of Force* implies " . . . the most advantageous distribution of one's forces. It does *not* imply a mere calculation of the minimum number of men required to win the battle, in order that the remainder of the army can rest behind the line. Its aim is . . . to ensure that every man shall play his full part in the struggle".[8] There seem to be three messages here. First is to seek the optimal distribution of resources; in turn leading to a balanced distribution — say between short and long term; finally one should constantly pursue economy and improve results.

What results and how achieve them? The purpose of business is meeting customer needs, for which profit is vital but not an end in itself: it measures success without itself constituting it, just as a thermometer measures temperature but is not itself heat. Profit may be increased more by spending than by saving money. The accountant tends to save cost when the goal is more profit — hence perhaps the view that he "knows the cost of everything and the value of nothing".

Tactical *Security* clearly needs a firm base, sound information, good communications. Strategically, there is a liberal interpretation: ". . . the highest form . . . is that obtained through the imposition of our will upon the enemy, through seizing the initiative and maintaining it by offensive action".[6] Fine and rather demanding advice!

Mobility is really the means to apply techniques like surprise and concentration. For war and for peace, flexibility and speed can exemplify the idea. Being quick on one's feet, to play the opportunist line without losing sight of one's ultimate aim, is to possess a nice and valuable balance. Flexibility is thus not being bound by an obsolete plan nor by what one wants to believe or have expected.

To the soldier *Co-operation* welds together different arms or services or countries. To him — but not apparently to the civilian— it is also self-interest, an aid to survival. To the industrialist it implies unity of command and aim: if the organisation emphasises to its members the interests that they all have in common and if individuals' incentives are consistent with the organisation's objectives, the temptation to pursue parochial interests may be suppressed. (But perhaps not eliminated. I have witnessed otherwise competent colleagues blandly behaving as though they belonged to different firms). Organisational sense comes from a climate that presses constantly for unity — but not necessarily uniformity; playing politics, parochialism, sheer awkwardness, must be seen to be unrewarding.

The Principles Applied: Interior and Exterior Lines

A centrally placed force faced by more than one enemy operating on the periphery is a scenario we shall frequently meet. How to deal with it illustrates some of the principles in action.

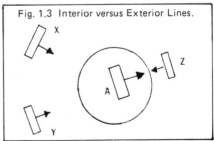
Fig. 1.3 Interior versus Exterior Lines.

In *Figure 1.3* the combatant A, placed centrally, fights X, Y and Z. A, being on 'interior lines', can move against one opponent and beat it with superior force if the others on 'exterior lines' do not co-ordinate well; as A has less far to go when he cuts the corner, even good collaboration may not save X, Y and Z from piece-meal defeats.

The rules for this game have been well thought out. Force A should: keep his enemies dispersed; keep for himself room for manoeuvre; attack singly and decisively; always attack somewhere. As a corollary, X, Y and Z should: weaken the enemy by universal pressure; maintain mutual support; retreat rather than be defeated; have superior numbers.

Warfare quite often sets opponents in these mutual relations. A 'war on two fronts' (which has been Germany's lot in two world wars) is simply one variant. The rules are quite simple but are not always easily applied. (Business has analogies. One company's product line may grossly overlap another's, when possession of an array of complementary products is a competitive weapon. The Boeing Aircraft Company is in this situation vis-à-vis Airbus Industries. It is an interesting exercise to think through what each firm should do. Are the guide-lines equivalent to the military ones?)

Military Management

In certain important respects the forces have different methods, styles, emphases, from their civilian counterparts — though it is unclear why business should have ploughed a new managerial furrow . . . In a previous career Austin Cartmell was Major Cartmell of the King's Regiment; now, after transformation from British Army infantry officer into manager with 35 years' line and staff experience in industry, he comments as follows:

> "The services start with a sense of purpose: life in them is a shared one. It is easy for all to see the value of unity. Senior commanders get killed! (The risks of industry are not perceived as shared. Is one of the objects of a corporate acquisition to benefit all employees, both of the predator and the victim?) Except for the professional, service life tends to be the consequence of national crises; nevertheless, the regular and the temporary soldier blend when in the common system — no doubt prompted by the cohesion bred by the country's readily perceived need.

The services' organisational design is dictated by the desired results. (The businessman argues from cost, that what he cannot afford he does not have; however, like most of us he tends to be able to afford what he wants.)

Military units, like components, can be used singly or in concert, and with maximum flexibility within the constraints of cohesion. Hence a variety of tasks can be tackled by the same force; conversely, units can be readily transferred from one command to another. For this manoeuvrability the half ranks, the joint commands, the powerless staff roles, so popular with industrialists, are anathema; the services see them as failure to make decisions. Instead, structure is pragmatic, little susceptible to individual whim, and senior officers relate organisational design to battle needs. Training in this important function is thought as necessary as in any other military affair. (Nevertheless, while the aircraft designer is — fortunately — trained for his work, the executive is too busy to study organisation professionally . . .) Services' organisation makes for unequivocal areas of accountability — i.e. with real risk — and of authority, for proper delegation and communication. Thus people can be readily told what they need to know to achieve their objects. Success demands a cohesion springing from common interest and mutual reliance: the infantry platoon, the air squadron, the aircraft carrier, work if their members are interdependent.

To staff this organisation a service, with few exceptions, has to make the best use of the people who are in it. There is no global pool of talent, and head-hunting within the service is not generally acceptable (but no doubt Montgomery — and others — did it!). Pay scales, common to all of comparable rank and service, are published; this concentrates attention on performance and, in the longer term, promotion. Performance review is standard and not secret and its outcome is embodied in a corporate-wide system; annual reports are not cross-checked but as they all move up through the command structure to the Military Secretary's Department some comparison is inevitable; they importantly influence promotion. But the confidential report is really only the outward and visible sign of

something that goes on all the time. I was not really surprised by any of mine . . . Successive reports after each
(frequent) posting confer a measure of objectivity. [But
both military and civilians would appraise more accurately more quickly if a person's peers and subordinates
could make their contributions! — CL.] A CO can post
away disfavoured people but this practice may rebound
on him so he has an incentive to improve his unit by
leadership and training.

The latter the services treat as integral: at all levels
resources are allocated for training, to increase effectiveness and promotability. A component of any service role
is the requirement to train subordinates, and an external
course is an adjunct to the process, not a substitute.
(There are well designed courses for industrial managers:
their usefulness is not enhanced by the shock student
learning on his return that he is often not expected to
practise what he has been taught). Training is viewed as
a pre-requisite for advancement and servicemen must have
been astonished at the need of the UK Government to
legislate for it. Of course, service training is (notoriously)
standardised but it works on the large scale.*

Putting the trained organisation to work is greatly supported by the service staff system, an integral part of the
whole, whose components can be recognised in an army
and in a battalion. The CO and his staff form a unit of
authority and accountability and it is implicit that the
staff issue orders on behalf of the CO. Though their authority is unlike the line's it is no less real; the effective
staff officer has to learn a style. Much time is saved, communication is unambivalent and things get done — usually.
(The civilian staff person may have no overt authority
over operations and is expected to give advice to harassed
managers ill-equipped to assess it; success may depend on
persuasiveness, not a recipe for cost-effectiveness).

The head of a military unit's staff** is trained under an
accepted code and all know who he is and why he is there.
He is accountable for converting the CO's plan into orders.
Any SO at any level knows how he fits into the structure
and what is required of him. So do the line officers! The
emphasis is reflected in the requirement for promotion to

---

*It is not that bad. As a sapper, I learned with many others in a matter of
days how to assemble a Bailey bridge. Starting with a heap of components,
we could readily bridge an 80 foot gap in 20 minutes. After 40 years I can
still remember much of the drill. CL.*

**See Appendix H for a discussion of the Chief of Staff role.*

higher command to have demonstrated performance in both types of roles. The command of regiments is rarely given to an officer who has not passed through the staff college.

Senior service commanders must marvel at captains of industry making life so difficult for themselves".[9]

One of the messages here is the power of making incentives work for one, of combining personal and corporate interests. Cartmell quotes Benjamin Franklin's advocacy — at the Convention to review the Articles of Confederation — of this point:

> "There are two passions that have a powerful influence on the affairs of men. These are ambition and avarice . . . When united in view of the same object, they have in many minds, the most violent effects. Place before the eyes of such men a post of honour that shall at the same time be a place of profit, and they will move heaven and earth to obtain it".*

*   *   *   *

Military technique is a long story, without an end and even from early times was complex. Generalship put it all to work. Every now and then it made innovations. We shall see that, as in business, its method sometimes matched its ambition — but only sometimes.

*   *   *   *

*Actually, Franklin was in his context worried about inappropriate motivation in government positions while my point is a general one: companies should consider what motives are operating and in what direction. But choice of motive will affect candidacy. What sort of people do we want to be attracted to which jobs? I personally would prefer members of parliament to be well-paid, to attract the money-seekers rather than the power-seekers. The current trend in British and US business to stress avarice may not add to its credit.

References

1   Professor Yigael Yadin, The Art of Warfare in Biblical Lands.

2   Dr. F W Lanchester, Aircraft in Warfare.

3   Peter Connolly, Greece and Rome at War.

4   Ed. James F Dunnigan, The Russian Front.

5   Quoted by Brigadier Peter Young, The Victors.

6   Major-General H Rowan Robinson, Imperial Defence.

7   Ed. M Windrow and F Wilkinson, The Universal Soldier.

8   Colonel A H Burne, The Art of War on Land.

9   A H Cartmell, Letter to the Author.

CHAPTER II

PROFESSIONAL MANAGEMENT: 'THE HANNIBALIC WAR'

"The purpose of an organisation is to enable common men to do uncommon things."

— Peter F Drucker

Part I: The Carthaginian Initiative and the Exhaustion of a Plan

Marketing: The System versus the Individual

Two companies may be destined to meet in mortal combat. Some personal whim or market force triggers the war. Success hinges on many factors. In this example tactical genius is matched against staying power. One 'company' has a strong-nerved Board sustained by popular support, so that dissent is confined to means, not ultimate objectives. In the past it has been hugely successful and the directors naturally repeat the time-hallowed recipe — stolid conventional methods backed by infinite determination.

Their opponent is as ruthless as they are, as well as being clever and crafty but lacking strategic vision. It is pushed almost against its wish into a decisive struggle for market share by the head of its oversea subsidiary. That executive is superb at marketing, winning selling positions with consistency, ease and economy. He has no repetitive drill, no facile or fashionable technique; he wins by the basic means of management — ingenuity, leadership, planning, control. Then he cannot exploit his dazzling success. His opponent evades receivership though half its home market is lost and bankruptcy looks inevitable. A generation later it repostes, prodded by a new 'marketing director' — young, far-sighted, creative, entirely ready to learn tactics from a competitor, yet appointed by popular vote while still unproved, almost as an act of despair.

49

With his Board's half-hearted backing, he carries the fight onto the enemy's home territory, thus taking the initiative and in the process the facility to dictate the strategic setting.

Thereafter, two master-tacticians must each make best use of their respective and differing strengths. In all, a case of straightforward, if inspired, professional management.

Prologue

The place? A sun-baked plain 120 miles south west of present day Tunis in North Africa. The time? 202 BC. The actors? In an isolated group are standing three men, talking. Within two miles of them are 75,000 others with 11,000 horses and 80 war elephants. All these wait on the debate, its outcome either peace and retirement or battle and probable mutilation. At stake for one side is its country's survival, for the other world dominion.

Of the three men, one is an interpreter. The others are the two greatest generals of their age. One is well known to us as the man who led an army across the Alps and brought near-lethal devastation to the Roman heartland; the other is known to history as Scipio Africanus, for reasons which will become apparent. They are meeting at Hannibal's request, to consider a negotiated settlement in place of the hazards of battle. Scipio gazes at the man who has been the scourge of his countrymen for a whole era in Italy. Hannibal remembers that his first Italian battle was against this man's father; now, fifteen years later, he is pleading peace of the son, himself winner of six battles with Carthaginian armies. He sees an apt pupil standing before him. The talk continues . . .

The careers that now converged at this meeting in Africa had already importantly touched each other. It was thus inevitable that these two professional soldiers should ultimately meet in confrontation.

Carthage and Rome

The "sea peoples" irrupted into the eastern Mediterranean in the 2nd millenium BC and those that settled on the Palestine coast were called Phoenicians (in Latin, Poeni, whence Punic) and were traders and sea-farers; they were also active colonisers and on the coast of north Africa, near modern Tunis, they established a city called Carthage in about 800 BC. It grew and prospered; by the 3rd century BC it was immensely rich and its citizens paid no direct taxes at all. They only numbered about half a million but their wealth paid for mercenary troops; these included excellent African infantry and Numidian (Algerian) cavalry, and formidable slingers from the Balearic Islands (who were paid not in gold but in women). The Carthaginian traders were whole-hearted monopolists: "Every foreign mariner sailing towards Sardinia or towards [Gibraltar], who fell into the hands of the Carthaginians, was thrown by them into the sea."[1]

Across the Mediterranean a young state with a sturdy rural population was already the strongest power in Italy; now Rome was extending its sway over Sicily, Corsica and southern France. Inevitably the two collided — in one of the dramatic struggles of history. Neither to us looks wholly attractive.

> "The Carthaginian Senate ... was based on a jealous control of administration by the government, and represented exclusively the leading families; its essence was mistrust of all above and below it."[1]

It ruled an aggressive people, greedy and cruel, given to wiles and deception, pagans practising child sacrifice. Unsuccessful generals were exiled or crucified though the survivors acquired — unlike the short-serving Romans — much experience over the years. The latter were a dour people, extraordinarily resilient and enduring and (sometimes) liberal administrators, but they were vengeful of defecting allies and over-keen on dominating all their neighbours. The states' systems varied as much as their psychologies. The penalty for Carthaginian military failure was of extreme severity and — one would have thought — inhibiting. In practice their generals were allowed considerable freedom of action, unlike their Roman counterparts, and they used it.

Very influential in Carthage was the Barcid family; its general, Hamilcar Barca, had been prominent in a recent war with Rome, the First Punic War. In that twenty-three year conflict the Carthaginians had lost important territory and 500 warships, the Romans 700; the latter also lost 150,000 men, perhaps one-third of their total man-power. Though extremely bloody it was quite indecisive, ending in a truce, not a peace. In 237 BC Hamilcar Barca left Carthage nominally to bring the North African littoral within the empire but actually to take control of and colonise Spain; it was a personal initiative as he sought a base from which to strike again at Rome. His far-sighted vision was of a new estate to reinvigorate the old, of new colonies with their commerce and soldiery to replace those lost. There he sired and educated a son, Hannibal, who duly inherited the family's influence as well as all its military ability, its enmity for Rome and its plans for a Punic revenge.

Rome meanwhile was rebuilding its fleet, subduing Celtic tribesmen in northern Italy and making threatening gestures at Carthage. With its Latin allies and its own robust peasantry it now had substantial man-power: most citizens were liable for military service until forty-five. It had always won its battles — well, nearly always — with the flexible, disciplined and aggressive legion and, preferring tradition to innovation, should go on doing so. It was to exemplify what Toynbee calls 'the Nemesis of success'. The Republic elected two consuls to rule it each year with great if short-lived power. The continuing influence in the land was the prestigious and experienced Senate, three-hundred strong, to which all public officials belonged. At first only an advisory body, it nevertheless could recommend generally acceptable and coherent policies. The Republic's politics were practical: the system bred some major mistakes but recriminations were limited (the Empire was to be very different). The attitude was for ultimately sinking differences and persevering through thick and thin, reinforced by a perhaps over-developed will to win. These attributes were about to be given their supreme test.

The Strategic Setting

Hamilcar Barca already controlled much of Spain when he was killed in battle in 228. He had long nourished a solution to the 'Roman problem'. Neither side could live with the other and Rome had already broken the peace treaty. He considered the Carthage government too corrupt and short-sighted to wage successful war, even if it had not already taken delegation to the point of abdication here in Spain. Rome had to be defeated in Italy; he would therefore build his own power-base, generating sufficient trade to keep Carthage quiet while training an army with which to invade Rome itself — but he died before he could implement this very ambitious plan. His son-in-law inherited his command but made no move, perhaps preferring local statecraft to foreign soldiering. He was assassinated in 220, when the army officers (by useful custom) elected Hannibal to the leadership. Though only twenty-nine, he was already rich in experience and distinguished in his father's camp: he was "... an excellent runner and fencer, and a fearless rider . . . He had commanded the cavalry . . . and distinguished himself by brilliant personal bravery as well as by his talents as a leader".[1] The family prestige, his technical prowess and the method of his selection, all combined to confer on him great authority. In character he seems to have been of his time, in no way inferior in behaviour and with distinctive mental qualities:

> "He combined in rare perfection discretion and enthusiasm, caution and energy. He was peculiarly marked by that inventive craftiness, [typical] of the Phoenician character . . . ambushes and stratagems of all sorts were familiar to him; and he studied the character of his antagonists with unprecedented care . . . History . . . attests his genius as a general, and his gifts as a statesman were, after the peace with Rome, no less conspicuously displayed . . ."[1]

This was the individual confronting Rome, a man then little known to her. The combatants were well matched in abilities — and in sharing the (quite common) trait of believing what they wanted to believe. To the Roman Senate the outlook appeared reassuring: its fleet now commanded the sea, the Celts in the north had been partly tamed, its southern ports were garrisoned and in a new war Sicily could be an invasion path to Carthage; Spain looked distant and unmenacing. Meanwhile, Carthage viewed Rome's power as patchy, its neighbours of marginal loyalty, particularly the Celts, so secession should prove contagious. Both sides ignored elusive yet crucial personal factors. The senators assessed the scene and the Carthaginian ability rightly enough, except for one subjective and imponderable power; one man's genius, which was to grip them in a desperate war for sixteen years, they could not discern. More understandably, Hannibal for his part could not foresee that Rome had just the resilience to sustain that appalling struggle.

Relying heavily on land power, Carthage had short-sightedly neglected its fleet and the Barcas were anyway land animals: this determined Hannibal's route. He had to evade any blocking force, invade Italy (by making the first ever Alpine crossing with an organised army) and detach the tribes allied then to Rome before the legions in Sicily could invade Africa; a whole new anti-Roman confederacy could thus be formed. In two swift campaigns

his Spanish base was consolidated and by 219 he was ready. Rome
was embroiled in an Adriatic conflict; his army was trained; the
legions were formidable but he had his African cavalry and Alexander the Great had clearly shown those willing to learn from the
past what that could mean *(see Chapter XII)*. It was time to go.
With an army of 90,000 infantry, 12,000 cavalry and 37 elephants, but without consulting Carthage, Hannibal set out from
New Carthage *(see Fig. II.1)* in the spring of 219. 'The Hannibalic
War' — Rome's grudging tribute to its most dangerous enemy —
had begun and the Ancient World held its breath.

Rome Invaded

Hannibal first besieged and, after an eight month siege, captured
Saguntum, a town quite arbitrarily declared by Rome to be under
its protection; on this hostile gesture war was declared. Hannibal
then sent emissaries to the Celt tribes in the Alps and the Po
valley to pave his way, despatched 16,000 men to protect a
Carthage now tacitly supporting him, left 15,000 with his brother
Hasdrubal Barca guarding Spain and — all foreseeable and necessary preparations made — himself marched into France with
50,000 foot and 9,000 horse.

Rome knew something of his movements but not his intentions
and sent a consul, Scipio, to Spain via Marseilles (blandly assuming
it had now, as previously, all the initiative) while a second army
was prepared in Sicily to invade Africa. For three weeks Hannibal
followed the coast and then crossed the Rhône against tribal
opposition, rafting over his elephants — with difficulty — and
turned north. He evaded Scipio by three days, who realised Italy
(now undefended) must be the target. This posed a conundrum.
He could either pursue this hitherto unsuspected invader or return
with his 24,000 troops to defend the homeland or carry out his
orders and continue to Spain, itself known to be important to
Carthage. He boldly decided to have his brother take the army on
to Spain while he himself hastened back to Italy. (There seems to
have been ample nepotism on both sides. For Hannibal this
conferred authority over co-operating units or armies on those
he could wholly trust; the Roman example in part reflects the
influence of the powerful Scipio family. However, as we shall see,
the practice also provided useful continuity.) The now aroused
Senate ordered the Sicilian legions instantly to northern Italy just
as the Carthaginians were approaching the mountains.

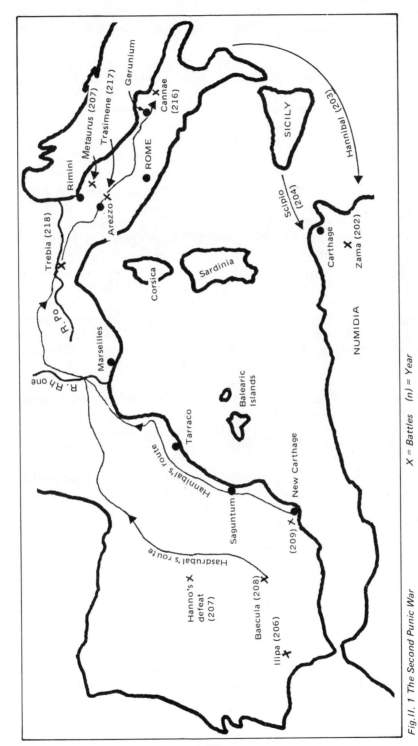

Fig. II. 1 The Second Punic War

X = Battles   (n) = Year

In a column perhaps ten miles long, the army marched up the Rhône and then the fertile Isère valleys; alongside the river Drac ravines made progress slow and very tedious. (We do not know Hannibal's exact route; for narrative convenience I adopt one plausible one, for which Appendix C provides a modest justification.) Further east the track narrowed; here hostile tribes laid an ambush, rolling down boulders on the attenuated column of men and animals. Only determined work forced a passage and then a slow and costly one. After modern Briançon the track zig-zagged up through the forest and snow and at the top of the pass the crudest path had to be cut out of the mountainside; it took two days to engineer a minimum way for the elephants. Hunger, ambushes, rockfalls, contributed to the agony. The descent followed a steep rock-face, then after three days' march the valley opened out. Shrunk to a force of 26,000 infantry and 6,000 cavalry after a fifteen day traverse, the army debouched in the late autumn of 218 into the Italian plain. Its morale quite unshaken by its ordeals, this heterogeneous but disciplined army looked down from the foothills into Roman territory. It could not foresee it was to be there for fifteen years.

While Scipio was hurrying to take command of the two legions in the Po valley, where he was to be joined by the two Sicilian ones after their march of 1100 miles in forty days, Hannibal had the time to build up his army and woo the local tribes. By the river Trebia he concealed a large force in ambush and, well aware of his opponent's impetuosity, lured the Romans before they had breakfasted into battle on ground of his choosing. Hungry, cold, wet and surprised, the legions were attacked on all sides and lost two-thirds of their number. Amongst the survivors was Scipio and his son, a young man set on learning his trade, and on becoming "Scipio Africanus". For unclear reasons Hannibal lost all but one of his elephants. This he now rode to his next Italian battle.

All these events electrified but did not dismay Rome: these local failures could be put right by simply repeating tactics with rather more competence. Legions were rushed to Sicily and Sardinia to counter any invasion while fresh ones were raised. In the spring of 217 the consuls for that year were sent north, Flaminius to Arezzo *(Fig. II.1)* and Servilius to Rimini. (For simplicity I mostly use modern names.) As often happened with such a system, they were not inspired appointments and Hannibal's strategy could unfold unhindered. He presented himself to the

Roman federation as a liberator; militarily he relied on fluid operations to trump the legions' strength with his tactics. With Celtic allies now welded into his army he moved south, as always by the unexpected way, crossing the barrier of the Appennines unopposed before Flaminius — who was a politician yet conceited about his military skill — could intercept him. Flaminius could usefully have improved the weak Roman intelligence system; he could have waited for Servilius' reinforcement; but Hannibal slipped by him and harried the countryside, making its official guardian look ridiculous. He plunged after Hannibal.

Near Arezzo there is a large lonely lake called Trasimene. Knowing his man, Hannibal hid his entire army in the hills above its shore. The pursuing Romans were marching without scouts and a morning mist further shrouded the trap. When the whole column was nicely exposed trumpets sounded the charge. The consul died with 15,000 of his men; probably the same number were taken prisoner while very few escaped. The Battle of Trasimene is probably the only instance ever of a whole army being placed in ambush. Servilius had sent 4000 cavalry to aid his colleague. Ambushed in their turn, none escaped. Rome had never known such defeats. Central Italy lay open. The Tiber bridges were broken down; more legions were raised; a dictator, Fabius, was appointed for an emergency period, while Hannibal marched to the Adriatic where, in rich farmland and with captured arms, he took the time offered by a paralysed Rome to rest, re-equip and re-organise his army.

Thorough in his intelligence gathering, Hannibal's spies informed him about his new opponent. Fabius was a cautious man who took firmness to the point of obstinacy. He would avoid a pitched battle but wear down this otherwise unbeatable foe by cutting off his foragers; attrition would replace combat. With more skill and political support it might well have worked but unpleasant remedies need prior commitment (and so require politics to be a general's business). The Carthaginians plundered widely but selectively while Fabius' army was made by the great moral courage of its general to watch impotently and Rome felt increasingly humiliated; furthermore, senators' farms were being burned — but not Fabius'. Finally an impatient Senate decided to divide the dictatorship between Fabius and his impetuous assistant, Minucius Rufus — who thereupon felt he had to justify himself. What happened to him is an example of the tactical art.[2]

His first camp was on
a hill and Hannibal, at first
distant, moved to a second
one better commanding an
intervening river *(Fig. II.2);*
he then sent an apparently
aggressive but small de-
tachment to occupy a hill
("A") close to Minucius.
As it was clearly valued by
his enemy Minucius would
occupy it himself — and
did so. Allowing himself to
be repulsed, Hannibal re-
treated to his first camp

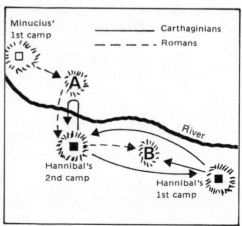

Fig. II. 2 The Humiliating of Minucius

and Minucius followed up, the better to crowd him. Without
having to force a river crossing, Hannibal now had him on his
own ground. Between them lay another hill ("B") with gullies and
hollows; at night 5000 Carthaginians were hidden in them. In the
morning Hannibal ostentatiously occupied the hill and again
Minucius responded — to be promptly ambushed. And to be
rescued by the watching Fabius. (There are echoes of these tactics
in *Chapter III.)*

Hannibal now went into winter quarters at Gerunium *(Fig. II.1).*
The temporary Fabian dictatorship expired and Paullus and
Varro were appointed consuls, which was influenced by the
demagogue Varro being an outspoken critic of the Fabian policy.
By a supreme effort two legions were raised and sent to control
the north, two to garrison Rome and no less than eight watched
the enemy. Thus arrayed, Rome faced the fateful year of 216.

The Battle of Cannae

Early that summer Hannibal broke camp and marched south, to
seize the Roman supply centre of Cannae. It was to give its name
to one of history's classic battles. On the Senate's orders the two
consuls followed, to offer battle by the river Ofanto. They were
joint commanders and to reduce indecisiveness (but not to
eliminate it) they held command by Roman practice on alternate
days. Paullus was the more cautious but neither could waste time:
a large army living off the country had to keep moving if it was
to find food and fodder. Hannibal, reading their minds, now

barred the way to their favoured terrain and harassed their foraging parties with his light cavalry. On Varro's day for command,
action was sought. Hannibal obliged him. Drawn up (very conventionally) so that its flanks were protected by the river and
by the Cannae hills, the Roman army looked both massive and
powerful. It numbered 80,000 infantry and 6,000 cavalry — the
largest force Rome had ever fielded — with skirmishers in front,
cavalry on each flank, in a line of battle extending for 2½ miles.
With armour shining and the standards surmounting the plumed
helmets it must have looked enormously impressive.

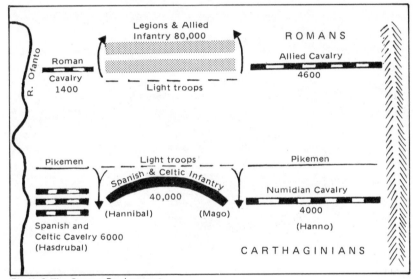

Fig.II. 3 The Cannae Deployment

Opposite *(see Fig. II. 3)*, screened by light troops, Hannibal
drew up his army — 40,000 infantry and 10,000 cavalry — with
much care. His superb Numidian horsemen could with their skill
equal the opposing cavalry on his right, and on his left he greatly
over-matched them; his out-numbered infantry, its weakest components in the centre, were deployed in a curve *convex* outwards.
A trusted general, Hasdrubal (not in this case a Barca) commanded
the left wing. Hannibal placed himself with his brother Mago
centrally: the weak point might come here.

Skirmishing over, both sides' light troops now retired; the
Carthaginian pikemen amongst them forming groups on each wing
— they had a role to play. The Carthaginian cavalry now charged

the opposing horsemen on their left to quick effect, and the Romans decided to advance their powerful infantry before its flanks became exposed. The legions charged forward, casting their javelins and following up to crash shield against shield while slashing and thrusting with their short swords; under the weight and shock the Carthaginian curved front began to fold in.

Meanwhile, the Roman cavalry fighting Hasdrubal was now in full flight, allowing him to give a timely and beautifully controlled reinforcement to the heavily engaged Numidians on the right wing who could then sweep their opponents away *(see Fig. II. 4);* in the meantime the Carthaginian infantry was being forced back until its line was becoming *concave* and being flanked by its fellow pikemen.

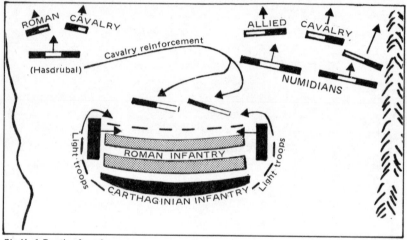

Fig.II. 4 Death of an Army

Having won their fight Hasdrubal's cavalry now fell on the Roman rear. The flanking pikemen faced inward. The entire Roman mass was funnelled into a cauldron. Increasingly compressed, many unable to swing their swords, the legionaries fought or died. By evening Hannibal had lost 6000 men. The Roman killed numbered about 50,000 and the prisoners 15,000: 80% of the largest army in Rome's history had been annihilated and 10,000 survivors only escaped — being rallied by one Scipio Africanus. The dead included Minucius Rufus and the consul, Paullus. Varro had to face the people of Rome. While the victor wondered what use to make of his masterpiece, a classic battle in the perfection of its design and execution, Rome lay stunned.

For a while the city was helpless. Five people were buried alive as sacrifices to appease the angry gods; every family mourned its dead; the Senate had lost 40% of its members. Then the insensitive but robust Roman spirit revived: nothing was to be yielded to the enemy, not a single Cannae prisoner to be ransomed (instead, they could be sold into slavery!), no peace made, no hope of winning to be lost, though much of southern Italy had defected. A new dictator was appointed, two new legions raised, slaves and criminals were enlisted; the survivors of the battle were organised into two legions and banished to Sicily in disgrace. Some loyal Italian cities maintained their defences.

Hannibal did not strike on the morrow of Cannae at the capital: lacking a siege train or put off by memories of the long siege of Saguntum, he felt unable or unwilling to press beyond a feint to test Roman resolution. He had won a great battle; could he now win a war? His army was small simultaneously to besiege cities, capture more territory and defend its foraging area. Against an ever-receding end-point this diverse beleaguered force had to be kept trained, supplied and inspired while the surrounding enemy reverted to the Fabian strategy, to wait on events. There were skirmishes and minor battles and three or four major ones — a long succession of moves and counter-moves, supported by enormous resolution on both sides. Hannibal's leadership could meet all the demands made of it and his immense tactical skill, defensive and offensive, remained always undefeated — but so also did the Roman state. It was, however, much the poorer: there were economic as well as military weapons. Much land went unfarmed, army pay was in arrears, inflation was ruining many smallholders: socially Rome was being debauched. Next year it doubled its taxes but in 214 it managed to raise six new legions. Later, manoeuvres centred round control of Sicily and southern Italy. The years passed.

Part II: The Roman Response — A 'Me-too' Strategy

A Spanish Inheritance

While Italy was being devastated Spain was in transition. With its silver mines, commerce and warlike tribesmen it was a natural Roman objective. Two Scipio brothers (one the survivor of the Trebia) led the first invasion but, lacking both troops and caution and after some successes, they were finally killed in 211 and the permanent command, rather naturally, lay vacant. Roman Italy was still recovering in the aftermath of Cannae: who would wish to be responsible for an outnumbered defeated army without allies or hope deep in the victorious Carthaginian empire? An ambitious aristocrat aged twenty-four, rather unRoman in his artistic taste, a soldier of lively if limited experience, offered himself for selection. In a dramatic public election the voting for him, stimulated perhaps by finding any credible candidate but concerned for his youth, was unanimous. The Senate concurred. (It is interesting that Rome left the filling of such a crucial post to such an accidental process: *see Appendix D).* "Never before in all the history of Rome had an authority so great been vested in a man so young and inexperienced." [3]

Publius Cornelius Scipio was born in 235, of an illustrious family. Nothing of his youth is known and little of his military apprenticeship. We do know him as cultured, self-confident and self-controlled. As an impressionable youth of seventeen he had seen Hannibal in action for the first time when in charge of a Roman cavalry troop at the Trebia battle and there he had rescued his father from the surrounding enemy by a lone charge. In 216 he was made a senior staff officer and he had survived Cannae where he was foremost in restoring his fellows' morale, earning further promotion. Tactful and with much charm, an accomplished speaker and a rational thinker, Scipio studied the art of displaying his gifts. A diplomat, who was also a calculating and far-sighted strategist, he was quite ready to imply he was helped by divine inspiration. Open-minded, he learned as readily from Roman defeats as from his own successes. ". . . Without his intellectual powers, his other qualities would have been of no effect; but without the simple human feeling which bound men to him . . . his intelligence would have been fruitless." [3] A great student, a master of 'PR', he would have been totally suited — but not necessarily selected — to run a British nationalised industry. Perhaps by accident, his country now managed to develop Scipio's innate talent.

> "The remarkable young man who commanded armies and ruled a province before he had filled any of the senior magistracies of Rome owed much of his startling individuality to the very fact that he had never been standardised

by passing through the regular offices. Rome had no difficulty in producing a Hannibal of her own; but she did so by reproducing some of the unusual circumstances which had created the original."[3]

Prodded in part by party politics, a by no means unanimous Senate gave this assertive young man two legions and sent him by sea to replace one Claudius Nero — of whom more will be heard — then in temporary command in Spain, and he arrived at the Roman base at Tarraco (Tarragona) in 210. He met the family connections, the local tribes who remained loyal, trained his army — in particular improving the equipment and organisation of the cavalry — and gathered information exhaustively before preparing his plan. The Carthaginians had three armies, all effective, all with quite able generals (one of them a brother of Hannibal) but all spread out; their base was the port of New Carthage (Cartagena) and it held much gold and war material and no doubt its excellent fortifications made them feel secure. Scipio's plan was based on his being seven days' forced march from the port while the nearest enemy was ten. The fortress might conceivably yield to a surprise assault. It was a bold and unconventional move. He blandly and very openly announced quite other intentions. (We are reminded again that information is the indispensable foundation of any plan and surprise its invaluable smoke-screen.)

> "This decision shows that Scipio had already made the advance from being a good General to a great one. A good soldier, seeing the enemy so dispersed would have planned to defeat them in detail; only a top-class commander would see the opportunity to cut right to the heart of the problem and have the audacity to put such a plan into operation."[4]

Within a week and without the slightest warning for the enemy, Scipio was encamped outside the walls of New Carthage. He attacked at once. Co-ordinated escalades defeated an over-stretched defence and the rich base was his. Strike one!

The Carthaginians still had numbers but the Romans had the initiative. Their communications were secure but they could threaten the enemy's. If he did nothing they could recruit Spanish allies. Thinking action the lesser evil Hasdrubal Barca, Hannibal's

brother, moved south with his army. Scipio mustered his ships'
crews into his army, equipping them from New Carthage's ample
work-shops. The armies collided at Baecula (near modern Cor-
doba, *see Fig. II. 1*), probably in 208. The Carthaginians suffered
severely but the wily Hasdrubal escaped into France where he
could recruit afresh before powerfully and perhaps decisively
reinforcing his brother in Italy. Like his father chasing Hannibal
ten years previously in very similar circumstances, Scipio decided
not to follow, believing pursuit through the mountains fruitless,
and Roman Spain would need re-conquering all over again if he
left it now. This has been criticised: the decisive arena was Italy,
so preventing Hannibal's reinforcement was surely paramount.
Scipio preferred foregoing the *possible* chance of frustrating this
in favour of the *very probable* chance of neutralising Hannibal's
base completely. Given the Romans' terror of Hannibal this logical
decision might well have appeared to them, but not to Scipio,
the risky one. It must have been a hard decision: he could be
damned either way. (Like all decision-makers, the military have
continually to balance risk against reward.)

Rome recovers the Initiative
Bribing the tribes along his brother's route, now free of snow,
Hasdrubal made a speedy passage over the Alps and, with probably
30,000 men, debouched unhindered in 207 into the Po valley
where there were only four legions under the consul Livius to face
him. He immediately sent messengers secretly (but curiously or
carelessly in only one party) to arrange a rendezvous with Hannibal:
they would meet, he was suggesting, at Narnia, north of Rome
(Fig. II. 5).

In this vital operation fate now intervened. The messengers were
captured and taken to the other consul, Claudius Nero (whom
Scipio had replaced in Spain), then watching Hannibal south of
Cannae. Nero was a member of the celebrated Claudian family,
able, bright, "a man who feared nothing — not even that terror
of weak men — responsibility." [3] Now at the crisis he did not
hesitate. Sending calls for food to be set out on the road north
and advice to Rome to mount a blocking force at Narnia, (but
without waiting for the Senate's necessary permission to leave
his province) he himself secretly slipped away from his post
and set off by forced marches with 7,000 picked men. The ordinarily stolid Senate was horrified: "All [their] misfortunes had

befallen them when the enemy had but a single general . . . it had become two Punic Wars, two mighty armies, two Hannibals, so to speak, in Italy."[5] Meanwhile, an unsuspecting Hasdrubal marched east, to meet his brother.

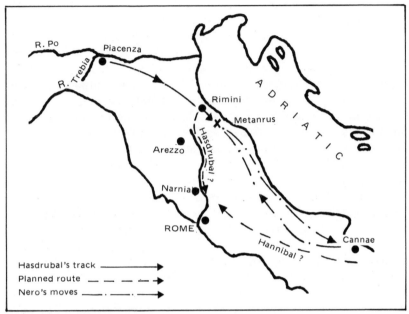

Fig.II. 5 Claudius Nero's Strategem

To avoid alerting the still dangerous Hannibal Nero travelled fast and by a circuitous route. Marching day and night, his men found food ready by the roadside; enthusiasts swelled their numbers. A week and 300 miles later they slipped unobserved into Livius' camp near Rimini, thus concentrating two armies at the point of decision. Next day, in haste before his brother could receive warning, they brought Hasdrubal, now out-numbered and misled by his guides, to battle. By the River Metaurus he was defeated and decapitated. A mere six days later found Nero returned to his station opposite Hannibal, to throw his brother's head into the Carthaginian camp: a brutal completion for a flawless operation.

A decisive point had passed. Brought by special messenger, the news made Rome deliriously joyful. And relieved. In Italy the defecting allies were gradually won back; henceforth Rome held the initiative; no reinforcements could get through to Hannibal, who yet remained immovable. No Roman army dared a pitched battle with the man whose tactical ingenuity and skill in contriving favourable conditions for himself seemed boundless, the Cannae conqueror of whom it could later be said, "What other General could turn an open plain into a gigantic trap in full sight of his opponent?"[4]

In Spain the Carthaginians raised a second army under the general Hanno; it and another were converging, Hanno from central Spain, the other from the south — not far from Scipio's links with New Carthage. What to do? It is a military principle not to split one's forces which, to the layman, can seem cramping; but the military very soundly aim usually to concentrate all their force (as did Claudius Nero) against part of the foe's. However, the superior general knows when rules should be broken.

Scipio detached his lieutenant Silanus, with 10,000 foot and 800 horse, to attack one force while he himself warded off the other. By moving fast Silanus won surprise and a victory. Hanno arrived too late to help but in time to be captured. The prisoner was sent to Rome while Scipio retired into winter quarters. (This for long was the invariable practice: lack of clothing, fodder, daylight and mobility made winter campaigning impracticable.)

Next year Carthage made a last attempt to hold their finest colony and with a fresh army their general, Gisco, confronted an out-numbered Scipio at Ilipa (near modern Seville). A Roman army when campaigning routinely and laboriously made a semi-fortified camp every afternoon; it consumed much time but boosted morale, gave protection and confined all troops in a controlled body. While so engaged, Scipio with foresight had prepared for a possible surprise attack: it was duly made and duly repulsed. The armies now faced each other across a hollow.

Each day, leaving his camp to invite combat, Gisco drew out his army in order of battle, always with his reliable African infantry in the centre and the weaker Spanish on the wings *(Fig. 11.6)* Each afternoon when there was little time to fight, Scipio responded. His order was constant and the mirror-image of Gisco's: the powerful legions in the centre, the Spanish allies on each flank. Several days passed.

One evening Scipio gave orders: troops were to be up, prepared and armed before dawn. At first light he led them out, fed, fresh and ready for battle. Gisco rushed out his surprised and unfed troops, automatically lining them up in their usual array — to find

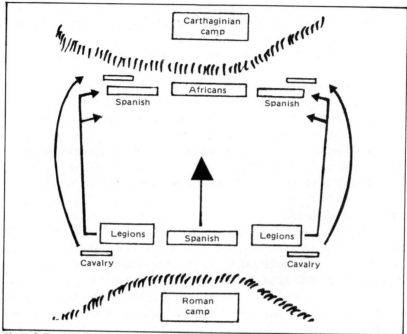

Fig.II.6 The Ilipa Manoeuvre

Scipio's reversed: the legions were now on the wings, the Spanish in the centre! Scipio advanced his centre slowly, 'fixing' Gisco's Africans in their position, while the legions deployed against each wing. Attacked in front and flank, these were easily routed while the Africans, necessarily inert spectators while in fear of their own flanks, had to wait their turn; inevitably it came and assailed on three sides they too retreated. A violent storm brought a brief respite before a pre-planned pursuit ruined them.

The country was now mostly Rome's but its general's mind turned to the future. He decided to risk a secret trip to Africa to form an alliance with a local king who could provide Numidian cavalry when he would want it. Carthage was militarily weaker in Africa than in Italy and there lay its heart: threaten that and it must conform to Scipio's moves and fight him on his chosen ground. Just as Hannibal had ignored Sicily in 218 and lunged directly at Rome, so Scipio now ignored Spain and aimed for Carthage. (By learning from No. 1 and catching him running 'out of steam', the copyist can be more effective as the No. 2.)

In 206 he rode in triumph to Rome and next year was elected

a consul. Its public adored him but older soldiers disliked his African plan. Grudgingly he was given charge of Sicily, where still languished the legions which had made the mistake of surviving Cannae. Many senators would have preferred him to follow a conventional strategy and fight the foe at the gate. After anxious debate he was allowed to make his indirect approach (often a better method for many sorts of problems than the 'frontal' or obvious one) but only on a voluntary basis. This does not appear to have worried him : self-confidence and an ability to cut through to the heart of a problem were his supports. In 204 he sailed with the two Sicilian legions and some volunteers for Africa, in all probably 28,000 men. The tide had turned.

The Battle of Zama

Scipio landed near Carthage in 204 and was promptly fenced in by Gisco with a fresh army. After buying time by spinning out negotiations on a pretended truce (and perhaps inspired by his reading of a very similar Sicilian move against the same enemy 80 years previously) he then set fire at night to the Carthaginian camps; in the resulting chaos most of their troops were burned, killed or captured.

Scipio was then free to move south, harrying the countryside as he went: to defend its food supplies the remaining and still numerous Carthaginian troops should be drawn away from the capital's formidable fortifications and the Romans could also make rendezvous with the Numidians in the long pre-arranged alliance. As Scipio had foreseen, Hannibal with his veterans was now recalled by a very anxious Carthage (but, lacking the transports, without his invaluable cavalry) and ordered to follow Scipio, who could feel only gratified. His precious allies were forthcoming; he had a firm African bridgehead; the immensely competent invader of Roman territory had been economically removed and his army drawn away from the fortress onto Scipio's own ground.

Hannibal collected both local troops and Spaniards and hoped too soon to secure some Numidians. A crucial battle was almost inevitable: Scipio's strategy was forcing decisive action and all now depended on tactics of which his opponent had a proved mastery. Every possible aid for the Roman side must be mustered. The two armies, each of which had strengths and weaknesses, were in presence near Zama *(Fig. II. 7)*, a modest town on the edge of a plain. Some scouts that Hannibal sent to reconnoitre Roman dispositions were captured but, instead of killing them, Scipio gave them a conducted tour and told them to report all they had seen to their general, who was reported to admire this opening gambit. Both sides camped on high ground near the plain, which should give Scipio's cavalry full scope; the Romans, arriving first, were much closer to drinking water. Two more points for Scipio.

In due course the two generals, for whom personally the stakes were as immense as for their countries, had their meeting, with Hannibal seeking a negotiated peace — or perhaps buying time for his cavalry to be reinforced; a deadlock over terms left the decision to force of arms. For this both now very carefully prepared. Short of water and inferior in cavalry, Hannibal could neither retreat nor wait long. "Before nightfall," says the Roman historian Livy, "they would know whether Rome or Carthage should give laws to the nations. For not Africa . . . or Italy, but the whole world would be the reward of Victory." [5]

Conscious of his cavalry weakness (but still hoping for its last minute remedy) and of the doubtful reliability of some of his infantry — in total perhaps 40,000 men — Hannibal arrayed them in three lines *(Fig. 11. 7)*; in front were no less than eighty war elephants — whose role was to be purely offensive — and the light troops. His Italian veterans formed the third line, a reserve. Scipio, with perhaps 35,000 men, deployed his infantry unconventionally — not for the first time — with the maniples in rows and columns instead of the usual checkerboard arrangement, leaving aisles between them temporarily concealed by light troops. The usual reserve was in rear and the dangerous Numidian horse on the right wing. This scheme was designed to absorb a severe central assault which, if survived, could precede a paralysing envelopment. "The whole business in any case would be touch-and-go, in which the victor (whosoever he might be) would creep home by the most desperate hazard." [3]

Fighting started with cavalry skirmishes and the elephants going for the legions. Scipio's light troops tried to deflect them and suffered severely before retreating between the maniples. Some elephants charged fairly harmlessly down the aisles; others were frightened off by the Roman trumpets all blaring out or by javelin wounds and galloped away, to confuse the Carthaginian cavalry. The Roman horsemen promptly attacked these, to chase them right off the field. (It has been suggested [2] that Hannibal

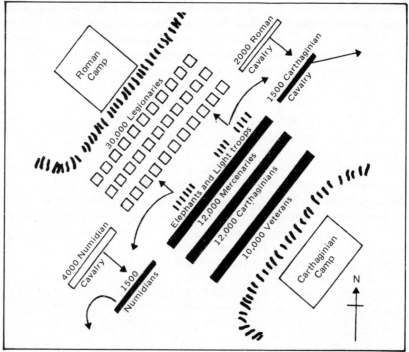

Fig.II.7 The Battle of Zama

deliberately lured Scipio's dangerous cavalry away from the main action.) Both Carthaginian wings were now exposed but the enemy cavalry was wholly engaged elsewhere — for the moment.

The massed infantry straightaway collided and the two front lines had a ferocious fight before the decimated Carthaginians retreated round their second line, who in turn went into the fray. They in due course were mauled in their turn and Hannibal marshalled the remainder on the wings of his third line, to prevent Scipio's encircling him. It was the final phase. The Roman infantry was weary and disorganised. Firm in his assessment and control, Scipio therefore coolly recalled it in the middle of the battle, removed his wounded who littered the ground, took the time to form the remaining maniples into one long line to threaten the Carthaginian flanks (and perhaps to give his cavalry time to return) and charged Hannibal's formidable veterans. (Hannibal's non-interference is a puzzle; presumably he had no choice; perhaps he was busy sorting out his own troops.) A violent and fairly even struggle ensued, only decided late in the day by the highly opportune return of Scipio's horsemen to take the veterans in the rear. It then became a Cannae in reverse.

The consequences were very similar. Carthaginian casualties were enormous — probably around 35,000 to the Romans' 10,000 — and Hannibal barely escaped the pursuing cavalry. (A few days later his own cavalry reinforcement, sufficient to have given him superiority, arrived, only to be bundled back to Numidia: another of life's little ironies.) Carthage sued for peace and the two generals agreed magnanimous terms. Scipio returned to Italy, to enjoy a triumphal procession through all the towns to Rome. He was still only thirty-two and at the height of his powers. His capacity to think and to learn had polished his tactical skill to match his strategic planning: the pupil now rivalled the master. His diligent 'intelligence' gave him information, his fighting methods were novel and foresight shielded him from the uncertain. It was this combination of far-sighted strategy and inspired execution which made him such a deadly opponent.

He was offered the dictatorship of the state for life; probably wisely, he rejected this heady but unsure prospect. His fickle admirers in time became uninterested, then turned positively cool. Later he was charged with embezzlement and corruption (like the equally victorious Marlborough 1900 years later) " ... beyond doubt empty calumnies ... although it was characteristic of the man, that instead of simply vindicating himself by means of his account-books, he tore them in pieces in presence of the people and his accusers ... "[1] Disillusioned, he exiled himself from Rome and died, a little over 50, a bitter man.

Zama was one of history's decisive battles, not just a supremely skilled contest between two of the world's greatest generals, though it is replete with tactical felicities. "The battle of Zama ... led the Roman people across the threshold of a united Italy to the highroad of world dominion."[6]

After sponsoring social reform but traduced by political enemies, Carthage's incomparable leader retreated from public life. Five years later he left the city for good, on hearing a Roman embassy was coming to demand his extradition: "The Roman only forgave his enemies when they were unsuccessful."[3] Carthage honoured its greatest son by declaring him an outlaw and razing his house to the ground. Thus, like Napoleon, he joined the ranks of the great failures but adorned with comparable fame. There is a pleasing legend that he met Scipio in after years in Ephesus, when both were in voluntary exile, and the Roman asked the Carthaginian whom he thought the greatest captain. Hannibal replied, Alexander. And the second? Pyrrhus (who had won several battles over the Romans a century before). So the third? 'Myself', said Hannibal. "On this Scipio laughed, and added, 'What would you have said if you had conquered me'? 'Then I would have placed Hannibal . . . before all other commanders'."[7]

He escaped continuing threats from the Romans but had to live eighteen years in exile and when these implacable pursuers finally caught up with him he committed suicide.

In the Third Punic War forced by Rome in 149, Carthage was defeated, the city utterly demolished and its population sold into slavery. It looked like final defeat. However, Hannibal had 50 years previously innoculated Italy with a wasting disease: a devastated country was now farmed by slaves in place of free citizen-peasants. This revolution ". . . increased for a time the monetary value of the produce of the land; but this was more than offset by the social evils it entailed . . . [which] gave the Roman people a shock from which they never recovered."[8] Perhaps in the end it was mutual destruction. Hannibal died in the same year as the alienated Scipio. Claudius Nero, the designer of the vital coup at the Metaurus, achieved no later distinction.

The effects of this enormous struggle echoed down the centuries. Rome, not very quickly weakened by its social cancer, went on to world dominion. But six and a half centuries after Zama, barbarian invaders from Asia were gaping at the ruins of Carthage, having sacked Rome a generation before.

*   *   *   *

Post-Script

The account of the battle of Ilipa and the defeat of Hasdrubal Barca is a simplified one. Actually Scipio's flank attacks on Gisco's infantry were unconventional, not to say peculiar:

> " . . . Scipio marched the legions off in column away from the centre . . . then had the two columns of legionaries turn at right angles towards the Carthaginians, and finally to deploy obliquely to cover the gaps between them and

the still advancing centre. The whole manoeuvre recalls the elaborate parade-ground movements of London's Trooping the Colour ceremony."[9]

What is intriguing is that one of the musical pieces always played at that British ceremony is Handel's "Scipio".

*　　　*　　　*　　　*

Annex : A Manager's Comments

Every manager will have recognised in this narrative analogies with his own trade : points about personnel selection, for example, or management development, or tactical skills, or others. But some aspects seem to deserve separate comment.

These necessarily fall in the shadow of the second Punic War's structure, itself striking enough : two ambitious, ruthless, competitive empires in search of Mediterranean supremacy. For its part, Carthage's strategy was short-sighted. After Italy had been invaded and Roman armies defeated, what then? It could not win without the defection of Rome's allies and the seizure of the capital. Rome's manpower and determination were almost boundless; it could not actually lose the war with them intact. Carthaginian intelligence failed to identify " . . . that central core of mutual trust and loyalty which distinguished the Roman state . . . The existence of this central core was the secret of the strength of Rome"[2] (And what a security for any organisation such a Roman-style social cement provides!).

But Carthage from the start had lacked any long range vision. There in Spain was its future to be made, when its leading general's son was rising to power and in his abilities already distinguished. Hannibal " . . . took to military life like a duck to water. He soon showed a genius for tactics, man-management, command, and leadership . . . his clothing and weapons were the object of his constant care."[10]

Acclaimed by his father's army he was the undisputed heir to the viceroy's dominion. He could pursue its ambitions. *He* was not to forego these for want of foresight. What problems and opportunities lay on his route to Italy? What problems and opportunities lay in his destination? There, 900 miles from base, how could supplies be found? (One staff officer suggested training the army in cannibalism.) Given the stakes — Carthage's survival — could not this ability have been recognised? To transform a local into a planned corporate enterprise was the first opportunity.

With Italy invaded there was a second. Stimulated by massive Roman defeats the Celts were in turmoil, Sardinia was in revolt and Carthage formed an alliance with Macedon. Timely application of all available force at the point of decision in Italy was thus invited. But Spain was the chief Carthaginian source of silver and Hannibal's political opponents were at work. His brother Mago, with a fresh army, was ordered to Spain.

Hannibal's early reinforcement, say after Cannae — or nearly three years into the war — was essential but was not pressed. As a result he found himself hedged around by "a mobile blockade [of small field armies and he] . . . drifted into the position of a chess player who plays simultaneously against many opponents . . ."[3] The plan had not been thought through nor serious contingencies allowed for. The conclusions are wholly unoriginal but deserve repetition :

— think through the implications of our plan to its underlying requirements : what do we need to make it work ?
— provide for its accidental undermining : what is our counter?
— underwrite the plan with good information and ask, what do we *not* know about the planned scenario ?

Of almost equal impact is Hannibal's tactical skill. His boundless ingenuity and adaptability we can readily accept but he went beyond this : he could read his enemies' minds and bend them to his will (e.g. at Trebia and Trasimene and with Minucius). He not only took advantage of Roman mistakes, he made them take them in the first place. So the example teaches. Scipio shows the reward for a simple capacity to learn. And what better instructor is there than your winning opponent?

Of course, Scipio had other attributes: he was not like some exam-passing university graduates, brilliant but without any feeling for his fellow men. He repeatedly demonstrated foresight, looking forward to the next battle but one. He had a talent for the grand design. But without the open-mindedness for learning he might never have survived to use these abilities.

Both master and pupil are noteworthy for another reason. Neither was wedded to a particular technique, to a simplistic kit of managerial parts, that purported to tell a manager 'how to win'. In the management profession there is still a penchant for fashions, for panaceas marketed as the universally applicable medicines for corporate ills. Examples are 'Management by Objectives', the 'Managerial Grid', 'OD'. Nothing could be more alien to the methods of Hannibal and Scipio. They relied on the elementary but basic truths: motivating leadership, the painstaking gathering of information, objectivity, imaginative planning, personal control where particularly needed . . . dull prosaic rules which someone somewhere in the organisation must apply.

It is not these guides alone but the glamorous aspects and the very personal satisfactions that drive people to the professional peaks, regardless of the dangers. Carthage dealt very summarily with failed generals and one would have expected the hideous 'downside risk' (of crucifixion) to abate the supply of volunteers. It did not. Many a manager is similarly wooed to sit in the hottest of seats. It shows the immense attraction of power, prestige and — to some extent — material prizes. This seductive effect puts individuals at severe personal risk (to health, home-life, reputation) while, conversely, the organisations are under no pressure to make their jobs reasonable. Is protecting people from themselves just charity?

At the end of it all one comes full circle, to the Roman state against Hannibal. One must respect the robustness of the one as much as the skills of the other. (The Carthaginian was a dazzling leader too and his style is discussed in *Chapter XII.*) That stolid resilient state was able, consciously or unconsciously, to breed and develop its own Hannibal and to give him the opportunity to do his work. Despite all its solidarity and discipline it could 'allow' (by a judicious mixture of regulation and discretionary authority) a Claudius Nero to leave his guard post opposite Rome's most terrible enemy, against clear senatorial orders, in order to try to destroy a menacing reinforcement. These managerial achievements are as admirable in their way as its opponent's thorough development, inspiring leadership and skilful use of his resources. The contest between state and individual is summed up for us by the classic battle, Cannae: national catastrophe for the one, fame everlasting for the other. The triumphant winner had cleverly encouraged the wretched loser, the consul Varro, in his actions and taken the most skilful and uttermost advantage from his tactical mistakes. This battle alone sufficiently attests Hannibal's genius for war. It also attests Rome's courage.

> "The Senate, after publishing the casualty lists, sent word to Varro to return to Rome. It was resolved to clear the slate and to begin the war afresh. Varro came. His return was a higher act of moral heroism than the death of Aemilius Paullus [his fellow consul]. Paullus had said beforehand that if they lost the coming battle he would never face his countrymen again. Varro showed a nobler if a more pathetic courage . . . [He] prepared to face the

justifiable criticism of Rome. He realized his irretrievable mistakes. He could not make them good; he could not offer any sacrifice or compensation. He could only come in person to stand before his fellow-citizens and confess that he had been wrong. His fellow-citizens realized that they also had been wrong. No scene in Roman history is more famous than that in which they met him with an official welcome, and thanked him for doing his duty and not despairing of the state." [3]

*   *   *   *

References

[1] T. Mommsen, The History of Rome.

[2] P Connolly, Greece and Rome at War.

[3] G P Baker, Twelve Centuries of Rome.

[4] T Bath, Hannibal's Campaigns.

[5] Livy, quoted by Major Gen. J F C Fuller, Decisive Battles of the Western World.

[6] J F C Fuller, Ibid.

[7] Sir Basil Liddell Hart, A Greater then Napoleon.

[8] A J Toynbee, A Study of History (Abridgement by D C Somervell).

[9] Dr. L. Keppie, The Making of the Roman Army.

[10] Sir Gavin de Beer, Hannibal.

Some Contemporary Events

290	B.C.	Rome completes conquest of central Italy.
264—241		First Punic War.
218–201		Second Punic War.
214		Great Wall of China begun.
183		Deaths of Hannibal and Scipio Africanus.
168		Rome conquers Macedon.
149—146		Third Punic War.
146		Rome controls Greece and destroys Carthage.
112?		Opening of 'Silk Road' between China and the Mediterranean.
64		Rome conquers Syria.
49		Julius Caesar conquers Gaul.

CHAPTER III

THE COMPLEAT CHIEF EXECUTIVE:

MARLBOROUGH FORCES THE LINES OF NE PLUS ULTRA

"The top-management function is singularly difficult to organise. Every one of the tasks is a recurrent task . . . They require a diversity of capabilities, and, above all, of temperaments."

— P F. Drucker, Management

"Marlborough as a military strategist and a tactician, as a war statesman and war diplomatist, stands second to no Englishman in history."

— G M Trevelyan, History of England

The Management of Size

Large organisations have large management jobs: size breeds sheer complexity as well as political pressures and social interests, and tasks in vast variety. More people are needed to help perform all the work, which in turn further complicates life. The big edifice has to carry what sailors would call 'top hamper'.

That little organisational problem solved, companies must earn their bread and butter. Most then meet more difficulties: if expanding, how do we manage a new and strange business? If at optimum size, how maintain vigour? If failing, what is the real reason? If necessarily static, how make the pursuit of excellence the substitute for growth? These problems may be extraordinarily intractable. Then the chief executive with imagination and ingenuity and inventiveness is the saviour. Often such traits mix ill with adminstrative and executive capacity, when resort is made to joint appointments, presidential assistants, committees or staff departments. These are always costly and never simple. Sometimes, but rarely, the leader has all the gifts. He can inspire his organisation, invent a marvellous plan, soothe governments and difficult colleagues — while simultaneously most competently setting the action, looking after his people and executing his designs. Examples are scarce but striking.

79

War with Louis XIV

England has always enjoyed its wars with France. The Duke of Wellington was echoing popular feeling when he claimed that, "We always have been, we are, and I hope that we always shall be detested in France." It was so in 1711.

The scene is north west Europe. The Britain of Queen Anne and its allies — the Dutch Republic, the Holy Roman Empire and Austria — have been in a war with the France of the 'Sun King' for nine years, called the War of the Spanish Succession. Though ambitious for his country, Louis XIV was easy-going, and an attentive ruler. "His pleasures — and they were many — never interfered with his state business, and he commanded his son to keep love affairs distinct from matters of government."[1] War started in 1702 and each campaigning season had seen manoeuvres, sieges and battles. These seasons were short as Europe was still in the 'Little Ice Age' with bitter winters, the River Thames iced over and cattle frozen to death in the fields.

The Allies' Captain-General was John Churchill, Duke of Marlborough, Sir Winston Churchill's ancestor. He was happily married to Sarah, a politically well connected and domineering woman. Churchill himself was finely featured and most handsome, and in his youth well favoured by several ladies at court. For much of the war he had been a leading member of a clique, a close-knit 'top management' group, ". . . the smallest and most efficient executive which has ever ruled England. Sarah managed the Queen, Marlborough managed the war, and Godolphin [their friend] managed the Parliament."[2] (This power group exemplifies one of Churchill's less well-known dicta: "It is in the nature of executive power to draw itself into the smallest possible compass.")

What sort of man was in charge of this war? Aged fifty-two on appointment, Marlborough still had limited experience and there were better qualified generals, but by 1711 his prowess in fighting and diplomacy ranked him the universally accepted 'supremo' in Europe. He knew his military technology, his troops' abilities, what his allies could do, what they would balk at. Though also venal and cunning, a professional soldier thus describes him:

> "Though his courage was of the highest, his imagination vivid, and his common sense profound, his master characteristic was self-control. Nothing unbalanced him, whether it was the stupidity of his allies, the duplicity of the

politicians, or the ability of his enemies . . . He possessed
the rare virtue of seeing the war as a whole, and of being
able to relate sea power with land power and strategy with
politics . . . A master of strategems, he consistently mystified his enemy; a master of details, his men were never
left in want. In the planning of a campaign he took infinite
pains, and in its execution infinite trouble . . ."[3]

A military historian is equally laudatory:

"Marlborough's talents had no flaw. As a strategist he saw
clearly and simply the great issues . . . As an organiser, he
made a nonsensical military system work. His care for his
troops . . . led to his nickname of 'Corporal John'. On the
battlefield his grasp of confused tactical situations was
uncannily clear and accurate . . . To all these qualities
he added unflexing will and resolution, and unflagging
energy . . ."[4]

Many generals have shared 'Corporal John's' capacity for organisation, and much appreciated it was by their men who liked being
well supplied and appropriately informed. (Life at the bottom of
the military dung-heap otherwise seems to consist of stupid orders
raining down on one from unreasonable men. The military consciously attempt to work at this, at its simplest as shown in the
admonition to officers: first feed your horses, then your men,
then yourself.)

Military talents of all were now to be tested. All Louis's generals
were competent and Marlborough's immediate opponent in the
spring of 1711 was typical. Marshal Villars was skilled and experienced. Though hot tempered and arrogant, he was no fool and
his army knew its business. These soldiers were working with
intractable materials which tried their management skills — and no
doubt their patience — to the utmost: the organisation and the
techniques worked against, not for them. The main weapon was
the 'flintlock' musket which only fired two or three rounds per
minute. Each man was only issued with twenty-four rounds and
the barrel life was about thirty.[5] Misfires were frequent; most
muskets after a battle would be found to be double-charged
because misfiring could not be heard! Marlborough had no official
control over funds and stores. He could influence artillery and
engineer services but only because by coincidence he was at the

time Master General of the Ordnance. (So much for those who think authority and responsibility must be coincident!) His total HQ staff numbered about forty, including a Surgeon General, ADC's and runners.[4] The Duke chose these aides with great care: they were required to sense a situation and report it accurately. It was their information which gave him control of his battle. Marlborough believed results came from fighting rather than fencing; manoeuvring could force offensive action but could also, by itself, sometimes secure an objective. In all this, casualties were inevitable. They were also unenviable: treatment in what passed for field hospitals was almost "a combination of magic and carpentry."[6]

Although Marlborough was Britain's Captain-General, the deputy one of Holland and an official of Prussia and Austria, his power was limited:

> "... although the highest title and general deference was accorded to the English general his authority could only assert itself at every stage by infinite patience and persuasiveness. He was never in a position to give indisputable orders as Napoleon was to do. He had to procure assent for almost every act from diverse and often divergent interests, and to establish his ascendancy by subtle and ever varied methods."[2]

"Marbrouk s'en va t'en Guerre!"

The whole struggle had begun in 1702 and each year for a decade continental people had a dominant cry: "Marlborough goes to war!" His political, military and diplomatic problems were immense and his role burdensome: he was "... carrying a heavier load of responsibility than any British soldier has carried before or since."[4] He was commanding German, Dutch and English troops, separated by language and scattered by geography. The Dutch were menaced by a powerful France keen on aggrandisement on their very borders and Austria seemed at the mercy of enemies all round it. His powers were heavily circumscribed, his political support erratic, the logic of his army organisation exiguous.

Undeterred by any of these difficulties, he quickly brought his allies into an effective group (the Grand Alliance) helped by Louis's thinking — for a time — that his was a court appointment.

Fig. III. 1   Theatre of War 1702 — 1713

In that first year a decisive battle was possible but was baulked at by the cautious Dutch (perhaps nervous because they had most to lose from a defeat on their threshold) and Marlborough had to content himself with capturing the eastern Meuse fortresses as far as Liège *(Fig. III. 1)*, a powerful preliminary to an invasion of northern France. A grateful Queen and country responded with a dukedom.

Anglo-Dutch argument next year inhibited capitalising on these gains and the opportunist French with their ally, the Elector of Bavaria, were permitted to win control of South Germany and the Upper Rhine. Was this a threat or an opportunity? The French sent an army to reinforce the Elector. Wearied of Dutch caution, Marlborough persuaded them early in 1704 to guard Holland while he campaigned with the rest of the army, just how and where he planned in the greatest secrecy. He aimed to present to the French a screen of alternative objectives while bodily marching right across their front. Meticulous preparation included the creation of a chain of depots across Europe; then the Duke marched with 40,000 men towards the Rhine.

The French hung in suspense. Was the Moselle valley, as Marlborough had already proclaimed, the target? They made ready. At Coblenz he kept on southward. The Upper Rhine? It looked likely — or were the bridging preparations a feint? Below Heidelberg the long columns of redcoats turned abruptly south east. Their progress to the valley of the Danube was wholly smooth and totally uninterrupted, when they arrived, due to perfect administration after a 250 mile march, entirely ready to fight — an astonishing feat by the standards of the time. Now they could aid Austria and threaten Bavaria. The French Marshal Tallard quickly responded and linked his army with the Elector's but Marlborough with Prince Eugene of Savoy, with whom he was to have, despite their equal rank, a lasting and productive partnership, risked much in the Battle of Blenheim to destroy it, inflicting 39,000 casualties to 13,000 of their own, thus restoring in one day's work the whole southerly position of the Grand Alliance. That evening a tired general pencilled this celebrated note to Sarah: "I have no time to say more but to beg you will give my duty to the Queen and let her know her army has had a glorious victory. Monsieur Tallard and two other generals are in my coach and I am following the rest . . ."

Never one to miss an opportunity for exploiting success, the Duke completed the settlement with Bavaria and then returned, by now in October, to secure for future use invasion routes into France: the capture of Landau guarding Alsace, and of Trier and Trarbach controlling the Moselle valley, did just that and rounded off the most dramatic campaign in British military history. "All Europe," says his descendent, "was hushed before these prodigious events." [2]

Marlborough's strategy for 1705 — an invasion via the Moselle to sidestep the French fortress zone (Lille to Namur, *see Fig. III. I)* — would probably have ended the war but after the Allies' procrastination it was still-born. He was forced towards a lesser objective — penetrating into the Flanders defences. Strong fortifications seventy miles long, the Lines of Brabant *(Fig. III. I)*, were cunningly forced with tiny loss. Louis, believing now that no defence could hold such an opponent, next year ordered action. Though with only equality in numbers, Marlborough

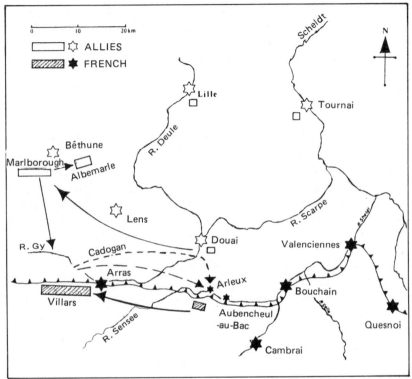

Fig. III. 2 The Arleux Fort Strategem

in his finest battle first pinned the French left before sweeping their right wing, then their army, right off the field of Ramillies and far away; in a remorseless pursuit the whole of Belgium and much of the fortress barrier fell to the Allies.

1707 saw Marlborough on the defensive in Flanders to let Eugene attack the French Riviera. (Not that the Duke was ordinarily defensive; as Sarah wrote, " . . . this day my lord came home from the wars and pleasured me twice in his top boots.") The following year his army leaped with enthusiasm into the encounter battle of Oudenarde; that won, the ten week seige of the "impregnable" fortress of Lille — a titanic operation of war — and the capture of Bruges, Ghent and Brussels, completed an heroic campaign. As Eugene, himself as experienced as any soldier in Europe, said: "He who has not seen this has seen nothing."

There was more heroism to follow. Tournai *(Fig. III. 2)* was taken in 1709 and, in a capricious surge of rage, both govern-

ments and armies sought close action. They found it at Mal-
plaquet and paid for it with 35,000 casualties. It was Marlborough's least inspiring battle. As if in reaction 1710 saw no
great encounters; simple slaughter was to make way for something
more subtle.

The Enticement of Marshal Villars

It was now 1711. Having captured Gibraltar and Minorca the
British navy was busy in the Mediterranean. The Allied army in
Flanders held most of the border fortresses; only a few protected
France so Villars had spent the winter fortifying a line from the
Channel to the Ardennes. Louis was playing for time; he knew
that the little executive had fallen apart, that Marlborough's
parliamentary support was eroded and that his political enemies
needed small excuse — like lack of results, much less a defeat — to
procure his head on a charger. (Like all managers he depended on
support; perhaps he had been too busy to work at it.)

Now Villars with 120,000 men manned his fortified line,
extravagantly named *Ne Plus Ultra*, meaning *Nothing further
is possible*. The line stretched from Montreuil on the coast,
through a succession of strong points, often along swampy rivers,
to Namur; beyond lay the hills and forests of the Ardennes,
very difficult to traverse for an 18th century army. Infantry,
horse-drawn guns and a long train of supply wagons, using rough
tracks, made a column great in length and small in speed. (Marlborough's army and train would have formed a column around
seventy miles long in marching order, and moved at about two
miles per hour.) Beyond the Ardennes the French frontier was
protected by the Rhine and the Vosges Mountains. The British
navy being elsewhere, Villars' flanks could not be turned.

With 90,000 men Marlborough confronted Villars. With
the season half gone he had to show results from this expensive
campaign; he had to restore his political base. He also wanted to
win the war. Heavy casualties, even in a victory, would have
undermined him. Meantime Villars was boasting his fortifications
were impregnable. Time passed; the famous Duke was jeered.
Quite unmoved, he took no precipitate nor very obvious action.
His attention was confined by his communications. The rivers,
much better than the tracks for moving stores and heavy equipment, could well supply him near the centre of the Lines. An
attack on their flanks was not feasible. His room for manoeuvre

was extraordinarily cramped. What to do? Marlborough now behaved like the archetypal entrepreneur: he devised a subtle plan and he himself set out to execute it in the way he wanted — one man setting the objective and making the decisions.

The approachable section of the Lines was from Arras to Valenciennes *(Fig. III. 2)*. Here nature's rivers, streams and swamps supplemented human ingenuity. There were two causeways through the swamps and leading into the Lines but these were guarded by forts, one at Arleux and one at Aubencheul-au-Bac. They could be stormed but that would have signalled Marlborough's intent; while opening up the approach to the Lines, Villars would have time to concentrate on his enemy. To use a causeway a fort had first, somehow, to be removed. If the Allies demolished it, their blow was 'telegraphed' and Villars would rebuild it. The ideal was for the French to demolish their own fort! To this remarkable task Marlborough now bent his ingenuity.

Leaving a garrison at Douai and detachments unobtrusively scattered around Lille and Tournai, he moved his army west to near Béthune, while detaching a small force to make a sudden assault on Arleux. This it did. He proceeded ostentatiously to strengthen his capture's fortifications. Villars at once responded by moving much of his army west, parallel to Marlborough's while the remainder attacked Douai, now seemingly and invitingly exposed. He was repulsed only with apparent difficulty. Marlborough being still forty miles away, further bait beckoned the French. An encouraged Villars laid siege to Arleux. Eschewing the use of the nearby Douai garrison, Marlborough instead despatched his right hand, Cadogan, with a modest force to its relief, with secret orders to hasten slowly. While Cadogan was still on his way from Béthune, Arleux fell.

Villars reviewed matters. Previously Arleux had seemed a well-guarded approach to his Lines but also an avenue through which he could attack the enemy. After Marlborough's seizure it appeared to be a dagger pointing into his own defences which Marlborough very obviously valued. Very well, he would frustrate him. He had the fort demolished.

A Free Passage

The Frenchman now confronted the Allies at Béthune with his own army in the fortifications west of Arras but his Arleux detachment remained where it was — for the moment. It seemed quite natural for Marlborough, who appeared publicly very irritated by his loss of Arleux (as reported to Villars by the ubiquitous French spies) to leave much of his army opposite Arras but have a moderate force east of Béthune under his lieutenant, Lord Albemarle, to cover Douai and his communications. After all, every army must guard its supply lines. It passed unnoticed that, mixed up in and shielded by this movement, much of the army's baggage and heavy artillery were moved back east.

Marlborough now thrust forward to confront Villars who, sure that no covert moves threatened, at once called in all his troops to oppose him. The two armies glowered at each other across the River Gy. Marlborough ostentatiously inspected the Lines facing him. Timber to fill in ditches was cut. On August 4th, with his staff, he rode forward in full view of the enemy, announced where his troops would assault and where his batteries would be mounted. His staff grew increasingly worried. A frontal attack on a well prepared position seemed determined, with fearsome casualties a certainty. Ten years of toil and worry appeared at last to have distorted the great man's judgement. The rest of the army was resolute but equally concerned.

It failed to notice that the field artillery had unobtrusively moved off east during the day. With but a small escort General Cadogan slipped unobserved out of camp and galloped away in the direction of Douai. That evening, also unobserved by all, the detachments in Béthune, Lille and Tournai moved to join forces with the Douai garrison — a combined strength of twenty-three battalions of infantry and seventeen squadrons of cavalry — all now within a comfortable march of Arleux.

Meanwhile at Arras, as darkness shrouded the scene, the last thing that Marshal Villars saw was what looked like Marlborough's massed forces opposite him, preparing as he knew for their advance onto his killing ground in the morning. On this he rested content.

As soon as it was dark word was passed down the ranks. The troops formed up, excitement growing. Officers were mounted and ready. Within half-an-hour the whole army was silently marching east. A very severe pace was set. Throughout the night only short halts were allowed. As dawn came up they were excited to see their artillery alongside them, moving east too and converging on their line of march. At 3 a.m. an eager messenger galloped up to the head of the column, where Marlborough rode in the van with fifty squadrons: General Cadogan with the Douai forces had moved stealthily forward during the night, past the razed Arleux fort, over the causeway and through the totally deserted French fortified lines.

Marlborough now sent his staff officers down the column, to inform every man in the army what was happening and the need to move fast: "My Lord Duke wishes the infantry to step out." The troops responded with all their strength. Thousands fell out of the ranks or collapsed; several hundred died from exhaustion. But they were ahead of the French — marching parallel but behind — even though their enemy had ten fewer miles to traverse and on better tracks. Precious hours had been lost to Villars by

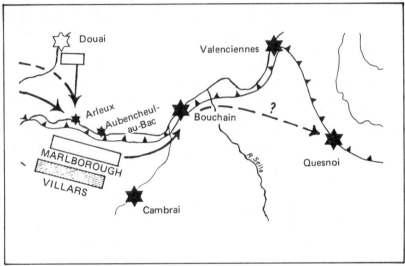

Fig. III. 3 France Confronted

Marlborough's camouflage.

The Duke, as usual placing himself at the decisive point, now rode ahead with his cavalry to reinforce Cadogan's bridgehead. The army followed. Stragglers were brought in. By the afternoon of the 5th, and after marching forty miles in eighteen hours, the entire army was drawn up in a defensive position, having forced the Lines of Ne Plus Ultra without an enemy shot being fired *(Fig. III. 3)*. Villars, humiliated and furious, dashed up, just escaping capture in the process. His army plodded after.

His opponent was now dominant. Marlborough's plan had been complex but wholly controllable and everything it needed had been thought out beforehand. By its perfect security — the Duke had explained it only to those who needed to know, himself and a few more — he had persuaded the French to accept the noose he proffered with which to hang themselves: those most in need of the Arleux fort would demolish it. (Only Hannibal's playing with Minucius — Chapter II — approaches this subtlety.) All the initiative was now Marlborough's.

He was pressed by his allies and his staff, though still outnumbered, to follow up his coup by assaulting Villars in a decisive battle. He resisted. His objective was the penetration of the Lines and the fortress barrier so that France would lie exposed with only Villar's army in the way. It could then be brought to battle in favourable conditions. In this he showed firmness and also consistency. The military principle, 'maintenance of the objective', reminds generals — unfortunately not always successfully — to eschew distractions. Overpowering France was the main aim and attacking Villars without better circumstances constituted deviation. More practically, he and his army were tired; after recovering their energy, flourishing a second example of military virtuosity would earn more political capital at home than a simple battle.

So Marlborough turned east and assailed the fortress of Bouchain, while covering the siege with part of his force to fend off Villars.

> "Like the bull-fighter who brings his adversary to a confused halt at his feet, he scornfully turned his back on Villars' superior army and set out to cap his marvellous feat of forcing the lines of Non Plus Ultra without the loss of a man to enemy action, by undertaking the siege of one of the most impregnable fortresses remaining to the French, daring Villars to do his worst."[7]

The French might have moved to protect Bouchain but would thereby uncover Arras: as in 1704 the Duke was threatening alternative targets, always a powerful tactic. Loss of Bouchain seemed the lesser evil. After a siege most ingeniously conducted by Marlborough in person, this stronghold was made to surrender and Villars to be further humiliated.

The Duke was now well placed to repeat the treatment on Quesnoi, which would have torn open the whole fortress line: nothing could then have saved France from catastrophe.

Nothing, except English politics. The Cabinet opened peace

negotiations with France on menial terms and tried to neutralise Marlborough's opposition by charging him with peculation. The accusation failed so instead they sacked him. The campaign ran out with the British army's having to desert its allies, who could wind up the war as best they could on their own. It was an abrupt and bitter ending to a feat of arms. One prefers to dwell only on what went before.

As in its first queen's reign, so now in its second, Britain's influence and power had surged to new levels. It had needed a Captain-General as the 'chief executive' of its European alliance with all the gifts, able to animate his cumbrous organisation, inspire his men, cajole hesitant partners, design a prodigious plan, execute it flawlessly — and at the same time most ably to look after 'pay and rations'. Lucky Queen Anne! Again Marlborough's descendant, himself a man of high talent, concisely sums up for us:

> "The whole operation was acclaimed at the time, and has since been held to be, an unsurpassed masterpiece of the military art."[8]

*   *   *   *

The Question of Optimum Size

Queen Anne really had no management problem. The military organisation on the continent, made up of British, Dutch and other forces, was big but, by dividing it (for most of the time) between Eugene and Marlborough, it was made manageable. The Queen, of course, was also lucky: her Captain-General possessed quite exceptional talent. What if he had not? Is size manageable only by genius? The difficulty can be eased, if not fundamentally circumvented, by sub-division — cutting up the whole into more or less self-contained units. (But if they are really self-sufficient, maybe they should not be within the same company?) The military use an additional technique: increase the top person's capacity by reducing her or his distractions. Devices like the chief of staff concept, a fruitful staff/line relationship, and standardised but flexible unit organisation, are aids we shall meet later. The business world mostly eschews such help while simultaneously over-loading top management.

We can start by challenging the inevitability of size. Companies grow because with better products they can increase market share or because with 'surplus' profit burning a hole in their pockets they want to grow. Why? One answer is 'diversification'. Why? 'To spread risks.' But the shareholders can do that for themselves. A pat phrase is, 'if you don't grow you stagnate'. No evidence is adduced for this; anyway, the Greeks were happy pursuing excellence rather than size, and they did all right. The unspoken motive may be management's *personal* ambitions: size means power, prestige, travel, publicity ... Whether the company's and the individuals' interests really coincide may well be totally ignored.

Tax policy can reinforce managers' instincts. If income from capital gains is less taxed than from dividends, reinvestment of surplus funds instead of distributing them to their owners will benefit the latter — if the investment is profitable. Too often expansion is not. Within one's business it may not be feasible; organic growth or inventing new products is lengthy and risky. The obvious alternative is, take over someone else. If he is already competent, this is labelled 'buying good management'; if he is not, it is called 'synergy'. But the acquirer is still at risk. By definition he does not know the new business and 'buying management' may not be a sufficient substitute; after all, how does he judge its quality?

My company, then deeply experienced in sugar refining, bought a starch company; the process technologies are very similar. We made our man its General Manager; he and I were trained production men and we thought the starch factory's performance terrible. Why? We thought it was due to lack of effort and application by its management but after eighteen months of trial and error, we discovered (with an outsider's advice) that it was not. It was plain technical incompetence. The solution? Bring in a starch production man. The point is, we could not diagnose the problem in a not unfamiliar area; equally we could not judge the quality of the saviour imported from outside but we solved that by getting private advice from a friendly retired expert — a totally informal arrangement available by accident.

This basic ignorance apart, the buyer of a company typically pays a thirty or forty percent premium for it; with the risks and uncertainties, can he really maintain that in his case, synergy — the only source of his recompense — is worth that much? In short, growth is risk.

It has been well said (I think by Peter Drucker) that growth is the process of becoming one's *optimum* size. (He has certainly said: "Absolute size by itself is no indicator of success and achievement, let alone of managerial competence. Being the right size is."[9]) No doubt this varies, depending on the technology, economies of scale, geographical spread and labour intensity, and little generalisation is safe. Except on the last one: a unit of five hundred to eight hundred people is a desirable maximum. An army battalion follows this guide; its Commanding Officer is thought not to be able to know personally and keep in touch with a greater number. Industry's accountants can argue strongly for breaching this rule; the saving in overhead by merging two factories into one is clear, quantifiable and substantial. Being computed in precise numbers, the move has a spurious attraction. The accountant typically ignores the losses. Poorer labour relations may reduce quality, productivity and the rate of innovation; one avoidable strike may offset all the savings; absenteeism and labour turnover may increase; the big unit's bureaucracy may reduce flexibility and customer service. None of these can be accurately predicted before the event — and can be discounted.

It is not the accountant's fault. If he were not precise he would not be a good one and equipped to monitor precious cash flows — the company's life-blood. Top management must confine him to calculating and measuring, and itself use his figures — as but one of its guides; otherwise he will wholly fulfil the definition of an accountant as "the man who goes on to the battlefield after the battle is over to count the dead and bayonet the wounded". [10]

*　　　*　　　*　　　*

References

1 Ed. W N Weech, History of the World.

2 Sir Winston Churchill, History of the English Speaking
   Peoples.

3 Major General J F C Fuller, Decisive Battles of the Western
   World.

4 C Barnett, Britain and her Army.

5 A Kemp, Weapons and Equipment of the Marlborough Wars.

6 R E Scouller, quoted by D Chandler, Marlborough as Military
   Commander.

7 D Chandler, Ibid.

8 Sir Winston Churchill, Marlborough — His Life and Times.

9 Peter F Drucker, Management.

10 Right Honourable David Mellor, quoted by the Financial
    Times.

Some Contemporary Events

1667	Beginning of French expansion under Louis XIV.
1683	Turks lay seige to Vienna.
1684	La Salle explores the Mississippi valley.
1693	Gold discovered in Brazil.
1700—20	Great Northern War, in which Sweden fights Russia, Poland and others.
1703	Peter the Great founds St Petersburg.
1709	Charles XII's invasion of Russia defeated at the Battle of Poltava.
1713	End of the War of the Spanish Succession.
1728	Bering explores Alaska.

CHAPTER IV

STRATEGIC MANAGEMENT: THE TRAFALGAR CAMPAIGN

*"By bearing plump down and passing through his line,
and raking him as you do so, then pelting him close on
his lee side, you strike a panic into him that he cannot
easily recover."*

— Admiral Charles Ekins *

A Company's Needs

Imagine a British-based international company locked in combat
with a continental giant, which not only has half that market but
wants the other half and the British one as well. The continental
finds exporting difficult but, once established in an area, its
resources, skill and speed make it formidable. The British finds an
initial export penetration easy but lacks the power to follow up.
It controls international trading through an array of dispersed
operating units, each with great delegated authority but of necessity fed erratically with information on what their associates,
their fellow units and their competitor are all doing. The limited
British resources are spread thinly but can be readily switched to
counter competitive moves. Companies in every major country are
involved, as associates or joint venture partners of one side or the
other. At issue is domination of the whole western world's market.

What are the British firm's 'critical areas' — those managerial
factors essential for success? First, obviously, inspired strategic
direction from 'Head Office' to allocate resources shrewdly
when its guides may only be surmise and deduction from scraps of
information. Second, an immaculate intelligence-gathering and
-dissemination service. Third, a gift for interpreting sparse intelligence and making locally sound decisions on life-and-death issues.

* *Quoted by P Padfield, Guns at Sea.*

Fourth, easy co-operation between operating units to share resources optimally. Fifth, the resilience to sustain harsh working conditions at a unique intensity for *decades* on end.

One might think this a list individually quite sufficiently formidable: if *all* aspects are critically important, might one term that company's life as inevitably brief? An example may suggest an answer.

Naval Warfare in Napoleonic Times

The French Revolution erupted in 1789. The radical threats to the social order it posed and the bloody excesses it encouraged generated a virtual crusade; like those against the Moslems 700 years earlier the response was not wholly altruistic — Austria and Prussia hoped to partition France, and Britain could see commercial advantage. None were to find these conquests easy. A revolutionary fervour reacted with the French spirit to recruit a large and volatile army despite an empty public purse, "a national army animated by a national spirit. Under leaders who knew how to exploit its spirit, it could display wonderful *élan*, and under those who could not, it was subject to panics and mutinies."[1] It defeated an invasion of France in 1792 and its reposte occupied Belgium. This threat to the Low Countries brought England into the war. In 1796 a French army led by a 27-year-old artillery captain from Corsica conquered northern Italy. Europe perceived a new power in the land.

Napoleon's career started fairly conventionally: he worked hard, entered a military college at 15 but was commissioned in half the usual time. He studied the great captains — Alexander, Hannibal, Caesar; he trained his memory and sharpened his analytical powers. Curiously, he spent two of the first four years of his service on leave or feigning illness, but thereafter promotion was rapid: Table I sketches the succeeding story, a depressing one for peace-lovers.

In 1798 Napoleon was at Dunkirk, thinking about England; he ordered invasion craft built. While local naval supremacy was awaited and meanwhile to weaken the island's eastern trade, he invaded Egypt with 35,000 troops escorted by thirteen battleships; while the army won the battle of the Pyramids, the fleet moored very close inshore, near Alexandria. Pounced on by a pursuing British squadron, all but two of the ships were sunk or taken after being heavily bombarded on both sides by envelop-

Table I: CHRONOLOGY OF THE NAPOLEONIC WARS

YEAR	MAIN EVENTS	LAND BATTLES	SEA BATTLES
1791	Napoleon a lieutenant		
1792	Napoleon a colonel; war against Austria	Valmy	
1793	War with Britain and Holland	Toulon seige	
1794	Napoleon i/c Artillery in Italy	Fleurus	1st June
1795	Napoleon a General	Loano	
1796	Italian campaign	Arcola	
1797	Napoleon Army Commander	Mantua	Cape St Vincent
1798	Invasion of Egypt	Pyramids	Nile
1799	Napoleon seizes power	Acre seige	
1800	War on Austria	Marengo	
1801		Alexandria	Copenhagen
1802	Peace of Amiens		
1805	War on Austria	Austerlitz	Trafalgar
1806	War on Prussia	Jena	
1807	War on Russia	Friedland	
1808	Spain invaded	Vimeiro	
1809	War on Austria	Wagram	
1812	Russia invaded; Britain fights America	Borodino	
1813	France invaded	Leipsig	
1815	'The Hundred Days'	Waterloo	

ing lines of ships. It was Admiral Horatio Nelson's neatest battle: his ships' seamanship had found just sufficient water to turn a tidy anchorage into a death-trap.

These battleships were termed 'ships of the line', that is, strong enough to be part of the line of battle by having at least two gundecks and sixty guns; the famous "Victory" had three decks and one hundred guns. They were to be distinguished from cruisers and frigates; too fragile for prolonged combat, these were used for patrolling, scouting, rescue-work and (most important) message-carrying. The battle of the Nile shows the fundamentals for action: seamanship and gunnery were decisive between basic-ally similar ships. "A French ship captured was not merely an addition to the British fleet; she was often a pattern on which new British ships were at least partially modelled".[2] Ships' cannon were numerous, with smooth bores firing solid shot; crews num-bered 600 to 800. "Victory" displaced about 3500 tons.

The British Navy was skilled, practised and aggressive. Its morale was high despite the high proportion of pressed crews and the harsh discipline. The Churchillian summary of British naval tradition — "rum, sodomy and the lash" — was not wholly mis-leading. Confined to their ports, French crews were unpractised, which was disastrous for smart seamanship and deadly gunnery, and their undemanding situation — waiting till something turned up — sapped morale. But the British custom of attacking had its risks. If two lines of ships are sailing parallel the aggressor is to windward because he can decide when to close. The admiral's signal to bear down on the enemy line may not be readily seen and is anyway obeyed with varying agility and some ships sail faster than others, so the leaders receive the defenders' full broad-sides to which they, being head on, cannot reply. (The "Victory" at Trafalgar, intentionally placed by Nelson in this situation, took fifteen minutes of gunfire before it could respond.) But of course the attacker has the moral advantage.

Sailing ships incur an obscure snag. If to windward, they heel towards the enemy lined up alongside, exposing their decks to grape-shot while their own lower gun ports may be under water and therefore shuttered. For this reason and to hinder any escape, the British tried to break through a French line and engage it from leeward. Ships were seldom sunk by cannon fire; they surrendered because they lacked guns or rigging and became unworkable. Casualties were often very severe before this was deemed the case.

Some ships at the Nile took 25% casualties. One Frenchman at Trafalgar, the "Redoubtable", fought three British with enormous zeal and suffered 522 casualties — 80% of her entire crew. Cannonballs splintered the woodwork, which caused hideous wounds; what passed for surgery extended the agony.

Most action was side by side. Gun range was up to 3000 yards (compared with 30,000 yards in World War II) but accuracy was poor. Best was to 'rake' the enemy. Sailing across his bow or stern every gun in your broadside could fire in turn and the shot might carry the whole length of the target. The result could be frightful; a Frenchman at Trafalgar took 40 casualties — 6% of the whole crew — from *one* raking cannonball. A variant was the tactic of 'crossing the T': steering your line across the head of the enemy's to fire in turn at his leading ships — an application of the principle of concentration. *(Fig. IV. 1)*. This manoeuvre was invariably effective and rarely accomplished. The Japanese managed it in 1905 and sank an entire Russian squadron. Jellicoe did it at Jutland in 1916 but the Germans turned away before he could reap his reward.

Sail propulsion severely constrained manoeuvring. A ship of the line could not sail closer than about 68° to the wind. Tacking and 'beating against the wind' were tiresome and slow. With a wind behind, a battleship could sail about 280 miles per day; the "Victory" could make about ten knots. The vagaries of the wind, the complexity of rigging, 'leeway' or drifting downwind in high-sided ships, tides and currents, all confounded mechanical movement.

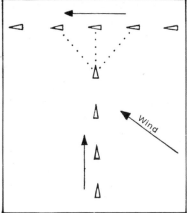

Fig.IV. 1 'Crossing the T'

The enemy's threats, gunsmoke, obscure flag signals, crew casualties, all compounded the problems, making confusion likely and control erratic.

Naval strategy followed general military principles, which was why Napoleon was good at it, but naval tactics, which he opted to ignore, were in part unique. On land concealing or defensible terrain and flanking moves assist concentration against a portion of the enemy. None apply at sea. Usually fleets are visible, the sea is homogeneous and 'rolling up a flank' impossible, as ships cannot move neatly sideways. Instead, 'doubling up' was favoured, massing two against one as at the Nile. Superior gunnery could be decisive: the British rate of fire was around 50% higher. They also had more three-deckers; one such was thought the equal of two others because, being higher, they could rake the vulnerable enemy decks and because they could always have at least two batteries in action regardless of their heeling over.

The Strategic Background

Evading British warships, Napoleon returned in 1799 from Egypt to France, then threatened by a coalition of Britain, Austria and Russia, and made himself a dictator. He moved fast. The battles of Marengo and Hohenlinden soon punctured the alliance and Napoleon again felt free to ponder the matter of Britain. Political manoeuvring intervened with a fourteen months' truce. In 1803 war was resumed. Immediately, Admiral Cornwallis took station with 20 ships (from now on this means 'ships of the line') outside the French naval base of Brest *(Fig. IV. 2)*. This was the key sea appointment. It not only watched the largest enemy fleet, it also guarded the Channel approaches. Cornwallis was soundly chosen for it — forthright, a leader rather than a driver, decisive in emergencies and always a man of action.

The whole of Europe became involved. Britain's role in this enormous struggle was based on her sea-power. Her population was around 15 million, compared with the French 25 million, but her navy was strong, though no more so than it needed to be. Its job was to stay close to the enemy, thus protecting the home islands, the colonies and her enormous merchant marine. It set up a close continental blockade, to hem in all the major enemy bases. Britain was playing for the highest stakes. Her invasion was possible — and would be instantly lethal. On the other hand a partial victory, a mere stand-off, would in the long run impoverish her, so the country had everything to play for. As was her habit, she tried to rely on (relatively cheap) sea-power, without more land forces than were called for by limited expeditions. She was to learn — and relearn in later wars — that there is no substitute for someone somewhere engaging the enemy's main land-power. (Not that sea-power was that cheap. By the end of the war 'defence' took 67% of total government expenditure, of which the Navy accounted for 20%.[3])

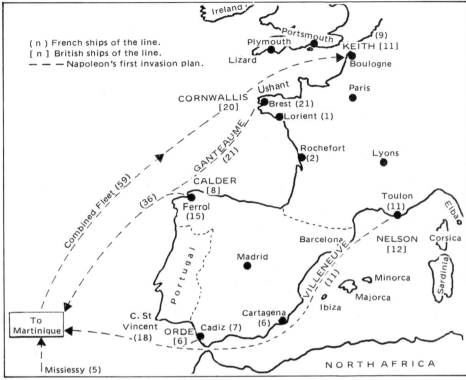

(n) French ships of the line.
[n] British ships of the line.
— — — Napoleon's first invasion plan.

Ireland

Portsmouth
Plymouth   (9)
                 KEITH [11]
Lizard   Boulogne

Ushant   Paris
CORNWALLIS
[20]   Brest (21)
          Lorient (1)

GANTEAUME
(21)   Rochefort   Lyons
          (2)

Combined Fleet (59)   CALDER
                       [8]   Toulon
          (36)   Ferrol   (11)   Elba
                 (15)
                       Barcelona   NELSON   Corsica
                                   [12]
          Portugal   Madrid   VILLENEUVE
                              (11)   Sardinia
                                   Minorca
                                   Majorca
          C. St   Ibiza
To   Vincent ORDE Cadiz (7) Cartagena
Martinique   [6]   (6)
          -(18)

Missiessy (5)   NORTH AFRICA

Fig. IV. 2 Warship Dispositions

Napoleon soon resumed his invasion designs, building transports at Boulogne and nearby ports. Napoleon's task was simple: "Let us be masters of the Strait for six hours and we shall be masters of the world". He had a large but dispersed fleet and in Spain a prospective ally; he had time and a strategy. Could he contrive the local naval supremacy for a short but critical period? *Fig. IV. 2* shows the ship deployment and the commanders. The British Admiralty's had been long thought out. The main fleet concentration was off Brest, commanding the Western Approaches to the British Isles, and it could normally ride out the winter gales, though very severe ones would blow it off station. The theory of the blockade was based on the fact that the prevailing SW wind that blew Cornwallis back to shelter in English ports would also pen the French in: the Brest channel is *west* of the harbour. A wind foul for the British was foul for the French.

Other detachments blockaded other ports. If any enemy

escaped, the guard was to fall back on Ushant (an island off Brittany) to protect the Channel. (The subtlety of the strategy is explored in *Appendix E.)* Cornwallis' orders nicely balanced guidance and discretion: when the Admiralty's instructions seemed inapplicable " . . . you must use your discretion and judgement for your guidance, giving us the earliest information of your proceedings". If the Brest squadron escaped, Cornwallis was to take post off the Lizard to cover Ireland and England. "While bodily present off Brest, Rochefort and Toulon, strategically the British squadrons lay in the Straits of Dover."[4] In effect the British used interior lines. With messages taking weeks in transmission thorough-going delegation was a pre-requisite for any effective action and it was managed admirably. The blockade plan was very sound but very demanding and "excited not only the admiration but the wonder of contemporaries."[4] The fleets' seamanship, fighting power and endurance under-wrote the strategy. They were essential to the close blockade system: "So severe was the wear and tear both to men and ships, that even the most strenuous exponents of the system considered that at least a fifth of the force should always be refitting, and in every case two admirals were employed to relieve one another."[5] Its value was summed up in Mahan's celebrated comment:

> "The world has never seen a more impressive demonstration of the influence of sea power upon its history. Those far distant, storm-beaten ships, upon which the Grand Army never looked, stood between it and the dominion of the world."[4]

The Play's Cast
On March 2, 1805 Napoleon ordered his admiral Ganteaume to sail from Brest, release the Ferrol ships and meet Admiral Missiessy already in Martinique; Admiral Villeneuve would join them from Toulon *(Fig. IV. 2)*. The combined fleet would sail to the Channel, defeat Cornwallis if intercepted and reach Boulogne in June, to escort the troops invading England. Detailed instructions covered delays and all obvious contingencies but everything hinged on unbroken sequence of successful evasions. The culmination of the moves thus initiated was a huge naval action eight months later off Cape Trafalgar, a rocky promontory 28 miles NW of Gibraltar. The excitement for observers of the chase

reflects, sadly rather feebly, the admirals' strain in conducting it. They were varyingly equipped to do so.

Though past his best and now preferring force to subtlety, Napoleon was still a giant. One of nature's dictators, he was also a born leader — decisive, understanding of his men, with prodigious energy and wide interests. He had a lightning eye for the tactical opportunity and an imagination for the strategic design. On land he had still no equal; at sea his general thinking was sound but biased by wishful thinking and contempt for his opponents; like Canute's courtiers he ignored the constraints of wind and tide. His most prominent admiral was Pierre de Villeneuve, now in command at Toulon. He was forty-two, a well born and therefore surprising survivor of the Revolution. Intelligent but lacking confidence, he had been a captain that evening near the Nile. It was a discouraging precedent.

The British admirals were very sound seamen, steeped in Admiralty strategy and, with one exception, able rather than brilliant. They were linked by their information system which was as good as the state of the art permitted. The fleets communicated fluently with each other and with the Admiralty; with its deductive powers supplemented by a spy system, in turn it fed them with intelligence and orders. When every scrap of news was precious and the theatre of war so vast, communication was critical. The navy was " . . . irradiated with an alert sympathy. . . by which admirals afloat seemed always to see into the mind of the Admiralty and the Admiralty to rest assured of what the admirals would do".[2] This still left them with burdensome responsibility; Nelson, as we shall see, became impaled on successive decision points and all must have felt the isolation of command. The loneliness of the far distant admiral was eased by having clear policies and decision rules; he knew his authority, the emphasis on mutual support, the contingency plans. All was explicit.

Nelson was then forty-seven and at the height of his powers. His had been the key role at the battles of Cape St. Vincent, Copenhagen and the Nile. His domestic life was erratic but he was a skilled naval officer and a courageous leader. Physically frail and a martyr to sea sickness, he could yet apply himself single-mindedly. For two years before Trafalgar he never set foot on land. Fuller thus sums him up:

"He was a bold and imaginative tactician, independent

> in outlook, ambitious, sensitive of his reputation, at times
> vainglorious and frequently violent in his dislikes . . . His
> pugnacity has seldom been equalled; nevertheless he was
> an indifferent strategist."[1]

His command style was participative. Before Trafalgar he met his
captains to explain his plan, and aroused more enthusiasm and
loyalty in weeks than his predecessor, the stern Admiral Collingwood, had in months.

One more actor deserves introduction. The First Lord of the
Admiralty (that is, the head of the Navy) had to resign at the
moment of crisis because public funds had been misused. In the
middle of a desperate war the British Navy was headless. No
successor had been groomed, nor had a conscious decision to
run the resulting risk been taken. Against Cabinet opposition
Pitt, the Prime Minister, asked an elderly veteran to take over.
Lord Barham, then aged eighty, agreed; he had been in his time
an excellent Controller of the Navy. It was to prove an inspired
appointment. He at once assumed operational control of all naval
forces. The play, as we know, had already started.

Atlantic Manoeuvres

In the same month as Ganteaume had received his orders from
Napoleon, Nelson had to take his twelve ships eastward to Sardinia
to reprovision. He had previously shown himself apparently
stationed to the westward off the Spanish coast and he left two
frigates to watch Toulon. On March 30 Villeneuve with an equal
fleet crept out, sailing south to avoid the British, as he thought.
Two days out a merchantman told him he was sailing into a trap
(a southerly track was taking him nearer Nelson.) He promptly
altered course, losing the shadowing frigates in the process. Four
days later they reached Nelson: when last seen they told him,
Villeneuve was heading south. Would he turn east or west? Nelson
thought the former — it had happened before — but resolved to
wait for better information. He set up a line of ships between
Sardinia and Africa to interrupt an easterly move and waited.

And waited with rising anxiety for twelve days. An Admiralty
message — the first guidance from London for five months —
informed him that an important and weakly escorted troop convoy of forty-five transports was soon to sail from England to the
Mediterranean, to co-operate with the Russians. On April 16 a

passing ship told him that Villeneuve had been seen off Spain sailing *west*. Two days later the convoy with two escorts sailed, quite ignorant of what lay ahead. It was leaving a confused London behind. The Admiralty was still leaderless; Napoleon had chosen his time well. It was to be five days before Barham took office.

It took Nelson three weeks against contrary winds to reach Gibraltar where he learned that Villeneuve had passed the Straits and extracted six allied ships from Cadiz, having driven Sir John Orde off his station there on April 9. This intelligence was energetically dispersed. A frigate captain, Lord Mark Kerr, had spotted the French battleships slipping through the Straits. He had instantly and on his own initiative hired a brig to warn Nelson and himself sailed to inform the Ushant, Ireland and Channel forces. Orde himself, following explicit blockade principles long established and clearly communicated, made to join up with the fleet off Brest — but left behind an elaborate system of scouts to keep track of the enemy; he also sent a shrewd report to the Admiralty, forecasting future enemy moves with considerable accuracy.

On April 25 Barham took office and immediately was confronted with the news: Villeneuve, with troops on board, was loose somewhere in the Atlantic; his destination was probably the West Indies but there were other possibilities *(see Fig. IV. 3)*. Missiessy was already there, threatening the British-owned sugar islands; the City of London was appalled to think a second fleet might be joining him. The Anglo-Russian offensive demanded protection but Nelson, *if* he was still there, should be able to guard the convoy. As the Channel was already protected, reinforcing the West Indies took the first priority and this was ordered. Barham hoped Nelson had followed Villeneuve but feared he might have gone east to cover Egypt. Five days later Barham heard that the Cadiz blockade had been lifted so his convoy was sailing into peril; if not beyond recall it would have to return. Orde certainly and Calder possibly were displaced from their stations and orders might well not reach them. To all these commands, orders and guidance had instantly to be given. A stream of lucid instruction, detailing all responses and contingencies, poured out of Whitehall to all commanders.

On May 9 Nelson, sniffing along Villeneuve's trail, was off Cape St. Vincent *(Fig. IV. 2)* and was informed that eighteen

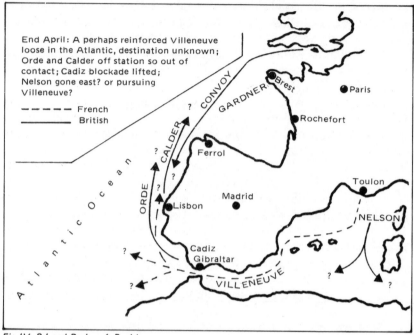

Fig.IV. 3 Lord Barham's Problem

Frenchmen had been seen heading in the direction of the West Indies and none appeared to be to the north. The aim now looked clearer; earlier Nelson had needed some assurance: "I cannot very properly run to the West Indies without something beyond mere surmise, and if I defer my departure Jamaica may be lost". Detaching a powerful three-decker to strengthen the convoy escort, he set sail to protect the islands. (One can note the priorities: the real objective was the army offensive; defeating Villeneuve was glamorous but defensive and not an end in itself.) To Napoleon Nelson had vanished. "In God's name! hurry my Brest squadron away, that it may have time to join Villeneuve." But it remained penned in by calms and by Lord Gardner, Cornwallis' alternate. (The Americans also alternated admirals, in their case to speed operations, in the war with Japan — *see Chapter VIII).*

On May 14 London received a letter from Lisbon written eleven days previously, saying (incorrectly) that Villeneuve had doubled back towards Europe. Admiral Collingwood with eleven freshly commissioned ships was despatched from Plymouth to rescue the precious convoy. With reinforcement from Gardner Collingwood could fight the Combined Fleet of French and Spanish ships. If they had actually gone to the West Indies he was to pursue them unless Nelson had preceded him.

This left only sixteen ships off Brest but nine were three-deckers and Barham told them and Collingwood to display their strength openly to Frenchmen on shore before the latter slipped secretly away. By the time that became known, reinforcements from home would arrive, so the risk was limited. It was also calculated. Closeted in his office, Barham was a severe delegator, who used his First Sea Lord (the senior naval, as opposed to government, official) as his chief of staff, treated cabinet meetings and attendance at court as inessentials and with extraordinary single-mindedness gave his time exclusively to the strategic dispositions of his fleets. "With the current affairs of the Navy he did not concern himself. The higher direction of the war was one man's uninterrupted work."[2]

More anxious waiting. While Nelson was searching the West Indies the Admiralty heard at the end of June that Villeneuve and Nelson were both there, so the convoy seemed safe (it had

Fig.IV. 4 Villeneuve's Threat

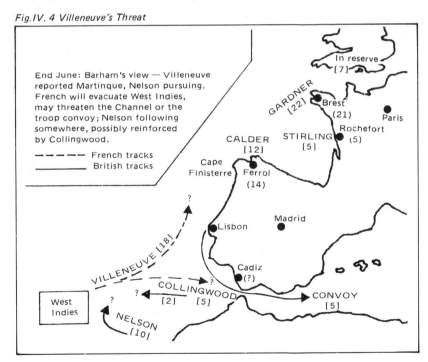

End June: Barham's view — Villeneuve reported Martinque, Nelson pursuing. French will evacuate West Indies, may threaten the Channel or the troop convoy; Nelson following somewhere, possibly reinforced by Collingwood.

––––––– French tracks
————— British tracks

actually taken refuge in Lisbon); the Combined Fleet was elsewhere; the sugar islands were getting safer. Barham thought
Villeneuve would flee from Nelson and return — but to where?
Fig. IV. 4 summarises the perceived strategic position. The return
of the prodigal sailor could threaten either the Channel or the Mediterranean offensive. Barham drew up a contingency plan — having
Calder and Gardner extend helping hands towards each other —
but it was still being drafted when fresh news arrived. Exaggerating
Nelson's strength, a nervous Villeneuve had left the Indies on
June 9, his tracker four days later. (Nelson had sent the brig
"Curieux" to inform the Admiralty of his movements, following
a northerly track in hopes of spotting the Frenchman.) Would he
and Ganteaume be able to combine? Napoleon too had laid
contingency plans but had not foreseen Villeneuve's fear of
Nelson. He was getting pessimistic about a Brest sortie. He hoped
diversions in the North Sea and elsewhere would disperse and dis-
tract the British.

On June 19 the "Curieux" sighted a fleet: it was steering
towards Cape Finisterre *(Fig. IV. 4)*. At its best speed the brig
reached Plymouth on July 7 and its captain London by 11 p.m.
next day, but the Admiralty staff feared to wake the First Lord.
Next morning, after a thus wasted night, an angry Barham dictated
his orders before dressing. By 9 a.m. messengers were galloping
to Portsmouth and Plymouth: Gardner was to raise the long-
established Rochefort blockade and send all its five ships to
reinforce Sir Robert Calder's ten off Ferrol; this fleet was to
cruise 100 miles west of Finisterre to intercept Villeneuve beyond
the immediate reach of his Ferrol allies. These orders were instantly executed. The stage was nicely set.

> "It is difficult to praise too highly the prompt and decisive
> step taken by Lord Barham, when so suddenly confronted
> with the dilemma of either raising the blockade of Roche-
> fort and Ferrol, or permitting Villeneuve to proceed
> unmolested . . . To be able to make so unhesitating a
> sacrifice of advantages long and rightly cherished, in order
> to strike at once one of two converging detachments of
> an enemy — shows generalship of a high order."[4]

Five days later a puzzled Napoleon heard this news: surely the
Admiralty "could not decide the movements of its squadrons

in 24 hours". They must have dispersed as he desired. On July 22
Calder was cruising with his fifteen ships as positioned by Barham.
They were in fog. It suddenly lifted — to reveal twenty Frenchmen! In a confused fight the British took two prizes but nightfall and fog parted the combatants. Neither renewed the battle
or maintained contact: " . . . less even than [Calder] could
[Villeneuve] rise to the height of risking a detachment in order
to secure the success of a great design".[4] (Calder's peers shared
this view: capturing only two ships when out-numbered three to
four was not the accepted standard of performance.) Villeneuve
moored in Ferrol, forming the very combination (of twenty-nine
French and Spanish ships) which Calder had been posted to
prevent. Indignant at colleagues' criticism the latter fell back on
Ushant, to help protect the Channel. Nelson joined him, to leave
his ships there and himself to sail to England, to which after a
two-year absence he was now summoned.

Cornwallis divides his Fleet

Napoleon now had twenty-one ships in Brest, twenty-nine in
Ferrol and five from Rochefort out commerce raiding. Cornwallis, back in command after sick leave, watched both ports,
knowing that if the wind was fair for one it was foul for the
other. On August 17 came news: the Ferrol force, twenty-nine
strong, was at sea! Cornwallis thereupon made the decision to
divide his fleet and to send Calder with eighteen ships towards
Ferrol: to win the war it was as necessary to press the Mediterranean offensive as it was to defend the Channel. Some have
criticised this dispersion of force as against the principle of concentration. As Cornwallis kept ten three-deckers with him the
effective odds at Brest were near equality. Nevertheless, some
risk was deliberately run in the interests of offensive action —
another principle of war.

Shortly thereafter, a neutral told Villeneuve that "twenty-five
British ships" were nearby. He promptly forgot his master's grand
design; he did not try to evade Calder and mass with Ganteaume
against Cornwallis. Concerned (not without reason) about ill-
found ships and a gale in the offing, he turned to Cadiz. As a
result the Combined Fleet there now numbered thirty-five ships;
outside, Collingwood and later Calder waited with twenty-six.
A second stage was set. The news brought immense relief to
London. At that moment a British convoy of twenty-nine

merchantmen from the East — valued at £15 million (equal to about five percent of the then national income!) — was plodding past a now confined Villeneuve. Its treasure apart, the convoy bore a passenger on his way from India to influence the history of Europe — and to becoming Duke of Wellington.

Thus Napoleon's concentration off Ushant remained remote. He seems not to have bemoaned his fate. By immediate decision the Grand Army broke camp and marched off from Boulogne to the Danube, to capture Ulm and 60,000 Austrians. It went on to other triumphs. The emperor's navy was equally, but less productively, occupied. Much of it watched Collingwood over the harbour wall of Cadiz and that was where Napoleon thought a change of command was needed. Admiral Rosily was despatched from Paris to take over. On September 14 Napoleon wrote orders for the Cadiz fleet to sail, link up with the Cartagena ships and support an attack on Naples. Next day Nelson, to popular cheers, sailed from Portsmouth aboard the "Victory" and reached Cadiz on the 28th to take command (for twenty-three days) of the thirty-three ships now massed there. On that same day both news of his arrival and Napoleon's orders reached Villeneuve, as did a rumour (not an official notification!) of a certain Admiral Rosily's commission. He decided it was time to depart.

The Battle of Trafalgar
Nelson's problem in his own eyes was more bringing the enemy to battle than keeping him penned in. He kept his fleet fifty miles WSW of Cadiz, to entice Villeneuve out, with a chain of scouts to keep watch *(Fig. IV. 5)*. There was thus a low risk of Villeneuve's escaping but a high probability of engaging him. Six of Nelson's ships were always provisioning at Gibraltar, leaving him with twenty-seven of which six were three-deckers, to the enemy's thirty-three, of which one was a four-decker and two three-deckers. Nelson envisaged Villeneuve's having a defensive posture and being in a long line of battle. His forecast was right; so was the Frenchman's prediction of British tactics! Nelson planned a quick attack, massing against part of that line after cutting it in two places with two lines of his own *(Fig. IV. 6)*, when one of them was to fend off the enemy van if it tried to beat back against the wind. Each line would be led by the three-deckers to mass the greatest firepower most quickly. The line ahead

formation would conceal his precise attack to the last moment: any section of the enemy was threatened. (Nevertheless, the tactics were risky: Nelson was deliberately having his 'T crossed', though to him, knowing his men and his ships, probably any dangers looked reasonable.) Nelson's captains were enthusiastic: though few had served long with him all soon adopted his attitude. Calder at this moment was recalled for a court-martial and a generous

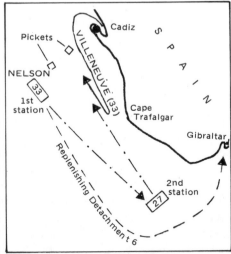

Fig.IV. 5 Manoeuvres off Cape Trafalgar

Nelson encouraged him to sail in his own three-decker, badly needed though it was for the planned battle. "The officers, grateful for his consideration to a fallen colleague, were flattered by Nelson's decision to discuss his battle plan with them. By the standards of the time, it was an extraordinary gesture of humility."[6]

On October 19 the inshore squadron made a signal: the Combined Fleet was putting to sea. To bar the way to the Mediterranean Nelson headed south-east *(Fig. IV. 5)*. By the 20th the whole enemy fleet was out, sailing for the Straits; on being confronted by the British Villeneuve turned north; on a very light wind Nelson followed. By 8 a.m. Villeneuve had marshalled his ships into a tolerable line of battle. Nelson formed his two columns, leading the northern one himself while Collingwood in the fast and powerful "Royal Sovereign" sailed parallel. With all sail set these two columns floated at two or three knots towards a wary enemy.

There was time for concern: would the wind last? Or the daylight? Did the swell portend a

Fig.IV. 6 The Attack Plan

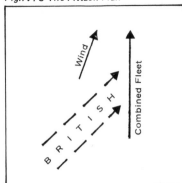

storm? Would the columns suffer as their T's were crossed? The leaders accepted the hostile cannonade as they approached, the two admirals in them ignoring the rule that commanders should be at the centre — to see and be seen — and made sure they were not overtaken.

As each ship reached the enemy line it typically forced a way through, raking one or both neighbours as it crossed their bow or stern, then pulled up on their lee to engage more closely. Four-and-a-half hours of continuous and violent fighting followed. Amid smoke clouds and the incessant thunder of the guns dismasted ships soon drifted downwind firing and being fired on, while fresh enemies floated out of the smoke to add to the storm. After two hours Villeneuve's flagship surrendered; a British marine officer described the prize: "The dead . . . lay along the middle of the decks in heaps, and the shot passing through these had frightfully mangled the bodies . . . More than 400 had been killed and wounded, of whom an extraordinary proportion had lost their heads".[1]

The Combined Fleet had been split by Nelson's columns and Villeneuve signalled his van to turn back; sheer dilatoriness and wind delayed them for a vital one-and-a-half hours while their comrades were gripped by equal numbers of British ships and by far superior gunnery. To Nelson, dying in the gloom of the "Victory's" Orlop Deck, the news of decisive triumph could be brought and, foreseeing a gale, he urged the fleet to anchor. By 5 p.m., of the huge Cadiz fleet eleven ships were fleeing back there, four were escaping seaward to be taken fourteen days later, one was on fire and shortly to explode, and seventeen were disabled. Darkness closed over a sea of widespread misery and confusion. The wind was rising and many ships floated only by pumping; 3000 wounded, many badly mutilated, awaited attention; prisoners had to be secured, rigging repaired, decks cleaned of blood, all by desperately tired men. Some ships, by Nelson's advice, anchored; others were towed seaward. Very close lay the shoals and rocks of Cape Trafalgar.

The wind became a gale. A sally next day by the Cadiz fugitives to rescue dismasted fellows in the bay, saved one but lost three of their own number. Thus, while *no* British ships were lost, the Allies after all their adventures had eight left, of which only two were fit to sail again. It was, as they said at the time, a famous victory. Apart from 94% ship losses, Allied crew casualties were

14,500 to 1650 British, 36% of the latter being taken by four ships — the two leaders and their followers.

While the British fleet mourned its leader, news of the battle reached the Admiralty and the man who had stage-managed it, Lord Barham, was (this time) instantly woken up by the Secretary. It was appropriate.

> "Barham . . . could face retirement with equanimity. He was in fact soon out of office, returning to an obscurity which long concealed his immense services to the country . . . He was . . . the brain behind every movement of the fleets, and to the conduct of the naval war he brought the experience of a lifetime, and a devotion to his profession which was not exceeded even by Nelson and Collingwood, who were his instruments."[7]

Nelson's body was prepared for its journey home; it was put in a cask of brandy and guarded by a sentry. It was not to be settled easily. Decomposition generated gas and raised the lid of the cask during the night, to the consternation of the guard. "The rumour was soon flying round the decks that the admiral was rising from the dead, angered, no doubt, that his ships were not anchoring."[7] He received an elaborate state funeral in St. Paul's Cathedral, attended — it is nice to know — by Villeneuve. A grateful country awarded an earldom and money to Nelson's family though his wife, from whom he was parted, received nothing; she later re-married. His famous mistress, Emma Hamilton, also missed any state generosity though both her husband and her lover had provided for her; in the year of Waterloo she died in poverty in Calais. Collingwood was made a baron and inherited Nelson's command. Having reached home in his 90 gun ship and heard about the battle, Calder wrote to claim a share of the fleet's prize money! The court martial cleared him of cowardice but he was severely reprimanded.

Though many Spanish sailors had been killed, ship-wrecked British crews stranded in Cadiz were treated with courtesy and kindness. Spain soon became an ally of Britain and they fought the Peninsular War together, which began two years later. *(see Chapter V)*. Rosily arrived to take command of what was left at Cadiz three days after the battle, no doubt secretly relieved that some insoluble problems had been taken care of for him.

So ended an heroic campaign and a model one, noteworthy for the equal and immense contributions of the British 'directorate, the management and the staff'. The whole naval war was of a similar standard: from 1793 to 1815 Britain lost seven ships of the line and seventeen frigates, her opponents 139 and 229 respectively![8] The army at the time was altogether less competent and it took a Wellington to make something of it, as we shall see. Why was the Navy's performance so immaculate? Did it in part spring from accepted standards of performance? Calder was court-martialled for losing contact with the enemy; Nelson described it as a lost opportunity and the Navy agreed. Informal standards may be more exacting than those imposed from above. The British love their Navy. "With the one the trade had to be learned from the bottom, while in the Army rank depended on what one could afford to buy . . . from the days of Alfred command of the sea was accepted as vital . . ."[9] The British Isles were left inviolate; a century of naval supremacy was born; Napoleon's ultimate defeat ten years later was rendered inevitable. Nelson's name has ever since been revered by posterity. Apart from its omission of Barham's, further justification seems superfluous.

*   *   *   *

Annex: A Company's Resources

We began by specifying a company's needs, in terms of its 'critical areas'. To carry out a task its capacity must equal its requirements — the equation is as simple as that. In this example, one of global conflict calling for an intricate strategy to allocate resources effectively, the strains were on both centre and periphery: no fashion for centralisation or its converse plays a part as both 'Head Office' and the individual units have to perform. Both are indispensable. It was a case of central policy and local execution.

The first critical area was the strategic direction of the organisation. This presupposes the selection of thinkers and decision-makers and organising them sensibly; they need authority, time and information to do their work. Britain's navy, in part by *accident,* found a central brain in Barham, who could work through the system and authority of the Admiralty and gave himself wholly to this single task. The obvious question is: can we for our part eliminate the "accidental" part of the process?

Barham's raw material was information. His 'products' were fleet orders and intelligence about the enemy. In theory information acquisition and display is simple. Police forces sift vast quantities of 'silt' for a 'nugget' of evidence. What useful information can *we* acquire by systematic detective work as well as by inspired intuition or from conventional searches? For Barham, continuous 'competitive surveillance' was essential for national survival; should we say the same?

Choice of local commanders suited to implement central plans is again obvious. But are ours "irradiated with an alert sympathy", steeped in our thinking (and we in theirs)? Do they have the authority and the decision-rules to make use of it? Being an array of linked fleets (or companies) they have to work with each other. Factors that castrate co-operation are professional jealousy and scope for playing politics. Positive ones are self-confidence, high professional standards, a formal system of assessment that rewards co-ordination and an informal one that recognises the common good and sound work for it. Do we consciously think through how to eliminate these adverse attitudes and foster these beneficial ones?

To rival our exemplar we have to maintain our standards over the years though office or factory may become wearisome — but never, surely, so harsh to live in for a decade as a ship of the line, on watch off Ushant, year in, year out, come sun, come storm? As

Dr Johnson said, "Being in a ship is being in jail, with the chance of being drowned".

*   *   *   *

References

1 Major-Gen. J F C Fuller, Decisive Battles of the Western World.

2 Sir Julian Corbett, The Trafalgar Campaign.

3 Prof. P M Kennedy, The Rise and Fall of British Naval Mastery.

4 Captain A T Mahan, The Influence of Sea Power upon the French Revolution and Empire.

5 Sir Julian Corbett, Some Principles of Maritime Strategy.

6 R Hattersley, Nelson.

7 O Warner, Trafalgar.

8 Prof. M Lewis, quoted by P Padfield, Guns at Sea.

9 A H Cartmell, Letter to the author.

CHAPTER V

THE HUMAN FACTOR: WELLINGTON'S PENINSULAR WAR

"Military organisations learned long ago that futility is the lot of most orders . . . [and] that to go oneself and look is the only reliable feedback."

—P F Drucker,
Management

The Resilient Manager

Managers want to be loved, but life may be against them. Their juniors may be critical or demanding or wayward. A senior may expect idiosyncratic behaviour, an autocrat may demand subservience. General and public opinion may clamour for quick results or painless medicine or the quiet life — or for miracles. The media may (will?) provide sensation, discredit, distortion. Meantime, there is still the competition outside. The pressures internal and external are numerous, their force severe, their continuance wearing. At the worst, the manager may be fighting a war on two fronts — the always active competition outside, unscrupulous sapping and mining inside.

Given all this the least a reasonable manager might ask for is a sound organisation, clear authority, competent supporting services, firm information, co-operative colleagues . . .

Or should he? What should he do if the company has dealt him a weak hand and is then a critical spectator? In our case the answer appears quite simple.

Prologue

The scene is a ridge in Spain; the time early in the 19th century. It is mid-morning: enter, frontally, a French army.

"About 1000 yards from the English line the men became excited ... The English remained quite silent with ordered arms ... Very soon we got nearer, shouting 'Vive l'Empereur!; the column began to double, the ranks got into confusion ... shots were fired as we advanced. The English line remained silent ... Our ardour cooled. The moral power of steadiness ... over disorder ... overcame our minds. At this moment of intense excitement, the English wall shouldered arms; an indescribable feeling rooted many of our men to the spot; they began to fire. The enemy's steady concentrated volleys swept our ranks ... then three deafening cheers broke the silence of our opponents; at the third they were on us, pushing our disorganised flight."[1]

Some years previously the man who designed this particular English line was waiting to see the Secretary of War. He had just completed a solid apprenticeship to arms in India. He was Major-General Sir Arthur Wellesley, within four years to become Viscount Wellington. "Also waiting ... was a naval gentleman with only one arm ... By the narrowest of margins providence had succeeded in bringing together the heroes of Trafalgar and Waterloo for the best part of an hour."[2] Their conversation entertained them. A month later Nelson lay dead in the cockpit of the "Victory". Thirty months later Wellesley sailed to Portugal to lead Britain's only army through seven years' campaigning against Napoleon's armies.

The Armies in Spain

It is 1808. Napoleon's France bestrides an unhappy Europe and this extraordinary man desires new adventures. Though wayward, he was not always unpredictable. In 1805, the year of Trafalgar, he appointed a Swiss military consultant, Antoine Jomini, to his staff; Jomini, later to be made a baron by a gratified master, was to join the French army on its campaign. Young[3] quotes the conversation:

"'If your Majesty will grant me four days' leave, I can rejoin at Bamberg.'
'And who told you that I was going to Bamberg?' the Emperor demanded ...

'The map of Germany, Sire.'

'How the map? There are a hundred roads on that map besides the Bamberg road.'

'Yes, sir, but it is probable that your Majesty will perform the same manoeuvre against the left of the Prussians as you did against Mack's right at Ulm, and as by the St Bernard against Melas' right in the Marengo campaign; and that can only be done via Bamberg on Gera.' [A town between Bamberg and Prussia — CL.]

'Very well,' replied the Emperor, 'be at Bamberg in four days ; but . . . no one must know that I go to Bamberg'."

Now, three years later and confined by British sea-power, Napoleon sought control of the continent. Much of Europe was under his rule and much of the remainder allied. However, the naval blockade had despoiled commerce; many French towns were depopulated and taxes were very heavy. French privateers harried British merchant shipping, but the Emperor, not one to think small, planned more serious remedies: India was to be threatened through Turkey while Sicily was invaded and Gibraltar seized to close the Mediterranean. Thereupon, 100,000 Frenchmen marched across the Pyrenees. As Portugal would not close its ports to British ships it was to be mastered. Napoleon forced the Spanish king to abdicate and be replaced by Joseph Bonaparte, the Emperor's brother, whereupon the Spanish people rose instantly in revolt, so becoming a natural ally and deserving of British support. The French Marshal Junot occupied Portugal, which also revolted.

In July 1808 Wellesley, then thirty-nine, landed at Mondego Bay with 13,000 troops *(Fig. V.1, p. 120)*; there awaiting him on the eve of his great expedition was a letter from London informing him that reinforcements, plus officers to supersede him, were on their way. (This presumably was the War Office's idea of how to win friends and influence people.) Undeterred, he felt that meanwhile a job could be done and, like all good generals, looked first at his opponents' problems — often larger than one's own.

The Iberian peninsula is mountainous country, hot in summer, bleak in winter, its roads few and bad, its people proud, tough and poor. The several French armies were dispersed, each seeking plunder, each trying to maintain its communications through a hostile country. Large escorts had to guard even one courier.

The French aimed to 'live off the country', which was a euphemism for gouging food out of starving peasants, if need be by torture. The Spanish guerillas, though erratic and ill-disciplined, attacked small targets ferociously. The invaders responded with reprisals and the savagery escalated; prisoners lived short and painful lives. Villages were raped and pillaged. Portugal was as bleak if slightly less hostile. There were two convenient roads into it and both were guarded by fortresses — Ciudad Rodrigo and Badajoz (*Fig. V. 1*).

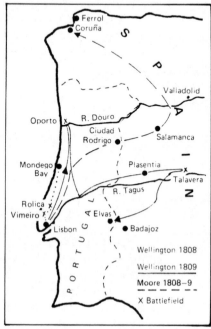

Fig. V. 1 The Peninsula, 1808 — 9

Wellesley, however, was not without his difficulties. His impending demotion apart, the army's organisation was grotesque: he had no direct control at all over his artillery, food and other supplies! (*See Fig. V. 2.*) It will be noted that for much of his resources the 'cross-over' point was the Prime Minister. Nevertheless, he made it work. His army would have looked quite familiar to Marlborough. The infantry was armed with the 'Brown Bess' musket which fired a ball with tolerable accuracy to 200 yards. Misfires were usual. Bayonets were seldom lethal as when charged, as they frequently were, troops tended to run away before they could be skewered. The men were poor, tough, disciplined with the lash and officered by brave and unprofessional aristocrats. The cavalry was well-mounted but wild, its officers wilful and arrogant; they tended to gallop uncontrollably off the main battlefield as if on a fox-hunt. For supplies of food, ammunition, forage and equipment there had to be collected hundreds of (the crudest) carts; mule- or bullock-drawn, they moved perhaps less than five miles a day. For breaching fortifications a siege train had to be hauled, with the shot and the forage for yet more draught animals. (Thus soldiering, like much industrial activity, is 10% glamour and drama, and 90% logistics and administration.) Staff officers were without experience; many officers had to be court-martialled for insubordination. There were no ambulances, no engineers, no intelligence system, no maps. Discipline was poor and desertion frequent.

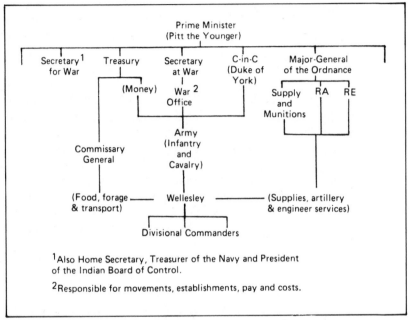

Fig. V. 2 The organisation of the British Expeditionary force. [4]

The British Commander
The lucky man commanding this impressive force was a young Irish aristocrat. Born like Napoleon in 1769 Wellesley grew up in Dublin and held political offices there. Aware that his background provoked comment he remarked, "Because a man is born in a stable that does not make him a horse". [2] He had learned the business of fighting and supply in the hard school of India, winning the major battle of Assaye.

> "He had reached his rank by a system of influence and favour impossible in modern times. But it is possible that, without such a system that gave generals a chance to learn their trade when young, his genius might never have flowered and the history of the world would have been altered." [5]

He was self-confident, intelligent, thorough, with a dislike for
humbug and show. His soldiers could dress as they pleased as long
as they were distinguishable from the French. He knew exactly
what they could do and to the best of his ability he looked after
them. With his horsemanship, his sense of humour, a braying
laugh and an enormous commonsense, he was not ill-equipped for
his job. Lawford and Young give us a splendid description of
the role:

> "The battle raged round the general . . . anything [he]
> could see was apt to be blanketed by thick clouds of
> smoke belched out by cannon and musket . . . excited
> officers would come galloping out of the murk with
> garbled and misleading messages; and while trying to dis-
> entangle the truth, the general might well find himself
> under . . . fire . . . In the midst of the chaos, the general
> would have to choose the right moment to feed in his
> supports . . . To be able to influence the course of the
> battle at all, he had to be able to look through its appalling
> disorder and . . . divine accurately exactly how the situ-
> ation was developing. Unless the general possessed this
> almost instinctive ability to 'read the battle' . . . the
> action, once joined, would become a splendid muddle . . .
> Over the years . . . great generals developed a special sense
> that gave them an uncanny quality of judgement; they
> could receive the most alarming reports unmoved, assess
> the truth . . . and then at the crisis intervene."[5]

Wellesley had in extraordinary measure this calmness in the
midst of chaos and could use to the full his ability to read the
battle. Stoical and self-sufficient, he seemed invulnerable. He did
not need to be loved; certainly his men thought he lacked warmth
and charm but they trusted him: " . . . that long-nosed bugger
that beats the French!" This confidence was sufficient and they
gave him their courage and endurance. In his fashion he offered
powerful leadership. The man's commonsense was famous. He
debated wintering in Portugal with his staff: " 'But we have eaten
nearly all the oxen in the country', interposed the commissary-
general pointedly. 'Well, then we must set about eating all the
sheep', said Wellington."[2] The corollary of this attitude was
reasonableness:

"Having explained to [the War Minister] exactly why he needed transports in the Tagus, he added that none of his reasons were worth anything if the ships were needed elsewhere. Such moderation . . . established a sense of confidence between Cabinet and general."[6] *

Throughout a battle his trim figure, simply clothed in a plain blue coat, cape and a cocked hat, would constantly be seen, watching his troops, assessing French moves, giving orders. Like a 3-star French restaurant whose management continually walk the floor, the general believed in intimate control: "The real reason why I succeeded . . . is because I was always on the spot — I saw everything myself". His command was small enough for that and he required from it not initiative but obedience.

Supersession and Reinstatement

As soon as Wellesley landed Junot sent a delaying force; at Roliça *(Fig. V. 1)* the British forced a passage but were attacked in turn at Vimeiro. Sound defence saw off Junot but his rout was foregone by one of the new commanders sent to replace Wellington who refused to follow up. They negotiated an over-generous armistice by which the French vacated Portugal and Wellesley put his name to it though he criticised it. So did London and all the commanders were recalled, all but one never to command again. The leadership devolved on the professional Sir John Moore. Napoleon was equally displeased by his generals and personally brought reinforcements, swept aside the amateur Spanish and lunged at Moore, who had bravely but rashly advanced to their aid. A harsh winter retreat to Corunna just saved his army, but not himself, after a hasty re-embarkation. Napoleon delegated this pursuit to his Number Two, Marshal Soult, and returned to Paris, believing the Spanish affair at an end.

The evacuation rankled with the British: attack and retreat seemed to be a habit; however, this man Wellesley had defeated the victorious French before so perhaps he could do it again. In April 1809 he was back in Lisbon to take command of all British and Portuguese troops. He had argued in a paper to the government that Portugal could be defended by a small army and he now had to live with his recommendation. His appointment lacked Cabinet unanimity and earned the opposition's hostility but his orders were unequivocal: " 'The defence of

---

* *Such rapport is critical for the commander or manager of a detached unit; see Chapter VI for a contrast.*

Portugal you will consider as the first and most immediate object of your attention'. Any combination with Spain would be left to his discretion, but he should on no account undertake it without the express authority of the British Government".[2] Though Wellesley's military inheritance was dismal, he still had two vast advantages: the objective was clear and he had considerable freedom to act.

The French aims were equally obvious. Napoleon wanted the British army speedily expelled. It numbered 23,000 British and German troops and also 16,000 Portuguese allies. Its situation was stark: Marshal Soult had ferociously sacked Oporto where he now lay with 23,000 men; Marshal Victor had 25,000 east of Elvas; General Lapisse had 6,000 at Ciudad Rodrigo, while in various garrisons were 200,000 more Frenchmen. Wellesley decided to use his interior lines to attack one army before the others could intervene. He marched rapidly towards Oporto where a relaxed Soult only guarded the seaward approaches, as a threat from across a flooded river Douro was ridiculous. Wellesley sent across a small assault force, covering it with a previously concealed battery; the French attacked the bridgehead repeatedly which, supported by the cannonade across the river, held on. More troops, held ready, were ferried over and they stormed the town, finding it filled with cheering inhabitants.

By afternoon Soult was in full retreat, having lost 2000 men to the British 400. Next day he found a Portuguese corps, previously sited by Wellington for the purpose, blocking the road to Spain. Not a marshal of France for nothing, Soult abandoned his sick and his guns and took to the mountains; after losing a quarter of the army, the disorganised remainder reached Galicia. The Portuguese, outraged by the sack of Oporto, took revenge on stragglers and the British "saw French soldiers nailed alive to the doors of barns and others trussed and emasculated."[6] For a time Soult was no threat to anyone. Wellesley now turned on Victor; while England cheered one victory, its modest army prepared for another.

Spain Invaded
It was June 1809. Some French troops had gone off to fight Austria; in northern Spain the corps of Marshal Ney, "the bravest of the brave", and Marshal Mortier were fighting guerillas; Soult had not yet full recovered and the Spanish were reforming south

of the Tagus. With this turn of events the Government sanctioned an offensive and Wellesley mustered 25,000 troops at Plasencia *(Fig. V.1)* near Victor's 23,000, who were also under threat from a Spanish group more or less commanded by General Cuesta. This "aged Spanish grandee ... who was as stupid as he was arrogant, and he was exceedingly arrogant"[5], proposed a united advance on Victor while the French under Joseph in Madrid were pinned there by a Spanish army under General Venegas. It was a grand scheme and assumed Victor's total immobility. Wellesley's necessary patience with an ally/colleague was about to be tested.

As always supplies were lacking. Much was promised by Cuesta but little arrived and he had little himself, while the British Treasury had delayed sending gold with which to buy more. It took Wellesley, a logistics expert, over a month to get ready. The chance to encircle Victor had passed — he had retired eastward — but he might still be caught. The British went to join Cuesta over parched plains, roasted by the Spanish sun; they were not over-impressed by their allies: talking, smoking, resting, these sprawled around under "the chaotic antiquity that overhung the Spanish army like a cloud of garlic".[6]

The armies closed on an outnumbered Victor near Talavera and Wellesley repeatedly proposed an attack while Cuesta repeated excuses. After the French had escaped towards Madrid, Cuesta announced his willingness, indeed his eagerness, to advance. Wellesley pointed out that they no longer had any advantages and they were running out of food. Nothing would deflect the old warrior; with his camp followers and his herds of livestock, he set off after the French. Wellesley refused to accompany him. With erratic allies and a renovated Soult reported nearing his communications, a retreat was more than justified — except by politics. His allies could fairly stress their own problems. London was far away and its opinion fickle: it could hardly understand an immediate withdrawal after an immediate advance. He decided not to retire without a fight. He found a tolerable defensive position and waited for Cuesta. A sound political decision was to prove a risky one.

Two days later the Spanish came streaming back. Venegas had held off out of pique so Joseph's corps had joined Victor and 46,000 Frenchmen were now chasing Cuesta. Wellesley lined up the Spaniards and his own men between Talavera and the mountains. Their options were limited. They could not tarry in a

wasted countryside; they could not move for fear of the strong
French cavalry. Only a successful fight could save them. "Scarcely
since the morning of Agincourt had a British army been in a more
perilous position".[6] Fortunately, there was little time to think
about it. An uneasy night disturbed by erratic shooting saw
Wellesley, lying in his cloak, sleeping soundly.

Dawn roused the Frenchmen for battle. Husbanding his troops
behind cover where he could, Wellesley countered each move.
Intense fighting went on until late in the afternoon of a very long
day, when the French, after losing 7000 men to Wellesley's 5000
and hearing that Venegas was at last nearing Madrid, called off the
battle. The guns fell silent while the grass caught fire, burning
many wounded to death. Nearby churches were turned into
hospitals:

> "Three hosts combine to offer sacrifice,
> To feed the crow on Talavera's plain."

Four days later Wellesley heard that Soult was marching on his
rear. It was time to go. The army retired westward. That same
month its general was raised to the peerage, which the opposition
attacked, and his family were vilified. The Talavera campaign was
over and a critical grumbling army returned to Portugal.

> " . . . throughout it all the Duke was immovable. With
> every officer in the army against him, he still held fast to
> his purpose of holding Portugal. When the troops grumbled
> at his inaction, and demanded to be led into battle, he
> steadfastly refused to indulge their wishes. He was betrayed
> into no outbreak of temper. As patient under calumny as
> unmoved by success, he treated his detractors with con-
> tempt, laughed at his insubordinate officers, and submitted
> with equanimity to the eccentricities of the Government."[7]

In October he took time off to ride with his chief engineer to
inspect the defensive possibilities of the Lisbon peninsula. As
usual, he was looking forward to the next battle but one. Very
satisfied, he gave him certain secret orders.

Outline of a War
The war had really just started. (To help keep track of the ebbs

and flows, *Fig. V. 3* shows a summary.) Irritated by his marshal's frustrations, Napoleon sent Marshal Masséna — a competent and cunning general — into the fray. London felt depressed but Wellington knew that all were bound by Peninsular rules — supply, communications, intelligence. He fenced with Masséna on the frontier *(Fig. V. 4, p. 128)*, then under pressure retreated towards Lisbon, pausing on a ridge at Bussaco for his practised and polished defensive battle and to inflict four times his own number of casualties.

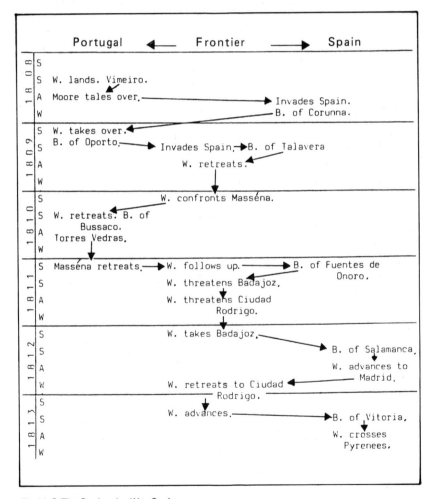

Fig. V. 3 The Peninsular War Cycles.

" . . . Consider . . . the French marshals when they found their cavalry checked at the foot of a long ridge. Except a line of skirmishers, half way down the slope, with a few batteries of artillery in support, there was nothing to be seen. It was impossible to detect the extent of the English line . . . There was nothing for it but to . . . launch the columns of assault, in the vague hope that they might encounter inferior numbers."[7]

The British resumed their retreat to near Lisbon and were astonished to file into prepared fortifications — the Lines of Torres Vedras — built by thousands of Portuguese by Wellington's orders in the months since Talavera. Masséna dared not assault such defences nor long tarry in a denuded countryside. In the spring of 1811 a starving army retreated and Wellington followed having ejected the French for the third time from Portugal. After more fencing on the border a still badly outnumbered general won another defensive battle (at Fuentes de

Fig. V. 4 The Peninsula in 1810 — 12

Oñoro) and Masséna retired to France and his rather demanding mistress, handing over his army to the young and capable Marshal Marmont.

Summer found the French dispersed and Wellington, if he moved fast, with an opportunity. With an *already prepared* siege-train he leaped at the fortresses of Ciudad Rodrigo and Badajoz, taking both by bloody assault — there was not the time for subtleties. The first opened the road to Spain, the second guarded his flank.* (The army's discipline, normally strictly enforced, broke down under severe pressures; after Badajoz was stormed with heavy loss the British thoroughly sacked it, committing many of the atrocities they had criticised the French for. But Wellington

*The French had to disperse in search of forage but should have guarded the fortresses. The Marshals were invariably talented but, for all their high seniority and responsibilities, usually conducted themselves to their own satisfaction when unsupervised. France's Peninsular War cried out for a supreme commander.

had not been able to select either his men or his officers.)

They now marched into Spain and Marmont with equal force met the invaders at Salamanca. After subtle manoeuvres by both sides, Wellington caught the French for a moment extended; the resulting battle was the Duke's best and Marmont's army disintegrated. He followed up with caution, being still much outnumbered. Would the Spanish pin the French? Would the marshals collaborate? These questions were unanswerable.

Wellington lunged around; he drove Joseph out of Madrid and chased another force east, then besieged Burgos for no obvious reason. "One is almost tempted to believe he began the siege in default of anything better to do."[5]   In the autumn he was warned of large French concentrations; Soult had evacuated the south to help hold the centre. Amid universal disapproval a prudent Wellington retreated all the way back to the frontier, his troops cold, tired, hungry and sullen. Another campaign had run into the ground — but the appearance belied the reality; the war had really been transferred into the heart of Spain, its guerillas were heartened, the French were shaken and Portugal was to see the British no more.

That same winter Napoleon, having lost half a million men on a march to Moscow, raided Spain for reinforcements. By the spring of 1813 he controlled little of the country, but Wellington had 81,000 men. Even the French judged him the foremost soldier in Europe after their Emperor. Now he could take the initiative but he divulged his plans to few. His engineers had spent months surveying routes through the northern mountains. He therefore transferred the bulk of his army north of the Douro to outflank the French, and ordered a sea-borne assault on Tarragona to pin one large French force there while himself holding a second's attention round Salamanca. Switching his (sea-borne) supply line to Santander on the north coast — in place of the long road from Portugal — while all the time threatening the French supply route from France, Wellington forced their retreat. At Vitoria (near Bilbao) he caught them, to win a major victory; the road to France lay open. (Supplies for an army, like raw materials for a company, are its basic nourishment. Wellington was here drastically shortening his lines of communication by making use of an outside resource; sea-power was supplementing, not just supporting, the land power, because the general was not too proud to eschew self-sufficiency.)

For the Duke success seemed now almost habitual and his men often applauded 'old Nosey'. He was not impressed. Perhaps it prompted a later remark to a girlfriend: " ... he told her how much he disliked cheering in the ranks — 'I hate that cheering. If once you allow soldiers to express an opinion, they may on some other occasion hiss instead of cheer' ".[8]

That autumn he crossed the Pyrenees. In April 1814 he captured Toulouse (and a Dukedom) while the Prussians, the Russians and the Austrians all eagerly invaded the country that had trampled on them. Despite a defence of exceptional brilliance Napoleon was overthrown. He abdicated and departed — unwillingly and temporarily — to Elba, a charming island close to the Tuscany coast. For a time no guns were to be heard in Europe.

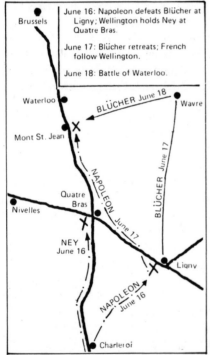

Fig. V. 5 *Napoleon's Last Battles.*

Epilogue

The 'Hundred Days' needs only a sketch. In the spring of 1815 Napoleon escaped and landed near Cannes. He entered Paris amid public acclamation, the old magic working, and raised a huge army. The Allies with haste marshalled their resources; the Duke commanded all the forces in Belgium, whither the Prussians sent an army. This was commanded by Field-Marshal Gebhard von Blücher, an immensely experienced and magnificent warhorse — who sometimes appeared a little touched (at one stage he had thought himself pregnant with an elephant). Napoleon crossed the border and concentrated his army with extreme rapidity nearly between the two Allied ones, to defeat them piece-meal. "Napoleon has humbugged me, by God!" said the Duke.

Wellington and Blucher held council, and promised mutual support. The Prussians were in a needlessly exposed position near Ligny *(Fig. V. 5)*. Inspecting this, the Duke was heard to say:

"If they fight here they will be damnably mauled". He returned to his army and "found his own dispositions even more damnable than Blücher's".[9] Bad staff work allowed the unsupported Prussians to be duly mauled; in a major battle they took 16,000 casualties to the French 11,000. Significantly, they were not disorganised, neither was their retreat followed up effectively.

Meanwhile, Wellington had fended off, with hasty reinforcements, an unaccountably slow Ney in an encounter battle at Quatre Bras, with an invaluable gain in time, and could retire unpressed to a preselected ridge at Mont St Jean near Waterloo; Napoleon belatedly followed. In the enormous and ferocious battle that ensued Wellington was his usual self — though he did leave, by a misjudgement or plain forgetfulness, a corps unused a few miles away when every man counted. Ubiquitous, superhumanly calm, always reading the whole battle, he dominated and controlled his army. Riding everywhere, exposed but seeing for himself, ordering every move, he fought Napoleon almost to a standstill, but the pressure was becoming too great and this despite the Emperor's inadequate reconnaissance of the battlefield, poor tactics and misguided delegation to his subordinates. When the loyal Prussians came that evening to take the French in flank, Wellington with relief could order a general advance.

This fearsome day had had its lighter moments, including what must surely be the most brash salesmanship ever recorded. "During the fighting an enterprising Cockney commercial traveller astonishingly solicited his custom,

> 'Please Sir, any orders for Todd and Morrison?'
> 'No, but would you do me a service? Go to that officer, (pointing), and tell him to refuse a flank.' "[10]

The day was bloody — 10,000 horses lay upon the field with 22,000 Allied dead and wounded to the French 33,000 — and infinitely exhausting for victors and losers. "I have never fought such a battle, and I trust I shall never fight such another." Worn out, Wellington left the cutting down of the fugitives to the Prussian cavalry and returned sadly and wearily to Waterloo. A remarkable military career was over. He had fought sixteen battles and sieges in seven years, losing none and taking 65,000 casualties to inflict 100,000 on the French. Yet it was not a flawless performance; "Asked . . . if he had his life over again, there was any way in which he could have done better . . . the Duke replied 'Yes, I should have given more praise' "[2]

Waterloo is notable for the simple mistakes made by all the commanders, even though all were experienced, meticulous and famous performers. Blücher's Ligny position invited — and got — needless casualties; Wellington could not discern Napoleon's plan nor anticipate the need to guard the Quatre Bras crossroads; Napoleon alternated (for health reasons?) between drive and torpor and seriously skimped the supervision and co-ordination of his corps commanders. Is the only realistic conclusion that uniform excellence is a forlorn hope?

Later, Wellington made a tour of the capitals of Europe, to be acclaimed its saviour:

> "Field Marshal, Duke — three times a Duke and once a Prince — he had dethroned an emperor and restored a King. His victories had saved Europe . . . and the greatest soldier in the world had fled before him. Monarchs accepted his rebuke, and respectful nations did as he told them."[8]

Fifty-one days after Waterloo, his great enemy was sailing down the English Channel on a British warship: "He was going to St Helena, a lonely island in the South Atlantic, his last exile, where there would be no sound of guns, but only the noise of the breakers".[11] Wellington used his enormous influence to forming a generous peace. With limited interruptions it was to last for a century — a very reasonable monument for a man of commonsense.

His entire attitude is perhaps nicely encapsulated in Churchill's account of his fighting a duel years later, when he was Prime Minister, with a political opponent who had accused him of dishonesty:

> "A full-dress challenge followed. The meeting took place in Battersea Park. The Field Marshal, now aged sixty, was most nonchalant, slow and deliberate in his movements. This was much more his line than smoothing the suscepti-bilities of politicians, or, as he once put it in a moment of complaint, 'assuaging what gentlemen call their feelings'. Turning to his second, who was also his Secretary at War, he said, 'Now then, Hardinge, look sharp and step out the

ground. I have no time to waste. Damn it! Don't stick him up so near the ditch. If I hit him he'll tumble in' ".[12]

Life has its simplicities.

＊　　　　＊　　　　＊　　　　＊

References

[1] Marshal Bugeaud, quoted by B L Montgomery,
    A History of Warfare.

[2] E Longford, Wellington. The Years of the Sword.

[3] Brig. P Young, The Victors.

[4] C Barnett, Britain and her Army 1509—1970.

[5] Col. J P Lawford and Brig. P Young, Wellington's Masterpiece.

[6] A Bryant, Years of Victory.

[7] G F R Henderson, The Science of War.

[8] P Guedalla, The Duke.

[9] Major-Gen. J F C Fuller, Decisive Battles of the Western World.

[10] J L Carr, The Duke of Wellington.

[11] Ed. W N Weech, History of the World.

[12] Sir Winston Churchill, A History of
     the English Speaking Peoples.

Some Contemporary Events

1788	British Colony of Australia founded.
1789	French Revolution begins.
1791	Mozart dies.
1805	Trafalgar.
1812	Napoleon invades Russia.
1818	Britain becomes effective ruler of India.
1819	US buys Florida from Spain.
1821	Greek War of Independence.
1828	Wellington becomes Prime Minister.

CHAPTER VI

POLITICS AND MANAGEMENT : THE AMERICAN CIVIL WAR

> *"Kings will be tyrants from policy, when subjects are rebels from principles."*
> — Edmund Burke, Reflections on the Revolution in France

> *"I have never believed that a group as such could manage anything. A group can make policy, but only individuals can admininster policy."*
> — Alfred P Sloan, My Years with General Motors

The Political Organisation

Managers in industry and commerce produce wealth, they are *useful*. Politicians play games, they are parasites. They also lack manners. Given their social superiority therefore, managers need not (should not?) be concerned with politics. "Yes, we have heard of 'Office politics'; yes, it does exist in some companies (i.e. not in mine), but managers need only concentrate on doing a good job; all else is at best distraction, at worst Machiavellian ... "

'Politics' here has two meanings: first, currying favour with those in top places and doing down one's fellows in the process; second, being independent of those who aspire to award state patronage to the point of ignoring them. Clearly, the latter ignores reality: politicians — or their commercial equivalents — decide appointments and so keeping them well briefed, while shielded from unpleasant surprises, is simple commonsense and courtesy. That politicians may have different standards of behaviour and a casual, not to say callous, way with people may be true but is in general irrelevant. In any case, industry's record is not spotless.

As for playing politics, many managers are human and hence over-ambitious or uncaring or self-centred. Trampling on colleagues is for them a not unnatural progression, but they must observe its rules: if they want to criticise the Board of Directors (and who does not?) they must be widely and profoundly informed; if they want to supplant their boss they must do better than him; if they want to displace colleagues they must view their own displacement with a good grace.

In the organisation they may do all this, faithfully obeying all these rules. Better by far that its leader drives it team-like towards an inspiring common objective, conferring individual satisfactions in the process, thus rendering 'office politics' a trivial game which its managers are too busy in valuable employment to play.

The Problems of Presidents

In 1861 Abraham Lincoln had to manage a war. It had started only six weeks after he took office as President of the Union. He was a lawyer, from the west. A tall gaunt figure, with an enigmatic face, he was withdrawn, intelligent, honourable, a son of the soil. He had neither military knowledge nor managerial training. He knew few generals. There was a general clamour in the North for action against the "rebels" of the South who sat on the defensive behind their 1600 mile frontier, guarding a territory of 800,000 square miles spread over ten states, all of them needing to be conquered. The regular Union* army was 16,000 strong, much of it out west fighting Indians. Its generals had limited experience, energy and skill. They faced a determined foe.

Jefferson Davis had to manage a league of nations — the "Confederate States of America" — of which he was the first and last President. He had served in the Indian and Mexican wars and considered himself at least the equal of his commanders. He had not wanted to be President; he had wanted to be an army commander. Now he had to defend a rural confederacy of nine million inhabitants against an industrialised one of twenty-two million. Rhett Butler (in "Gone with the Wind") said: "All [the South] have is cotton and slaves and arrogance. They'd lick us in a month" — an understandable exaggeration. Like Lincoln, Davis had his problems.

Politics: North and South

In 1783 America held some three million people, mostly in the east; twenty years later it had doubled its area (by the 'Louisiana Purchase', which bought much of the central USA from France for $16 million!) and by 1826 settlers were crossing the Mississippi. The Southern states grew cotton for world markets on

*Both sides had several names. The secessionists were variously called the Confederacy, the South, Rebels; their opponents the Union, the North, Federals. East and west, often used in the text, are invariably geographical terms.

slave plantations. An argument started about the extension of slavery to the west; Lincoln, a candidate in the 1860 presidential election, advocated limiting slave owning and this issue became entangled with a second, equally emotive — states' rights. Should the Federal government coerce states on 'local' concerns? A furious debate within the Union formed the alignments: the North — industrialised, commercial, bustling — against the aristocratic agricultural South. The division was moral, economic and social: "The South felt a class-superiority to the . . . North. The Puritan stock of the North regarded the elegant gentry of the South with something of the . . . censure of Cromwell's Ironsides for Rupert's cavaliers".[1]

The South was determined to keep its way of life and to resist

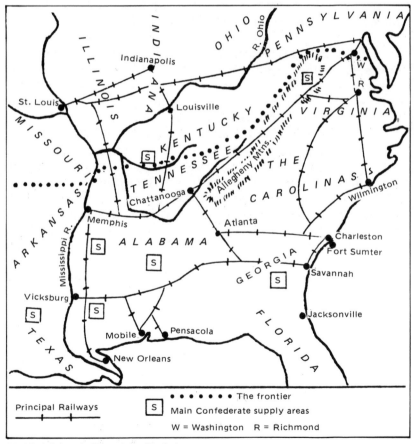

Fig. VI. 1 *Strategic Map of the Confederacy*

interference passionately. The North felt bound to cure a moral wrong. "I believe this government cannot endure permanently half slave and half free. I do not expect the Union to be dissolved . . . I do expect that it will cease to be divided. It will become all one thing or all the other". Thus Lincoln made an uncompromising stand. He won the elections. The South then seceded from the Union and formed the Confederacy *(Fig. VI. 1)*.

Lincoln ordered the re-supply of a Federal outpost, Fort Sumter, in South Carolina and deep in Confederate territory. Davis demanded its capitulation. After a two days' bombardment in April 1961, its garrison surrendered unharmed: "No blood had been shed, but the awful act of rebellion had occurred"[1] Thus began a war, to be waged with passion for four painful years.

The Military Setting: Blue and Grey

Neither side was ready. The regular army contained both Northerners and Southerners; the latter, mostly forsaking the blue-uniformed Federal army, went off to don Confederate grey. On paper the North looked supreme, with thrice the wealth production and thirty times the arms output. But the South was vast with few railways and roads. Invaders would have to bring most supplies with them. There were political factors. The Federal capital, Washington, was just across the Potomac River from seceded Virginia while Davis made Richmond, a mere 100 miles to the south, his capital. "Thus the two capitals stood like queens at chess upon adjoining squares, and, sustained by their combinations of covering pieces, they endured four years of grim play within a single move of capture."[1] The populace, eager but ignorant, demanded quick action and looked naturally at the eastern theatre close by.

But not the Federal General-in-Chief, Lieutenant General Winfield Scott, an elderly and experienced warhorse. He wanted to blockade the South's coast, train a competent army and send it with gunboats down the Mississippi; meantime, to capture New Orleans at the river's mouth with an amphibious expedition, thus gripping the whole river line and dividing the Confederacy, cutting off some cotton-growing and recruiting areas, and establishing Union river communications to support a thrust at the Southern heart. It was a clear and coherent plan but political vision was mesmerised by the east. Scott presupposed patience and vision so few people, of which Lincoln was one, favoured it: it could not fit with the cry, "Onward to Richmond!" The seizure of the strategic axis in the west was delayed for two costly years. The North hurried into battle in Virginia.

Lincoln had a standard management situation; he did not know the technology of the business; he had to learn on the job without a teacher. As was inevitable he made some overly political appointments and sometimes bent to popular clamour; unsuccessful generals, of which there was a superfluity, were given no opportunity to learn from their mistakes. No Union generals at the war's end were in high commands at its start. They naturally looked over their shoulders. The President was in effect commander-in-chief with commensurate power; how to use it was none too clear.

The South was decentralised, which means some states' outlook was parochial, and its President was not the man to secure teamwork. Davis, tall and trim, at fifty-three a year older than Lincoln, had been trained at West Point. He mostly chose his army commanders well and supported them but his strategic judgement was flawed. He wanted a purely defensive war, with the east and west theatres self-contained despite the South's being on interior lines. Critics think his choice of capital unsound. Fuller[2] has argued that choosing Atlanta would have focussed attention on the decisive west; he would have screened Virginia economically while fighting an offensive/defensive war around Chattanooga to protect the rail network *(Fig. VI. 1)* linking the supply states, the Mississippi crossings, the supply ports and the armies. Such a plan would have called for a high order of strategic direction but Davis was no Barham: he reacted to events and made no general plan. His later opponents would do just that though their army at first lacked aptitude: Fuller[2] quotes a contemporary:

> "The army was weighed down ... by venerated traditions ... by the firmly tied red-tape of military bureauism, and by the deep-seated and well-founded fear of the auditors and comptrollers of the treasury ... "

He himself comments:

> " ... the less military side was the more soldierlike; free from shibboleths, the Confederate soldier could expand with expanding events, whilst the Federal sought to overcome difficulties by text-book rules."[2]

(It sounds like accountants versus the entrepreneurs.) Technology favoured defence. Both armies started with muzzle-loaders but later acquired some magazine rifles. These breech-loaders were to have two great attributes: they fired seven shots a minute instead of five and they could be reloaded by men lying prone under cover. Their range, about 500 yards, out-distanced cannon. The rifled muzzle-loader was accurate to 300 yards and though fire was slow each hit made a fearsome wound. With that other weapon, the spade, one protected rifleman could take on three attackers with equality.

Geography was an influence. The Allegheny Mountains divided the frontier though the transverse rail links allowed some inter-theatre movement. Virginia's mountains, forests and rivers favoured the defence. Simple lack of communications stopped dead in their tracks moves that seem at first glance obvious. A Federal army could surely have out-flanked Richmond by traversing south from West Virginia, to roll up the rebels' positions? Not a bit of it: lack of roads or rail would neuter such a move; no army could stay in supply after an advance through the mountains. The sea girdled the Confederacy. The North's superior navy could not only blockade Southern ports, cutting the export of cotton and the import of arms, but could launch amphibious attacks — the classic use of exterior lines allied to superior numbers. (The coast was and is ideal for 'boating': you can sail from New York to Savannah, Georgia, on inland waters without ever touching the sea.)

Even in retrospect the strategic issues do not look simple. At the time clear thinking must have been difficult. It was certainly not forthcoming. While American soldiers had studied Napoleon, at his peak only fifty years before, they could not practise their trade except against the Indians and the Mexicans. Now there were many innovations to master: the rifle, troop trains, wire entanglements, flame throwers, observation balloons. A small cadre had to equip, train, lead, supply and control forces expanding twenty-fold in a matter of months. Organisation was a Confederate ally. The Union soldiers mostly stayed in their old units and raw recruits formed the new ones; Southern sympathisers resigned from the Union army and took command of new Southern units as they were formed so the professional yeast leavened the entire military dough.

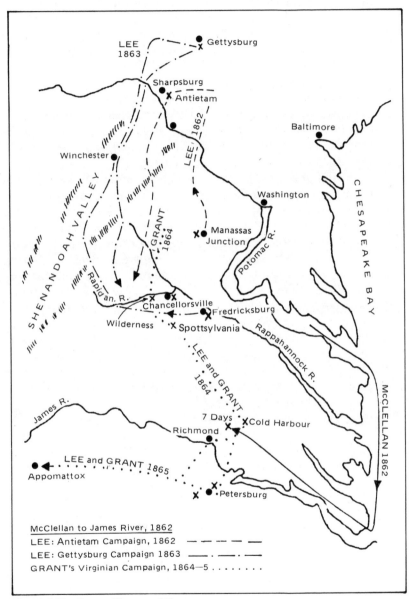

Fig. VI. 2 The Eastern Theatre of War

The Eastern Theatre : The Campaign before Richmond

Despite all difficulties, the combatants appointed leaders, formed armies and sent them off to war. (We concentrate now on the east where our interests are best exemplified.) The first moves were to capture the border states for their supplies, recruits and strategic positions. Missouri and Kentucky were secured to the Union side: "I should like", said Lincoln, "to have God on my side, but I must have Kentucky". West Virginia was a prized communication link. Nudged by Scott, one General McClellan captured it, becoming the North's first hero. (A possibly confusing number of generals are named in this narrative as many were chosen and few survived — a selection process to be noted.)

The South marshalled its small army in northern Virginia, under General Beauregard, standing on the defensive as weapons were scarce. The Federals, urged on by the press, agreed that time was passing — it was now July; anyway, the short service militia should be used before demobilisation. The Cabinet pressed Scott who against his better judgement ordered an advance. General Irvin McDowell led the Union army to a messy battle at Manassas *(see Fig. VI. 2)* called First Bull Run and fought incompetently by both sides. The Federals were routed. Congressmen and their ladies who had come to watch a spectacle fled to the safety of the capital's entrenchments. (The diagram in *Fig. VI. 3* summarises for clarity the oscillations of fortune.)

By Davis' order the Southern follow-up was cautious. Some generals felt they could have rushed Washington; it was a possible decisive move but with hindsight probably an impractical one. Anyway, the chance passed, untried. Success demoralised the Confederacy; the troops thought they had done their duty and they could go home till the next battle. Its lack of cohesion, its being a collection of equals, led to a paradox: the Confederacy had seceded from the Union on the issue of state sovereignty; could it now relax that enough to defend it? It watched while Federal strength grew faster than its own and found an occupation for itself. Beauregard wrote to his President that political interference had prevented his capturing Washington; the letter appeared in the press before it reached Davis.

General Joseph Johnston, the other commander in Virginia waxed status conscious. He was an amiable but touchy man, better liked from below than above, and nicknamed "the gamecock". He wanted to outrank other generals because he had done so in the Federal army. Davis disagreed: previous line, not staff, rank should determine present levels. The controversy will not be unfamiliar to managerial readers. (A Confederate general commanded an army, a lieutenant-general an army corps of two or three divisions, and a major-general a division. Except for the General-in-Chief the highest Federal rank until 1864 was major-general, the title for all three levels.) The South had some colour-ful soldiers. Innately independent, they took naturally to detach-ment work. The Virginian cavalry commander was Jeb Stuart, a great showman and an equally great commander of light cavalry. His cloak was lined with scarlet and he had a personal banjo player on his staff. His success was assured.

The year ran out. Davis left the west unorganised; he urged no exploitation of the eastern victory and troops were switched

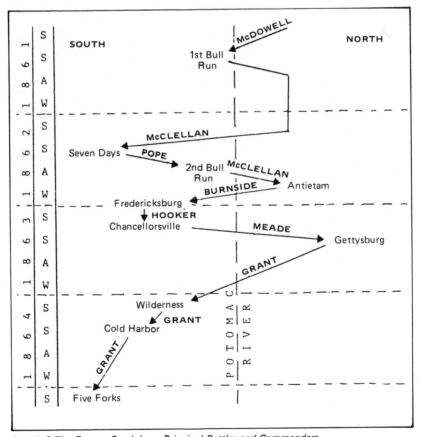

Fig. VI. 3 *The Eastern Pendulum: Principal Battles and Commanders*

to garrison duty. He sent a General Lee, of whom more will be heard, to 'co-ordinate' Virginian defences though their commanders outranked him. Johnston and Beauregard wanted to invade Maryland while Union morale was low and its levies raw but Davis refused to reinforce them and the South relaxed; recruiting fell off.

But the Federals were quite busy. Lincoln sketched a broad plan — imperfect but at least a thought-out program. It implied an eastern defence followed by a western offensive. The day after First Bull Run McDowell was moved out and Major-General George B McClellan, thought to be the tested hero of West Virginia, took command of the "Army of the Potomac". McDowell was thought ill-starred rather than incompetent and was merely demoted. His successor was then thirty-five and was " . . . a short man with a barrel chest, a handsome face, and the air of one who knew what all the trumpets meant, he won — without trying much more than was necessary . . . the lasting affection of some very tough fighting men . . . He had too much . . . too soon . . . For a time he served his country most ably".[3]

He disciplined his levies and built up a corps of competent officers. All liked him because he made them a self-respecting cohesive force, but his relations with his superiors were erratic. His bearing earned the nickname "Young Napoleon" and when his political masters expected action they encountered an incomprehensible deliberateness. McClellan resented interference and did not lack self-reliance: "I shall . . . crush the rebels in one campaign". Nevertheless, he preferred parades to anything more aggressive. He complained of his superiors' ignorance and did not confide in them as too ill-equipped to direct military men. Meanwhile Washington lionised him: "President, Cabinet, General Scott and all deferring to me . . . I seem to have become the power of the land"[3], heady stuff for a man after one day in town. Puffed up with pride, he wooed politicians and intrigued against Scott, who contemplated a court martial. In November, he resigned and McClellan replaced him; he now had to perform. After some weeks' illness he presented his plan: to take Richmond by flank attack from the sea. Provided Washington was in no way exposed Lincoln approved it and the army was to be ferried down Chesapeake Bay to the James River east of the Southern capital *(Fig. VI. 2)*. Meanwhile, out west the Federals were for a time active, attacking key forts on the main rivers; an amphibious assault secured New Orleans and closed the mouth of the Mississippi. These were potentially menacing moves but Davis' attention was elsewhere.

However, Lincoln's summer had been a frustrating one. His generals in the west were now busy "re-organising"; if they had plans for further action they were not telling him nor had they provided for mutual co-operation. The President wrote: "It is exceedingly discouraging. As everywhere else, nothing can be done". While McClellan was ill Lincoln convened a 'management meeting' with, amongst others, two of the general's own subordinates. Lincoln "remarked quaintly that if General McClellan . . . did not plan to use the army right away he would like to borrow it, provided he could find out what ought to be done with it"[3] His feeling was understandable. The generals were quite unable to comprehend the pressure for action; McClellan's debt to the politicians for his promotion called for prompt deeds and time was not on the Union side. Internal politics or external intervention could alter the balance of power. Behind Lincoln's "clumsy White House conferences and his almost frantic messages to the generals . . . lay the conviction that time was running out. The government could win the war if it struck immediately. If it did not, the future was all but unimaginable."[3]

McClellan managed to sail at the end of March 1862, leaving 70,000 troops near the capital. He ceased to be General-in-Chief, being now far from centre, but no one replaced him except in part Stanton, the Secretary of War. He landed north of the James River *(Fig. VI. 2)* and heard that Lincoln was now retaining one of his corps to help guard Washington: "most infamous", he said. He was soon to face a new opponent, General Robert E Lee, who was given command of the "Army of Northern Virginia" in June. He was a Virginian of gentle birth, already distinguished in the service. Scott had originally offered him command of the Federal army which after heart-searching he declined: he could not side with an attack on Virginia even though he opposed slavery. He resigned his commission and sadly rode down to Richmond. There he was immediately given high rank and, understandably, exercised much influence:

> " . . . he understood the processes of war as few men
> have ever done. He knew, apparently by instinct, the
> risks that must be taken . . . the way to impose his will

> on his opponent, and the fact that . . . a general must be
> willing to move in close for a showdown fight regardless
> of the cost. Because he was what he was, the war lasted
> much longer . . ."[3]

His military outlook verged on the egocentric: a natural leader,
he never waited, he only initiated; he could only see opportunities
for himself, never chances for his opponents; a cool calculator,
he pushed risk-taking to the point of rashness — but he had all
to gain by so doing. Other qualities will become apparent in Lee's
actions. He had need of them. The enemy was a mere five miles
from Richmond and with 20% more troops. Lee recalled General
Jackson — his partner to be in many an enterprise — from a daring
diversion in the Shenandoah Valley which had kept Washington's
nerves usefully on edge. Manoeuvres to procure a local superiority
of force culminated in the Seven Days' Battle, a mutual blood-
letting. Inexperience and the frictions of war spoiled Lee's designs
but McClellan was penned into a corner sufficiently far from
Richmond. The two armies had lost 36,000 casualties and
McClellan the confidence of Washington.

He was defiant. His senior, Stanton, was "the most deformed
hypocrite and villain that I have ever had the bad fortune to meet
with". Lincoln ". . . would relieve me tomorrow if he dared to
do so. His cowardice alone prevents it". The President was aware
of these generous sentiments; in July he appointed Major-General
Henry H Halleck, one of the cautious western commanders,
General-in-Chief; from above he looked successful when actually
he had been partly carried by a subordinate and, with McClellan,
he shared "a singular genius for making war in low gear".[3] Under
him was a new commander of the forces in northern Virginia (the
Army of the Potomac was still on the James River), General John
Pope, an aggressive and self-confident man who expected to see
only the backs of his foes.

Nervous of Lee's now obvious pugnacity, Halleck wanted to
concentrate all his force for a direct approach on Richmond and
McClellan was sharply ordered back from the James to join Pope,
a perhaps naive adherence to the concentration principle as well
as dispensing with surprise. McClellan slowly complied, being more
concerned with restoring his own authority than maintaining
Pope's. He found excuses to halt, which Halleck described as
disobedience. McClellan requested detailed instructions as "it is

not agreeable to me to be accused for disregarding orders when I have simply exercised the discretion you committed to me". What Lee had done was to transfer the war from the outskirts of Richmond to the approaches to Washington.

The Campaign before Washington

At the Second Battle of Bull Run in August 1862 Lee, running great but calculated risks, brought Pope to battle near Manassas before McClellan ran out of excuses, inflicting 15,000 casualties for his own 9,000. This Northern defeat can be compared with the Seven Days' Battle. Like McClellan Pope had been mystified by Lee; both victims criticised colleagues' unhelpfulness; both argued their own efforts had minimised disaster, which anyway reinforcement would have transformed into victory.

> "Because these battles had been lost the crisis of the war was at hand . . . and the administration in Washington had to face a baffling problem in leadership."[3]

Pope had failed and the search for a scapegoat and a successor began; Halleck evaded responsibility; McClellan tried to cover his back while Stanton argued for sacking him with which the Cabinet agreed. Pope now intervened: McClellan's army (though personally loyal) was disaffected because of its withdrawal from the James, he said, and this called for action at the top. But time had run out; Lee was about to invade the North and Lincoln, not normally reluctant to face changes, had no choice if McClellan's men would only work for him. His officers wanted no other general, perhaps because his security was theirs. At Lincoln's prompting McClellan asked them to co-operate with Pope. Lincoln by stages insinuated McClellan over Pope; only then was the Cabinet informed. Lincoln's power was manifest and so was McClellan's. Lincoln then hinted to Halleck that he should personally command the army against Lee, a message which he transposed into a similar one for McClellan! Pope, bitterly protesting, was sent west to fight the Indians.

During these dignified proceedings Lee was moving into Maryland, like Marlborough always seeking the decisive battle but, weakened by straggling and ill-supplied men, he was outnumbered. He planned a risky deception but a document detailing it was captured. A severe battle called Antietam took place at Sharpsburg *(Fig. VI. 2)* which for Lee was a pyrrhic victory; having lost the initiative and some prestige he retreated. McClellan adopted an engaging modesty. With 17% of his army laid low he wrote to his wife: "Those whose judgement I rely on tell me that I fought the battle splendidly and that it was a masterpiece of art".

He forebore from following up this masterpiece. He invariably felt, invariably incorrectly, that he was outnumbered. (He employed the founder of Pinkerton's Detective Agency as his intelligence officer; this gentleman seems to have been a better businessman than staff officer.) Thereupon, McClellan applied himself to politics, disparaging Stanton and Halleck, and to his other preoccupation — reorganising. After that he might advance "on whatever line may be determined". Lincoln made just such a determination for him yet it took him a month to cross the Potomac. Lincoln, Halleck and McClellan all expressed disgust with each other and Lincoln came to a decision: the command was passed to Major-General Burnside. McClellan went home and the war saw him no more.

But for Lee, recovering from Antietam, no invasion was over: if reinforced he could force the Federals to fight again on their own land. "To his uncomplicated but tenacious mind it was the other man's army, not his, that had just brushed the edge of disaster."[4] Desertion underminded his ambitions but he still stood between the Union army and its goal. He wanted to stand further south where the terrain favoured both defence *and* a deadly reposte. The less far-seeing Davis opposed "needless" giving of ground and Lee had to fight the next battle at Fredericksburg, where defence was easy but a counter-stroke not — another Southern opportunity missed.

His new adversary, Burnside, had command thrust on him; a justifiably modest man, he was likeable and with an unusual humility. He made a good plan, cleared it with Halleck, who took it to the President though it was within his discretion. It might have worked. It needed a pontoon train to bridge the Rappahannock River, which was delayed; Burnside persisted with his scheme in new circumstances and reiterated attacks on Lee's position above the town piled up the dead in front of impregnable defences so easily that Lee remarked: "It is well that war is so terrible — we should grow too fond of it".

One of Burnside's divisional commanders was General Joseph

Hooker. He combined an aggressive reputation with a total lack of loyalty to any but himself. To him patronage began at home. (He has the distinction of originating by his athletic womanising the term 'hooker'.) An erroneous newspaper report "which should have read, '(still) fighting — Joe Hooker' came out in print as 'Fighting Joe Hooker' "[4], and the name stuck. His superiors deserved better of him. Burnside shouldered all responsibility for failure.

In the new year displeasing questions obtruded. The army's morale sagged and its officers' ambition clashed with frustration. Several of them criticised Burnside's new plan to the President and counter-proposed their own. Burnside wanted them all cashiered. Lincoln asked Halleck very properly to examine Burnside's plan and either confirm or forbid it. He would do neither; instead he tendered his resignation. As commander-in-chief the President was now alone. Joe Hooker made his contribution. All he said was that his boss was incompetent and the Cabinet ridiculous and they needed a dictator. His colleagues wanted McClellan to be army commander while he simply wanted him to be Joe Hooker. Meanwhile Burnside tried some action but weather and disaffected men frustrated him. He switched to the political front: Stanton and Halleck, he told Lincoln, had lost the army's trust; they should be moved somewhere else and himself to private life. Lincoln would not immediately accept his resignation; so Burnside recommended the dismissal of nine senior officers, Hooker topping the list. The President did not accept this either. Instead, three days later, the army commander was fired and sent to the Ohio River. Joseph Hooker replaced him.

What happened to him deserves a slight diversion.

The Battle of Chancellorsville
It is January 1863. "Fighting Joe Hooker" has welcomed his appointment. He has also received a letter from President Lincoln:

> "I have placed you at the head of the Army of the Potomac ... upon what appears to me to be sufficient reasons, and yet I think it best for you to know that there are some things in regard to which I am not quite satisfied with you. I believe you to be a brave and skilful soldier ... You have confidence in yourself, which is valuable ... You are ambitious, which, within reasonable bounds, does good rather than harm; but I think that during General Burnside's

> command of the army you have taken counsel of your
> ambition, and thwarted him as much as you could . . . I
> have heard, in such a way as to believe it, of you recently
> saying that both the army and the government needed a
> dictator. Of course it was not for this, but in spite of it,
> that I have given you the command. Only those generals
> who gain successes can set up dictators. What I now ask of
> you is military success and I will risk the dictatorship . . .
> I much fear that the spirit which you have aided to infuse
> into the army, of criticising their commander and with-
> holding confidence from him, will now turn upon you. I
> shall assist you to put it down as far as I can . . . Beware of
> rashness, but . . . give us victories."[5]

A classic statement of the position. Hooker was a professional,
had served in the Mexican War and in all the major eastern actions.
Handsome, an able administrator, "he shared with McClellan the
knack of *looking* like a good general"[3] He restored the army's
morale. For himself he was tolerably confident. "My plans are
perfect," he announced; "May God have mercy on General Lee,
for I will have none". He had 130,000 troops to Lee's 65,000. The
auspices looked favourable. (However, a question remained: was
the rule my father propounded being obeyed? "You don't promote
a man because he's good in his present job but because he's going
to be good in his next one.")

We have met Lee already. A pious, restrained fastidious man, he
was a knight-errant, a passionate adherent to a cause: not to abstractions but the basic verities — motherland, fellow countrymen,
kindness to others. Though austere he could be impulsive, though
modest daring, though detached decisive. One of his staff wrote:
"He looked at everything as unrelated to himself . . . He had no
favourites, no unworthy partialities . . . A victory gave him pleasure
only as it contributed to the end he had in view . . . He was the
ruling spirit of his army." This aloof religious knight, both cautious
and audacious, had an equally striking partner — General Thomas
Jackson, seventeen years Lee's junior, also a professional soldier,
in 1861 an instructor at a military institute.

> "His character was stern, his manner reserved . . . his mode
> of life strict, frugal, austere . . . he slouched in his weather-
> stained uniform a professor-warrior . . . gifted with that

strange power of commanding measureless devotion from the thousands whom he ruled with an iron hand."[1]

The two men were a trusting complementary pair; Jackson with his determination was the natural instrument of Lee's audacity in manoeuvre and he suited Lee's management style. Lee was a delegator, quick to conceive a plan, resolute in ordering — in general terms — its execution. All then depended on his subordinates. Jackson normally — he had been known to halt all movement on the Sabbath — had all the drive.

Hooker's army was gaining strength and he assured Lincoln it was a question of when, not if, he would take Richmond. He bypassed Halleck; having in the past criticised his colleagues, they now watched him. The Army of Northern Virginia was less happy; a quarter of it was away foraging and some men were demobilised to man 'essential' industries, but who says what is essential? Lee suspected political influence and resisted it though this was not his main worry. He believed his army was invincible but even it needed supplies. For once he had to wait on the North.

In April Lincoln reviewed his army; it looked all right but he could be forgiven for harbouring the shadow of a doubt; he liked the hen "because she never cackles until the egg is laid". Under his prodding things were happening and looked well. Things always looked well at the start. He said to Hooker, "I want to impress on you . . . in your next fight put in all your men". An interesting but clearly necessary lecture of the professional technician by the untaught civilian.

They now went to work. Hooker's army was north of the Rappahannock River at Falmouth *(Fig. VI. 4)*; opposite, lining the heights above Fredericksburg, Lee manned strong defences. Hooker's plan looked sound; his predecessor, Burnside, had assaulted Lee frontally here and lost over 12,000 men: not for Hooker such foolishness. He would feint a left hook downstream while throwing the bulk of his army around the Confederate left. Lee must then retire or face destruction. Meanwhile the Northern cavalry would have cut Lee's communications with Richmond by a wide sweep, when Lee would obviously detach his own horsemen to restore them. At the end of April, each man carrying sixty rounds and eight days' rations, four corps crossed the river west of Fredericksburg while three assaulted on the east and their commander felt able to say. "I have Lee in one hand and Richmond in the other."

At a crossroads the Chancellor family had built a large house. Between it and Fredericksburg is pleasant farming country; to its west was heavily wooded ground, the Wilderness. Lee soon learned the enemy were around Chancellorsville and their cavalry in his rear, but he kept his own to scout hostile moves while screening his manoeuvres — the opposite of what Hooker intended. He watched and waited. Hooker aimed to march his right pincer towards his left; he could attack Lee front and rear or if he retired, the likely course, spear his flank. Whatever happened Lee would be in great trouble. The Union troops massed in the right pincer while the left under Major-General Sedgwick jabbed at Lee's front.

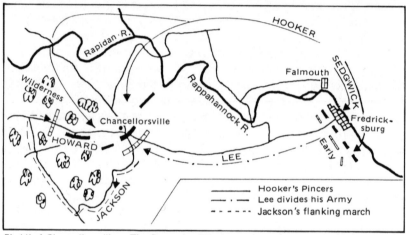

Fig. VI. 4 Chancellorsville — The Rewards of Daring

By that evening Lee had decided that Sedgwick was feinting; the real enemy was coming out of the west. He considered a quick attack on Sedgwick but it looked too costly; he disliked a retreat, if only because it was expected of him. Taking his whole army towards Hooker would be orthodox. He did none of these things. Leaving 9000 men under a tough general, Early, to ward off Sedgwick's 47,000, he took the remainder west. Hooker's plan seemed to be working. Now, when closing with the enemy, the general's responsibilities became all too clear to him; now he should be pushing east to box in Lee, in the process uniting his own forces. And now he hesitated. Not till noon next day did he order his army to move, when it discovered that the Rebels were not where it was thought they were. Having barged into a small but alert force the Federals on the spot prepared to sweep it aside. To their commander in rear things looked different; here was not a fleeing foe but an ordered attack; a prepared defence was best. His troops were to retire to Chancellorsville. They were astonished and argued the matter. Hooker confirmed his order: "I have got Lee just where I want him; he must fight me on my own ground".

Their commander apart, the Federals could still rejoice: Lee had a major army on each flank, his communications were cut and he was completely outnumbered. He searched for some initiative; joined by Jackson that evening, he wondered how to get at the enemy. Jeb Stuart's cavalry reported that Hooker's line ended "in the air"; a corps under Howard was lined up along the road, its right flank exposed. Suppose a flanking march could be made? A path through the woods was found and a local to act as guide. At four a.m. Jackson with 28,000 men marched away, leaving Lee with 14,000 to keep Hooker's 70,000 in play for the whole of a long day. None knew better when to apply the concentration principle and when not; now he was shielded by forest but if Hooker pressed the matter Lee would be ruined.

Jackson was screened from view except at one point and there he was spotted and Hooker advised Howard to prepare for a possible attack. But he had expected Lee to retreat; probably he was now wisely doing so. Howard agreed though his pickets reported a hostile presence. His men were preparing supper. (Their pious general was not over-popular; a colleague said, "At West Point he talked nothing but religion. If a young lady was introduced to him he would ask her if she had reflected on the goodness of God during the past night".) By five p.m Jackson had his men carefully marshalled in line of battle astride the road and facing east. While Howard's men were resting, yelling troops rushed at them out of the forest. By dusk they were all scattered, having taken 2500 casualties, but their assailants were in disarray and very tired. In the gloom sporadic firing continued. A conventional general would have paused to reorganise but an elated Jackson could think of nothing but keeping the fight going which might trap Hooker's whole army. Wishing to see for himself he scouted through the shadows. Returning, his men mistook him for the enemy and he was fearfully wounded. He was carried to the rear as the night at last fell silent.

His hand was no longer on his corps; no one knew his plan.

Stuart took temporary command but Jackson could only tell him to "... do what he thinks best". Perhaps both sides now missed their chance. Hooker, with most of his troops still fresh, could have successively destroyed the separated Confederate forces but he was already in his mind a beaten man. Stuart and Lee attacked next day and were reunited, having pressed Hooker into a perimeter by the river, when there was news from the east: a Federal corps was marching on Lee's rear! For the third time Lee divided his army. A minor force kept Hooker occupied while the remainder with Early herded a now surrounded Sedgwick across the river. Again Lee turned on Hooker, who asked his corps commanders to vote on fighting or retreating. A majority wanted to fight so he ordered a retreat. Back in Falmouth his army glowered at a victorious Lee across the river they had forded ten days before. The only difference was that Hooker had given away 17,300 casualties and his job.

Four days later Jackson was dead, saying as he went, "Let us pass over the river and rest under the shade of the trees". He was buried with all honours in Richmond in the presence of thousands of his countrymen. With him went a measure of their hope. For Lee Chancellorsville was a brilliant hollow victory. He had wholly confounded the enemy, inflicting 30% more casualties than he received while outnumbered one to two; in the process he had lost his right hand, leaving a lasting weakness: "I know not how to replace him". Having taken 12,800 casualties this great battle left the South a little weaker, its problems unchanged.

The Gettysburg Campaign

A breathing space had been bought. The North had its difficulties. In May came the report on the erstwhile offensive against Richmond: the Army of the Potomac, Hooker announced, had retired and was now "safely encamped" at its starting point. "My God!" said Lincoln, "What will the country say!" He and Stanton agreed Hooker must go but meanwhile he could continue reorganising the army while Lincoln sought opinions on his successor. Two corps commanders refused the job, one counter-proposing a third, General Meade. (Consulting the team on its next head is an informative method — *see Appendix D.*)

While the east was retreating the west was advancing. A certain General Grant was investing the vital Southern fortress of Vicksburg on the Mississippi; the whole river artery and the state of

Mississippi were threatened. The South needed to make decisions: should part of Lee's army with the man himself be sent west? Worried that Hooker was being reinforced, Lee wanted to pre-empt him, invade the North and force it to strip troops from Grant. Davis must choose: lose either Mississippi or Virginia. But he could afford neither; no fresh ideas were adopted. The President wanted both and ended by losing both. When all options are unpalatable compromise beckons and an 'hors d'oeuvres' policy — a bit of everything — looks the least distasteful. As Wolfe, the captor of Quebec, said, "War is an option of difficulties".

Left to his own resources, Lee moved into Pennsylvania, marching round Hooker to entice him away from Richmond, and a rich countryside gave him much needed supplies. Strategically the operation was defensive and its aims realistic — to start with, but before the swelling current of events the objectives receded beyond Lee's grasp.* He thought his army could do anything which was only nearly true. Both armies, whatever their seniors thought, believed a showdown was near. Hooker followed Lee as Lincoln wanted to trap him rather than try a thrust at Richmond, so converting a Southern threat into a Northern opportunity without excessive 'downside risk': at worst the North could lose another battle but the South could lose its whole army. Hooker sensibly argued for one commander for all the forces moving against Lee. Lincoln cut him short. Halleck and Hooker argued until the latter, feeling himself without authority, resigned. (He was later sent west where under a strong leader he performed well. Like some managers, he was a good Number Two.) The resignation was promptly accepted and Meade named as his successor; as he was expected to object an instant handover was ordered. "I suppose I shall have to go to execution!"[5] said Meade as a good soldier. He was also a tough one, describing his business as . . . "the pleasant task of sending people to eternity". So the Army of the Potomac acquired a little known chief on the eve of a major battle.

Four days later the armies converged on a modest town in Pennsylvania. Gettysburg was simply a useful road junction. Almost by accident an encounter fight occurred and escalated to total involvement. Lee did not press his corps commanders who were irresponsibly slow; Jackson's absence was perhaps decisive. Three days of unimaginative battle fought the combatants to a standstill with 50,000 casualties. Lincoln prodded his army to cut off a spent Lee, who just managed to extricate his damaged

*The STC set-back in 1985 appears to be a commercial equivalent.

force into Virginia. He "... had lost only five guns, and the war".[1] The day after Gettysburg Vicksburg surrendered to General Grant.

The rest of the year was spent in sparring. Grant was now in charge of all Union troops out west. Southern hope declined as foreign intervention in its favour was discounted. But 1864 was election year; if Lincoln lost, war weariness might breed a negotiated peace; anyway, Federals might make some great mistake. After all, "Hanging on waiting for something to turn up is an important branch of the military art".[6] And of others.

Grant against Lee

The North hung on too. There was pressure to appoint a new General-in-Chief; the search for a war winner had been ceaseless and now Grant's western record singled him out. In February 1864 he was appointed and immediately went to work. Then forty-two, Ulysses S Grant was a West Pointer; he had fought in the Mexican War but resigned in 1854 when menial jobs occupied him up to the Civil War. He was businesslike, commonsensical, quick to accept responsibility, unafraid of hard decisions. Like Lee he was ready to order a showdown and both men could make necessary if costly moves. Like his President he favoured bluntness and clarity and he seldom confused anybody. He kept his controls in proportion. A Quartermaster asked him to decide a matter costing millions of dollars and Grant quickly approved. Asked if he was sure he was right, he answered, "No, I am not ... but in war anything is better than indecision ... If I am wrong we shall soon find it out and can do the other thing. But *not to decide ...* may ruin everything". A colleague said that Grant's men "...knew him and trusted him and he knew them. He could stand any hardship they could stand and do their thinking besides"[3]

A robust Meade offered to serve anywhere Grant wanted; impressed, Grant confirmed his appointment but decided to have his HQ with Meade's, leaving Halleck in Washington as chief-of-staff to handle administration. The new man was as much concerned with perfecting the political situation as the military one:

> "This army had been beset by politics from the beginning, but Grant understood what many of the army's officers could never understand — that the political fetters were partly self-imposed ... It struck Grant, looking back,

that when an officer was crippled by politics it was usually the officer's own fault: 'What interfered with our officers more than anything else was allowing themselves a political bias'."[7]

Grant made a plan: he wished to apply general pressure on the South. His formidable successor in the west, General William T Sherman, was to drive into the Confederacy's heartland. Meade was to march south: "Lee's army will be your objective point. Wherever Lee goes, there will you go also". It was what Lincoln had long advocated — extensive sustained pressure by superior force using exterior lines. He gave Grant full support, writing to him thus:

> "The particulars of your plans I neither know or seek to know. You are vigilant and self-reliant, and, pleased with this, I wish not to obtrude any constraints or restraints upon you. While I am very anxious that any disaster, or the capture of our men in great numbers, shall be avoided, I know these points are less likely to escape your attention than they would mine."[3]

The general knew what he had to do about Lee: "... to pin [him] down and make him fight the kind of war he could not win ... the simplicity of this concept being tarnished only by the difficulty of finding some way to make it operative".[7] The advance through Virginia began.

Lee was not wholly ready. He lacked supplies and numbers but as always sought the initiative, suggesting moves in Kentucky or Virginia to unbalance the Federals. He never lost this cast of mind: "... his idea of the way to parry a blow was to strike before the blow could be delivered. Any Federal General who began a 'forward to Richmond' campaign was apt to learn ... that his chief concern had suddenly become the defence of Washington."[3] But the shadows were lengthening. In May Grant sent troops under General Benjamin Butler by sea to the James River, two days' march from Richmond. Butler was politically influential but a military ninny and Grant gave him good subordinates and reckoned surprise and numbers *must* overbear such incompetence. A force under General Sigel was sent down the Shenandoah Valley. Grant himself accompanied Meade in the main thrust and 120,000 men crossed the Rapidan River to do battle with Lee's ragged 65,000. It looked like a deadly pincer movement.

In practice, Butler did manage to snatch defeat from the jaws of victory; a fortnight's shuffling around left him penned in, showing that propping up a senior may not work. After one battle in the Valley Sigel was in full retreat. But the main operation was not to be so lightly deflected. A year after Chancellorsville a battle was fought in the Wilderness; using superior numbers, Grant sought to turn Lee's flank. Both generals were thoroughly competent, the fight was a draw and Grant was not halted. Though the Army of the Potomac took 18,000 casualties it said afterwards, "Lee no longer commands both armies. We've got a general of our own". That general reviewed his plan and, having nothing to learn about 'maintaining his objective', made no change. He moved round Lee's flank who had to conform. They left an appalling battlefield behind, as the Wilderness undergrowth caught fire and many wounded were burned to death. A repeat occurred at Spotsylvania and again Grant turned Lee's flank while his numbers guarded his own communications and absorbed his losses. He wrote to Halleck, "I . . . propose to fight it out on this line if it takes all summer". June found them only ten miles from Richmond; the city was fortified and a siege began. Despite a brilliant defensive campaign by Lee, the action was now permanently shifted from northern Virginia, though at the cost of 60,000 Federal casualties to Lee's 30,000.

In the west Davis changed his commanders — and lost Atlanta, the second city in the Confederacy, which influenced Lincoln's vote in the coming election, another disaster for the South. It had a brief rally. Lee sent Early, of Chancellorsville fame, via the Valley to lunge at Washington. Never was it so close to capture! With the South apparently sinking fast, here was a razor at the North's throat. Hasty reinforcement just saved the day.

In November the Union went to the polls; Lincoln's opponent was a certain George B McClellan! That gentleman again lost and the South's last hope was gone. A week later Sherman left Atlanta to draw a harrow of destruction for 300 miles to the Atlantic coast: "War is hell", he so rightly said. Lee's army was wasted by illness, casualties and desertion.

By the spring of 1865 Sherman had bifurcated the Confederacy and was moving north (*Fig. VI. 5*). Lee thought of a quick lunge at

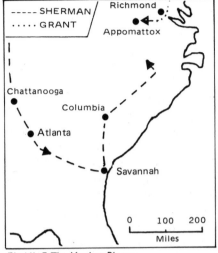

Fig. VI. 5 *The Yankee Pincers*

him before turning back on Grant, who gave him no chance. Again the flank was turned and on April 3 Richmond was evacuated. What was left of the Army of Northern Virginia dragged itself west. Surrounded by Grant at Appomattox *(Fig. VI. 2)*, Lee surrendered on April 9.

The war's complex moves were completed; three million men had enlisted to fight; the Union had taken about 600,000 casualties, the South 400,000. Though bloody the conflict "... must upon the whole be considered the noblest and least avoidable of all the great mass-conflicts of which till then there was record".[1]

With their immense prestige and large natures the two generals could quickly agree honourable peace terms. "Lee when he left Appomattox — a paroled soldier without an army — rode straight into legend ... The cause that had failed became The Lost Cause ... taking on colour and romance ... but never again leading to bloodshed. Civil wars have had worse endings than this."[3] Technically I believe Grant exceeded his authority in offering the terms but his vision prevented a bitter guerilla war. He was a generous and large-minded victor, worthy of his opponent, who was himself "... cautious, magnanimous and bold, a very thunderbolt in war ... self-contained in victory but greatest in defeat".[8]

Five days later, Abraham Lincoln, the re-confirmed and victorious President, with a fresh mandate and his vista of a generous peace, was assassinated. Within a fortnight his killer was dead, shot by the police. Two weeks after that Jefferson Davis was taken prisoner. The Civil War was over.

Five years later, one autumn morning, Robert E Lee said, "Strike the tent," and died of natural causes. Ulysses S Grant went on to serve two terms as President of the United States of America.

*   *   *   *

Management Notes

We have seen how two states, both unprepared, had to wage instant war, 'learning while they were earning'. Though neither was ready, both felt so passionately about their quarrel that a fight for survival was the chosen path with small consideration given to other less dangerous ones. Thus can chance throw up an issue and the resulting current of events and emotions convert it into a matter of suicide. Beware such subjectivity. I knew a company which became — for good reason — obsessed with defences against loss of market share. There was a broad and powerful sweep of opinion favouring, even obsessed with, buying out competitors. While not a stupid policy, its perceived attraction closed the minds of its adherents to anything else.

The Federals and the Confederates learned rapidly 'on the job'; they had to. Placing the right general in the right place tested their Presidents to the limit when they had simultaneously to devise appropriate strategies for complex situations. These tasks, on top of more routine ones, overwhelmed them (though Lincoln's innate talent was later to give him mastery of his job). One wonders, looking at companies' failure rates, whether there are too many taxing jobs chasing too few supremely talented men. This would force us to a new policy: instead of trying to improve people, we should design out some of the load on them. (Chapters X and XI sketch some ideas.)

Lincoln had more to learn than the ex-soldier, Davis. It can be argued he should have left military matters alone but how could he judge the quality of his general-in-chief without understanding the business? Winfield Scott, being senior and objective and about to retire, could have been a teacher. Instead of being allowed to graze the pastures of retirement, the old can be used — before and after they depart. They can have two attributes: being out of the race, they are independent and, having spent years in the business, are soaked in its principles. This combination can be put to use, at the technical or the managerial levels. Sugar refining is not a very esoteric chemical engineering process but it has its lore and its fundamentals; 'old sweats' know these backwards and no newcomer, however talented, can exactly replace them. Every refinery needs one.

The battle of Chancellorsville illustrates some simple but serious points. Beforehand, the (amateur) Lincoln had lectured the (professional) generals, because he felt it necessary. How right he was. It can be rash to assume that one's technical people are supervised well and performing well. Sugar refineries have large bills for fuel and all record its consumption and their boiler efficiencies, yet an inspection of the boiler house in one of his three refineries disclosed to the Managing Director that its efficiency was two points down — worth then 5% off the company's trading profit.

Hooker's record was quite good, he had drive and a sound enough army, he had an excellent plan with which to fight at Chancellorsville. There was really no reason to fear he would fail. But he did. Either things are always liable, even if rarely, to disaster or continuous monitoring is called for: not a palatable choice. Conversely, from the Confederate point of view, all things are possible: 'never despair' is the moral of their story.

The piety of Howard, one of Hooker's corps commanders, was remarked on. A subordinate with a private line to his Maker may have an assurance not given to his fellows and which may or may not be well founded. I had one such; his self-confidence was boundless and it took a lethal amount of time to test its substance.

Chancellorsville attests Lee's generalship and his men, though often ill-supplied partly because quarter-mastering was not their leader's strongest point, were devoted to him. As we saw also at Waterloo, even great men have their days off but Lee had a weekend. The battle of Gettysburg sealed the fate of the South. For if Lee's reconnaissance was dismal, he was ill-served by some of his chosen subordinates, he left too much to their discretion and failed to follow up on his orders and check on their implementation. Kind as a man, Lee was too kind as a commander:

> "He was too anxious to avoid giving offence — a fault from which his great rival Grant never suffered — and refrained from forcing his views upon unwilling recipients ... At Gettysburg Lee was at his worst ... "[9].

In the event he suffered 37% casualties to the Union's 26%.

But the man's general qualities and abilities were marvellous, which gave the South a much longer life than it had any right to expect. Surely the conclusion is this, that we cannot expect an invariable level of performance (though investment and newspaper analysts and commentators seem to) and must agree with Schiller:

"Let no man measure by a scale of perfection the meagre product of reality".

This chapter has been — in considerable part — about managerial politics. For a forthright and highly practical guide to winning at the game Michael Dixon, who writes a regular and lively column in London's Financial Times, has a winsome summary which takes some beating. He is referring to Dr Virginia Schein, a US management consultant:

> "When teaching about the workings of company politics, Dr Schein takes an attitude resembling that of an experienced biology teacher discussing the natural functions. She cannot see that there is anything to be ashamed about. No matter how rational a company's organisation chart may be, managers continually have to work against political opposition, she says. To be effective, especially in getting changes made, they must know their political power bases and how to use them — even to the extent of deceiving colleagues likely to frustrate their aims. The power bases are of seven main kinds, each having risks as well as advantages.
>
> First comes expertise, or being seen by the company as the only person who could cope with some type of crisis. Expertise can be exploited politically if it is supposed to lie in some area which the organisation has recognised as a problem or opportunity. . .
>
> Dr Schein's name for the second power base is "assessed stature'. It boils down to having a general reputation as a winner. Its flaw is that, like the rainbow, it comes and goes. While achievable by deftly publicising personal successes, it is made hard to maintain by the near impossibility of keeping secret inevitable failures.
>
> The third base, credibility, depends much on attaining prominence outside the company . . . The snag is that the value set by the employing organisation on external activity depends on the attitudes of senior management, which are prone to change. What was credibility last Friday night may be absurdity on Monday morning.
>
> Next comes the base of mobility, or the possession of skills readily transferable to some other jobs. But if managers make their mobility too visible, their chiefs may

decide to dispense with and replace them quickly rather than risk having them leave at some later and less convenient date.

The fifth base is control of information. A good way to build it up is to develop external sources of data which few, if any, colleagues are likely to get. The outside intelligence can then be sat on, traded with colleagues for further information, or passed on to them in accurate or distorted versions . . .

The sixth is called political access. It is attained by cultivating an undergrowth of friendships by tit-for-tatting with colleagues in other sections, no matter how low their rank . . . The danger is that managers who too obviously cultivate a wide network of friendships might be seen as insufficiently loyal by their own departmental colleagues.

The result could be the loss of the seventh power base — group support. It consists in having the manager's domain united in unswerving pursuit of his or her important aims. A particularly effective way of achieving group support is to convince everybody in one's department that the rest of the organisation is plotting their ruin.

Once the most appropriate power bases have been built, they can be exploited in ten main ways. The first is to develop well-advertised formal links with whichever departments are important to the manager's schemes. Such links can serve as a deterrent to the use of isolating tactics by opponents. *

The next is to present a conservative image. Enthusiasm in a manager needs only a little unwanted aid by adversaries to be seen by senior levels as near-lunacy . . .

The third is to bring identifiable opposition into the open. If opponents are obviously invited to air their views at a meeting of all involved, their strength can often be dissipated.

'Allying with powerful others' is fourth . . . From that follows spearheading one's own proposals with measures ostensibly designed to reduce colleagues' difficulties, expecially if these are trivial. To paraphrase the rugby football maxim: get your reciprocation in first.

Sixth comes striking while the iron is hot. Politicking through one proposal successfully can often ease the

* *One is reminded of the outside expert called in to advise a British government. He was effectively castrated by civil servants simply omitting him from the distribution lists for departmental memoranda. — CL.*

passage of another . . . This tactic, Dr Schein's seventh, is called using a neutral cover. An allied tactic may be to limit the outflow of information about the scheme. Plans which would call forth determined opposition if revealed in their full glory frequently go through on a series of nods if unveiled piecemeal as a series of apparently self-contained parts.

The ninth ploy is research. It consists in setting up a study of one's proposed scheme to produce 'hard data' which, whenever practicable, should be true. Either way, discussion of the data with other people should always be introduced with the words: 'Well, here is the evidence. I am not inclined to believe all of it myself. But we cannot just ignore it, I suppose.' Sometimes a manager who has brilliantly politicked a pet scheme through to approval will suddenly be faced with strong competition from someone else to take the project over. In that case Dr Schein thinks it may be best to use the last of her tactics — withdrawal. If there is any appreciable risk that one's scheme will turn out a failure it is usually wisest to try to manipulate someone else to volunteer to take it over. Of the various ways of preserving a power base, few are better than leaving others to compete for the right to catch a tartar."[10]

What more need one say?

*   *   *   *

References

[1] Sir Winston Churchill, A History of the English Speaking Peoples.

[2] Major-Gen. J F C Fuller, Grant and Lee.

[3] Bruce Catton, The Centennial History of the Civil War.

[4] J P Cullen, The Battle of Chancellorsville.

[5] Quoted by H Hansen, The Civil War.

[6] Alfred Duggan, Conscience of the King.

[7] Bruce Catton, Grant takes Command.

[8] General C F Adams, quoted by Col. A H Burne,
      Lee, Grant and Sherman.

[9] W B Wood and Brig-Gen. Sir James Edmonds, Military History
      of the Civil War.

[10] Michael Dixon, Management Education — Financial Times,
      October 4, 1985.

Some Contemporary Events

1846	Mexican War begins; US conquers New Mexico and California.
1854–6	Crimean War. Commodore Perry forces Japan to trade with US.
1857	Indian Mutiny.
1859	Franco—Austrian War.
1860	French expansion in West Africa.
1861	Outbreak of American Civil War.
1864	Prussia defeats Denmark.
1866	Prussia defeats Austria.
1867	Russia sells Alaska to US.
1870	Franco-Prussian War.
1875	Disraeli buys control of Suez Canal for Britain.
1877	Russo-Turkish War.
1879	Chile, Bolivia and Peru at war.

CHAPTER VII

MEANS AND ENDS: HITLER'S WAR WITH RUSSIA

*"Objectives are not fate; they are direction. They are not
commands; they are committments ... they are means to
mobilise the resources and energies of the business for the
making of the future."*

— Peter F Drucker

*"I wouldn't believe Hitler was dead, even if he told me so
himself."*

— Hjalmar Schacht

Purpose and Achievement

"I'm in business to make a profit", says the company director.

"Oh, really? Why do you want to make a profit?"

"Well, to reward the shareholders who provide my capital and
to finance expansion and to find better products and to . . ."

"So profit is *not* the objective, there is another or several others
behind it?"

This bit of dialogue is not imaginary; I have heard it often in
seminars but very rarely in Board rooms. If industry is unclear on
its purpose, why should its enemies not assume its aim is simply
(and selfishly) to make money?

Let us step round this little difficulty for the time being and
assume a valid, measurable, realistic and continuing objective is
established and can in turn guide ancillary aims. These are set to
be achieved — by designing a suitable strategy and managing deftly
its execution. The whole of this strategic planning process is a
mountain of waste paper if it lacks high level thinking, which at
the corporate level is abstract and conceptual in nature. The
implementation depends on team work and on the person at the
coal face: how it all looks to him and to his manager may be two
different things.

Truisms? Of course; but just as business can often mishandle or

166

even ignore them, so can others — even when life hangs on them.

"A World in Flames"
Chancellor of Germany, Führer of the Third Reich, warlord, madman plenipotentiary, Adolf Hitler led his resilient talented aggressive nation to war in search of world dominion, in the process to annul past defeats and present injustices. For the second time in his generation the lights of Europe were to go out, extinguished by the costliest conflict in history. The consequent disturbance to the human race was staggering. Most of the world's nations were involved; they mobilised 100 million people into their armed forces; untold numbers made munitions and equipment; the total killed was probably fifty million and a greater number wounded[1]. Further millions were evacuated, made homeless or enslaved.

The main determinant of the war's outcome was the Russo-German War and this climactic struggle arose from one man's mind — Hilter's: "No man of the twentieth century, except Stalin, can more richly have deserved hanging".[2] The man in question described the war's end, even if he did not anticipate it: "We shall never capitulate, no never! We may be destroyed, but if we are we shall drag the world with us — a world in flames".[3]

A Search for Objectives
Friedrich Barbarossa, the Holy Roman Emperor, died in 1190. Legend held that he was only sleeping, ready to rise up if Germany needed him. Conscious of Aryan tradition Hitler named his eastern venture Operation Barbarossa. "When [it] commences", he said, "the world will hold its breath and make no comment".[4] Only the first part of that statement proved correct. On 22 June 1941, 129 years to the day after Napoleon advanced on Russia and to his own ruin, Hitler launched 3½ million men and 3500 tanks at his then ally. Four years later, after twenty million of the combatants' civilians had died and over fifteen million of their soldiers were killed or taken prisoner, Berlin was raped by the Red Army and Hitler lay dead in his bunker.

All this decided the war. Total German casualties were probably ten million;[5] no less than two-thirds occurred in the east. In the first seven months alone, when Barbarossa was going relatively well, the Germans had 930,000 casualties. It was the gloomy forests and the boundless steppes of Russia that saw the German army bled white and whence came the hordes to overrun half the Reich. Given Napoleon's awful example, why was the invasion attempted? What was its purpose? Where did it fail? These simple questions throw some light on intelligent peoples' thinking and actions.

Only two years previously, after dividing Poland with brutality between them, Germany and Russia had signed a non-aggression pact. One may assume both signatories were equally cynical about its purpose. Stalin feared Germany, did not yet feel strong enough to attack it and was not above appeasement. Hitler, liking 'lebensraum' and hating communism, was buying time. He went on to conquer most of Europe while Stalin waited on events, though the Red Army did simulate in war games a German invasion and start to set up the defences these exercises indicated. Early in 1940 Hitler pondered on an eastern initiative, a pre-emptive strike. The idea appealed.

Nazi Germany controlled Europe from the Pyrenees to the Vistula but, not far enough away, stood a hostile Britain, an unfriendly USA, a suspect Russia; strategic security seemed still elusive. Neutralising the most accessible and most alien of these threats seemed both natural and timely; and in its feasibility appearance greatly exceeded reality. Russia had five million men under arms. Space was at a discount. The Ukraine was a rich but a spreadout agricultural prize. The main industrial centres were scattered *(see Fig. VII. 1)*, even as far as the Ural Mountains — 1300 miles from Germany. To tap these resources would require a vast occupation of territory. The front would be like a fan — the further the advance the greater its length. Objectives were spread laterally: Leningrad in the north, the Caucasian oilfields 1300 miles to the south east.

Hitler's planning directive said the Wehrmacht "... must be prepared to crush Soviet Russia in a quick campaign ... The first goal of operations is protection from Asiatic Russia from the general line Volga — Archangel". This implied seizing most of the Soviet economic base as well as battles of annihilation. The aim of neutering Russia had to be set in a wider context: winning the world war — at an acceptable cost. Then the political purpose, to whose gain that military victory was contributing, could be achieved. Thus he had a hierarchy of objectives — like companies who earn money, not for its own sake, but to finance their ultimate purpose. These politico-economic aims had to be supported

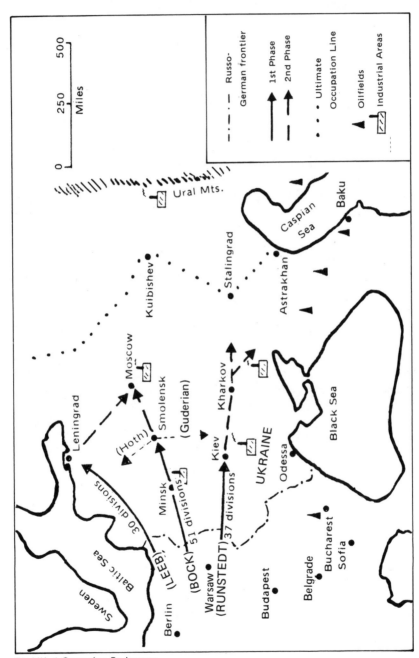

Fig. VII. 1 Operation Barbarossa

by clear military ones, but strategic thought needs strategic thinkers and these were lacking. An expert on the German Army, Colonel Seaton, writes:

> "The waging of war . . . was echeloned into four separate levels of command. The highest of these was . . . the war economy and the overall conduct of the air, land and sea battle . . . this activity was the province of the head of state and war cabinet . . . Then came grand strategy . . . conducted by war ministers, commanders-in-chief . . . Below strategy was the field of operations . . . The lowest activity was tactics.
>
> The ability of military commanders . . . obviously varies widely. The strength of some lies in tactics, that of others in operations or strategy . . . many a distinguished field-marshal would be lost if placed at the head of a regiment. A few officers, the gifted, are equally at home in all military fields, but these are rare * . . . It appears that [Hitler's] military ability lay only in the field of operations . . ."[6]

Initial plans sketched a central thrust along the traditional invasion route to Smolensk, while a southern arm scooped up the Ukraine's wealth and a northern one threatened Leningrad. Thereafter there was vagueness. Encircling the Soviet armies close to the border was an objective. There were others. Moscow? Though his generals were keen, Hitler was then unsure. Leningrad? Hitler wanted it before Moscow, perhaps (though this is not clear) for its history, and to link up with the allied Finns. Hence the powerful central drive should halt at Smolensk and help its neighbours. After that the Führer would decide what to do. In effect, says Seaton, ". . . Hitler launched Germany into the unknown with nothing but a six weeks' campaign plan in his pocket".[2]

Leadership and Organisation

The German adventurer had his virtues as well as his all too evident vices:

> ". . . restless energy, an inquisitive and active brain, great will-power, a clear memory and a good head for detail and technicalities . . . by attending demonstrations and

The implications of this, if true, for predicting the future of juniors is to be noted.

exercises he soon acquired the necessary military voca-
bulary and a grounding in war planning. He checked and
cross-checked the information and opinions given to him
by his advisers, and was not above encouraging ambitious
or disloyal officers to criticise their absent seniors."[6]

Between them Hitler and the General Staff had to decide
strategy and direct operations.* Between them were communication gaps. Total army strength was 208 divisions, each with
about 16,000 men, but a quarter of this force was garrisoning the
west. German intelligence under-estimated Russian strength which
actually included 15,000 tanks and 7,000 aircraft. The Wehrmacht
lacked petrol, tyres and winter clothing — which Hitler ignored:
"He could be far-sighted on scarcely relevant matters, yet on
subjects vital to the Reich he often could not see the wood for the
trees".[6] Over the years the General Staff had become staid and
corrupt, its officers able to take refuge from harsh political matters
in a narrow professional world, though it too was distorted by
ambition and personal disputes. This in outline was the 1941
organisation:

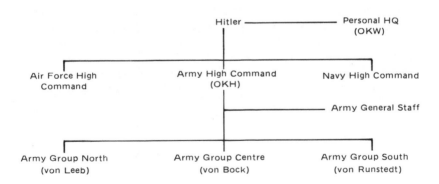

While in theory sound, the head of this organisation and too
many of its staff played politics. OKW had very different views
from those of OKH — second guessing probably provided self-
justification. Clarity of thought was further obscured because
Hilter, though a strong personality, could be got at by the schemers
and the designing, and this at a time when the General Staff's
standards had declined. "Hitler well understood the effect of promotion in seducing men's judgement and producing compliance.

* *On Hitler's talent at operational level Seaton comments: "Such ability is rarely innate.
It is more likely that the dictator's mind was conditioned to this particular level by his
talks with the leading officers of the panzer troops. . ."[6] A case of abilities being
sponsored by an example, perhaps.*

Professional ambition rarely resists that form of temptation."[2] *
Divisional strengths on the eastern front were as follows:

	Infantry	Motorised Infantry	Cavalry	Armoured	Total
German and allied	135	16	3	20	174
Russian	118	24	8	47	197

(There is uncertainty about the Russian figures: Fugate[7] gives the total of 230 divisions but many of these were at half strength.) 77% of the Germans walked into battle and had mostly horse-drawn supplies, when with a not impossible increase in vehicle production they could have been fully motorised and perhaps won the war, especially given more tracked vehicles — a case of failing to anticipate the needs of even the main campaign. Much depended on German speed and quality; a long war was probably not winnable. On the other side Stalin seems to have made what defensive preparations time permitted: reserves were held back to provide a defence in depth and the frontier screen was deliberately (and secretly) left to absorb the initial shock, kept uninformed and treated as expendable,[7] though Stalin appears to have doubted sometimes if Hitler would ever indulge in a two-front war. Had Hitler looked further eastward he would have seen his mirror image. Stalin too lacked military experience but wished to practise 'hands on' management. He had both the power and the desire to exploit it; he was —

> "... within the limits of his dogma, essentially practical. . . He knew how to use people by deceit and trickery . . . He was capricious and cynical and had a biting, sarcastic tongue; he never admitted to an error . . . He [exploited] for his own purpose only the lower instincts of human nature, by provocation, terror, demoralisation, corruption and blackmail."[6]

Not an obvious candidate for the chairmanship of ICI — or of General Motors. But, Colonel Seaton continues, "Stalin had . . . common sense, a ruthless and brutal determination, a good head for detail and a lively and inquiring mind . . ."; in fact, excepting the first point, very like his opponent. Like him he had shortened

---

*I remember my then company's debating a change to a centralised engineering service for its several factories. I opposed this. The Managing Director said, "What if you were in charge of the new central department. . .?" It was a dangerous temptation.

the chain of command to tighten his grip on it. Two committees received front line reports and directed grand strategy and operations; Stalin chaired both. He had personal representatives at each main front, quite apart from the normal political control of the Red Army — the network of commissars. There was also the NKVD* secret police reporting system. Thus Stalin had five separate information systems; no wonder he could frighten his subordinates.

1941: A Confusion of Aims

At dawn on June 22, thunder fell on the Russian lines. Within days they were ripped apart and armoured divisions, followed by plodding infantry, poured through huge gaps, and the Red Air Force lay shattered on the ground. Many Russian positions signalled: "We are being fired on; what shall we do?", to which one reply from HQ was: "You must be insane. And why is your signal not in code?"[8] Army Group Centre, commanded by the capable but over-bearing Field Marshal von Bock, took 290,000 prisoners after winning its encirclement battles round Minsk *(Fig. VII. 1)*. Within three weeks a further 300,000 were trapped and Smolensk, 350 miles from Moscow, captured. The southern drive, led by the highly experienced aristocrat, Field Marshal von Runstedt, made much slower progress towards the Ukraine. The northern arm, directed by the cautious over-methodical Field Marshal von Leeb, was half way to Leningrad but meeting counter-attacks.

In July Hitler ordered von Bock to release one Panzer Group under Colonel-General Hoth to reinforce von Leeb and one under Colonel-General Guderian, soon to become the most insubordinate and best known Panzer leader, to help von Runstedt execute a vast 'Cannae' near Kiev. Von Bock violently resisted and an extended argument developed. OKH wanted to keep part of Guderian's Group for refitting in preparation for a drive on Moscow. The Group Commander, talking directly to Hitler, said he would divert himself southward — provided his Group was kept intact; a deal was done. Guderian's superior, von Kluge, favoured the Kiev diversion, in part because it would place him under von Runstedt in place of the difficult von Bock (personal feelings thus influencing strategy). The latter and his other group commanders disagreed. Should not Moscow be taken first? The road was open and the weather fair. Hitler, attracted by the Ukrainian bread-basket, resisted contrary arguments; while 200 miles from

*Now the KGB.

the capital he sent Hoth and Guderian 400 miles north and south, a justifiable strategy only if consistently followed: Kiev's capture could lead on to the wholesale possession of southern Russia's rich resources.

Meanwhile, the Russians did not lack for problems. The Soviet opponent to von Bock was General Pavlov. His troops had been caught badly deployed while Moscow itself had to sanction any retreats. His senior told him his armies were surrounded, having heard it on Berlin radio. The luckless general found he was superseded when his replacement arrived at his HQ; he and his chief of staff were arrested forthwith and shot, maybe because he had made the mistake of discerning that his front was being treated as expendable — which was poisoned knowledge. The south found Stalin less prompt; he was pre-occupied by his over-riding wish to protect Moscow. The local commander was Marshal of the Soviet Union S M Budenny, an old crony of Stalin's with a large beard and a small mind. Now he wanted to retreat; when Stalin finally allowed this, it was too late. Von Runstedt, aided by Guderian's Group, completed a vast encirclement and a further 660,000 prisoners went into the cages. Another advance trapped 200,000 more. The Germans were well on their way to their final bag of five million prisoners, of whom perhaps only a million survived the experience. (This, the worst Soviet disaster of the war, is not of itself a criticism of centralisation. Stalin's spies told him OKH were aiming for Moscow where his reserves were massing; he could not reasonably have imagined that politics could switch this aim. When their master was proved wrong, four Soviet armies had to slow up the potentially lethal German southern thrust as best they could — before they were killed or captured.)

Von Bock had reached Smolensk on July 17. A, to the German mind, surprisingly effective Russian defence and arguments about objectives had occupied Hoth and Guderian until August 23. Not until September 5 did Hitler decide that, after all, Moscow should be taken when the Kiev pocket had been cleared. This reversal of aim was due to the Führer's being a 'soft touch'; the optimistic Göring and the OKW got at him, only too successfully — and the Soviet Union was saved. A broad front advance was resumed because "... Hitler was opposed to very deep operational thrusts but preferred closer objectives ... and he over-exaggerated the importance of Red Army concentrations ... *he altered his strategy merely to counter the tactics of the enemy*"[6] (my italics

— CL.) The contrast with Grant's single-mindedness is sharp. At Hitler's HQ the territory won looked enormous on the map. "No *Schweinhund* will ever reject me from here", he declared. All the ex-military attache in Moscow, who knew his Red Army, could manage in reply was, "I hope not".[8]

All this meant time was passing, which would have been less precious if Hitler had set out to win the co-operation of the disaffected Ukrainians and other dissidents. A Hannibal would have found ready allies while Hitler's savage treatment of the *Untermenschen* ensued their enmity. (It is ironic that the Allies' demand for 'unconditional surrender' was likewise unhelpful. An invader or acquirer must seek allies where he can; negotiations are lubricated by conciliation, retreat paths and face-savers.)

Kiev fell on September 18 and the advance on Moscow only began in early October, when the weather breaks, the countryside is flooded, the tracks — called 'roads' — turn into channels of slush. Grey skies and interminable rain become uniformly depressing. The German infantry could not physically march near to Moscow till mid-November; the army with remarkable tenacity battled on, to be at last halted in the capital's suburbs by bitter weather and stubborn defences. Then the full winter fell on them with its deep snow and day temperatures of $-30°C$ ($-22°F$) and icy Siberian winds. Was one more heave justified? The senior generals were unsure. "Von Kluge decided that he would gain the opinion of the front-line troops themselves — he was a very energetic and active commander who liked to be up among the fighting troops — so he visited the forward posts, and consulted the junior officers and NCO's. The troop leaders believed they could reach Moscow and were eager to try."[9] But in the end adversity defeated the enterprise of the men at the 'sharp end'.

Both sides were worn down, but the Germans were now overextended and exposed. A Russian counter-offensive lapped around German strong-points and regained substantial ground; continuous fighting allied with 'General Winter' drained away a dangerous proportion of German strength through battle casualties, frost-bite and sickness. This spasm faded out in February. Total German casualties were now 1.6 million, of which permanent losses were about 660,000 (assuming 2/3 of the wounded and 4/5 of the sick would return to duty). Russian casualties had been of the order of five million, of which over three million were permanent — but these could be replaced.

1942 : The War is Decided

Hopes of a short war were fading and the debate on strategy and objectives was resumed and the German leadership proceeded to sow the wind. Had it been single-minded either the Ukraine or Moscow might now be under SS 'supervision'. It should have admitted that, ringed with enemies of growing power, time was running out and 1942 had to be decisive. If a tolerable peace could not be negotiated quickly the future would become unthinkable. Some generals favoured a retirement to their start-point, others a limited or tactical offensive — which was really masking shallow thinking with a cloud of activity. Hitler demanded ". . . breaking the power of [the Red Army] in the south, capturing the seat of their economy and taking the option of either wheeling up behind Moscow or down to the oilfields of Baku". OKH made a plan aimed at Stalingrad, a major manufacturing city on the Volga, with limited moves towards the Caucasus, without stating what should follow, while Hitler and the OKW speculated about scouting towards the Urals and grabbing Caucasian oil. The organisation reflected these discords; a special 'Army Group A' was to handle a drive to the Caucausus while its co-ordination with 'Army Group B' aiming at the Volga was purely informal.

By May large German forces were deploying at Kharkov *(Fig. VII. 2)*. Spring after a terrible winter renewed confidence and despite the hideous losses the Wehrmacht was still dangerous if used in a way to capitalise on its strengths. The Russians had about 300 divisions of very mixed quality and were short of tanks; the invasion had about halved production but a moderate reserve had been accumulated and it was decided to use it in three spoiling attacks, which were persisted in despite their increasing uselessness. So 400,000 precious men and 700 more precious tanks were sacrificed to pride and ignorance. (The incompetent without luck have to preserve flexibility : the guide, 'maintenance of the objective', is a sharp weapon for the able but a double-edged one for the weak.)

In June the Germans themselves attacked, bursting open the Russian front with consummate ease and advancing rapidly under huge dust clouds over the sun-baked steppes. Some resistance on the northern flank caused Hitler to form a defensive shoulder against Voronezh while the central and southern axes were strengthened on the often sound principle of reinforcing success; at Stalingrad and the Caucasus Mountains these were finally halted. Hitler now 'lost sight of his objectives and redoubled his efforts'; Stalingrad's capture became an obsession. The defensive shoulder was soft. The Russians, glad to be accommodated, counter-attacked, encircled and destroyed the 250,000 Germans at Stalingrad and very nearly cut off the whole of 'AG A' east of Rostov. After a most skilful retreat, the most physically difficult of military and morally difficult of managerial manoeuvres, it just escaped.

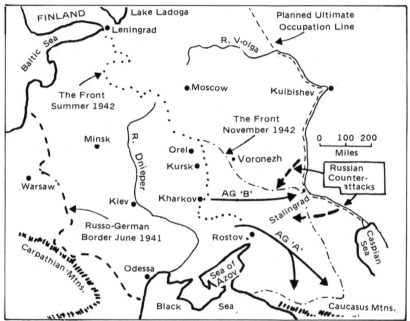

Fig. VII. 2 The 1942 Offensives

So ended the German initiative in Russia. Like better men before him the Führer was defeated by his inability to make Russian dissidence and space his allies and to link consistent objectives to rewarding strategies. In retrospect, it appears that he missed by so little . . .

Alternative Thoughts for the Führer

So Hitler deserved to fail. By the winter of 1942, if not before, he had lost the war: as Fugate[7] puts it, "A single mistake in strategy cannot be made good in the same war . . ." He goes on to argue that Germany could have had *either* the Ukraine *or* Moscow in 1941 but it could not have had both; concentrating on taking the whole of the southern economic basin would have constituted a strategic victory. Hitler's compromise constituted defeat. This argument is backed up by the German casualty rates. The graph shows that the winter advance to and retreat from Moscow cost 854,000 casualties of which 450,000 were sickness and frost-bite. A conservation policy after the Kiev success could have made some 400,000 extra men available to help take the capital in 1942.

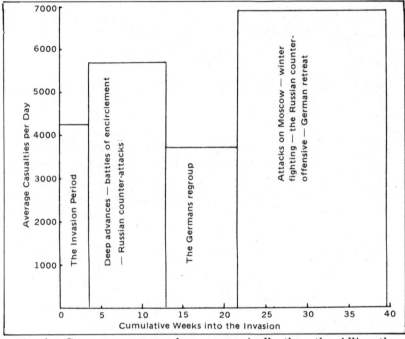

As the Germans were weaker economically than the Allies, they had to adopt the 'blitzkrieg' technique; they were simply not geared to wage the lengthy war that ensued. Could they have won it? With the advantages of a calm impersonal atmosphere and a moderate amount of hindsight, we can sketch what might have been thought.

Hitler's continuing objective was 'success' for the Third Reich and power for himself (not necessarily in that order). His strategy required the physical control of rich (hostile) countries. If their incorporation in the Reich went peaceably, the process continued; if not, then war. The objective for that would be to establish a military condition conducive to a satisfactory peace: i.e. control of an undamaged Europe without excessive German losses. For this the strategy should have been either a holding operation in the east (with Russia staying peaceful) while defeating its western allies *or* the converse. (His plan should also have taken account of the economic balance of power by covering time, resources and the scope for industrial mobilisation. There was, in fact, a story current in Germany that bears on this theme. A simple German peasant was being shown a map of the world; he was visibly impressed by the perceived physical size of America and of all the areas coloured red. He looked up and solemnly asked: "Has anyone told the Führer?")

Hitler assumed that Soviet Russia was the ultimate enemy whose basic hostility required a pre-emptive strike. (Stalin probably contemplated attacking Germany sometime, perhaps on his opponent's own reasoning, and the Germans could have awaited such an attack: their defence would surely have been relatively much stronger than the current NATO one on which the West now relies apparently happily?)

His chosen plan could have been to hold in the west, avoiding antagonising the USA, setting his economy into high gear, while effecting either the permanent neutering of Russia or its destruction, depending on the actual feasibility and cost — if a stout defence was not to be the strategy. The objectives then become the capture of the Red Army's economic foundation (South Russia and the Caucasus) and of its political and communications centre (Moscow), again with a detailed strategy to match.

The procedure involves working one's way down by hard thinking from abstract concepts at the highest strategic level, through each lower level, to increasingly detailed and more immediate objectives, each with their corresponding strategies. Managers and businessmen, being highly practical and geared to action, are no more inclined to adopt this discipline than was Hitler. I have seen a Board of Directors debate as a formal agenda item their company's strategic plan as proposed by the senior management: it moved as quickly as it could from discussing — quite incompletely — the abstract and generalised mission and objectives of the company to considering operational matters — and this was a Board of highly intelligent, articulate, experienced men.

Stalin against Hitler

So much for what might have been. What actually happened was that the war's outcome was determined, and Russia's future was secured. Its dictator had always tightly controlled its war effort. Isolated in his Kremlin fortress, primed by his multiple information systems, armed with power and ruthlessness, his Russia had to make war by centralised decision-making and local obedience. It was this calculating harsh autocrat who fed reinforcements with judicious parsimony into the Stalingrad cauldron, while building the reserves for a deadly riposte. He always kept the strategic reserve under his personal control, doling out frugal allocations to his generals as he alone thought necessary.

> "No Armenian or Jewish usurer ever safeguarded his capital so diligently, or called in the loan so swiftly when it was failing to bring him advantage . . . Front commanders were deliberately starved of men and materials until the need for allocation should arise . . . For, in spite of his lack of military experience [or because of it? — CL], Stalin was able to divorce himself at will from the detail of the tactical battle and see the thousand mile theatre, even the Soviet Union's titanic war effort, as a whole."[6]

The results were laudable though the methods were unattractive. Stalin and his senior colleagues interfered freely with the generals who in turn abused and ordered their juniors readily on the whim of the moment. General Zhukov, who became Stalin's trouble-shooter, for example, had ". . . the Russian's inborn respect for brutal authority . . . He felt himself in no way answerable to his subordinates or his troops. The only criterion was success, and it was immaterial how this was achieved. He . . . was frequently a bawling, raging tyrant in the field . . . For he was over-bearing and contrary with his inferiors".[6] An awful example of a manager looking much better from above than from below, although one must wonder if, given the situation and the Russian mentality, more humane methods would have sufficed. Stalin, too, suited the Russian character (remember the saying, 'scratch a Russian and you find a Tartar'?) but his interferences could be counter-productive. (Interfering in place of demanding performance can encourage people to play games, when scoring points becomes a not infrequent substitute for useful work.) Officers looked over their shoulders. Costly attacks were persevered with in case commanders appeared to lack "determination". Orders had to be rigidly obeyed and rules scrupulously followed. A German corps commander, who repeatedly saw off massive attacks, said: "The Russians usually made about three tries a day — the first about 9 a.m. . . . the second between 10 and 11; and the third between 2 and 3 in the afternoon".[9] Perhaps they then had tea. If you really want initiative you must encourage it.

After the German escape from the Caucasian salient, the recluse Stalin went on to beat with alternating punches exposed portions of the vast front in ponderous offensives and Hitler, lodged in identical seclusion and isolated physically and mentally in his bunker in a Prussian forest, obliged him: retreat was forbidden or too delayed and interference was continual. Thus did this otherwise shrewd erratic gambler sacrifice his Wehrmacht's competitive advantages — its mobility and tactical power — and continue this policy until it was proved to be literally suicidal.

Even so the Reich was a long time a-dying. In the spring of 1943 with the terrifying Caucasian retreat behind it, the German High Command once more debated the options. The generals wanted either some pre-emptive strike to weaken Russian offensive power or a mobile defence. Hitler vacillated. His staff advisers, none of whom had any overall responsibility, unsurprisingly adopted parochial stances. (A not dissimilar debate was going on in the Kremlin where a Stalin nervous at German preparations also wavered and the strain of waiting reduced him to rage and abuse.) The Germans chose a final fling — a massive attack on the Russian salient round Kursk. Any attack was questionable, much less one on strong fortifications; Hilter thought it a gamble but it was better than retreating.

For this enormous battle Hitler collected all his reserves but doubts continued. Guderian asked him: "Why do we want to attack in the East at all this year?" and his master answered, "You're quite right. Whenever I think of this attack my stomach turns over". The battle of Kursk — "the largest tank battle in history" — opened on July 4; 18% of all Germany's divisions and 51% of all its tank strength was committed to a struggle which could be won or lost in a matter of days. The assaults penetrated quite deeply but even deeper defences ground them to a halt and Hitler called off the battle. Casualties in the merciless fighting were very heavy and included 3000 tanks, of which about 1,000 were German, the latter being irreplaceable. Thereafter it was only a matter of time.

All strategic initiative had been lost but it took time to reap the whirlwind. From 1944 on, the USA and Britain hammered at the western front with its guard of forty more or less burned out German divisions and at the Italian side-door immobilised another twenty-six, while 160 weak German ones held off perhaps 400 Russian divisions; it took Stalin twenty-one months after Kursk to enter Berlin. In the midst of this holocaust, it may be noted that the German General Staff demanded that training courses for officers would not be less than eighteen months:

> "... with three months of 'on-the-job' training in field units. Even in late 1944, as the shortage of junior officers became critical, they stuck to their guns, and ... refused to accept Hitler's demands."[5]

An interesting order of priority.

Even though German tanks for much of the war were inferior to Russian ones and overall the army was outnumbered by around 2 : 1, its manpower casualties were only 1 : 2. Generalship, tactical skills, officer and NCO training, the troops' toughness, all combined to dilute Hitlerian fancies. How fortunate for their opponents that they were not led by an Alexander or a Scipio.

*   *   *   *

Neither Stalin nor Hitler are quite text-book examples of the manager-as-leader. But in their fashions both were effective. At the end of 1944 some 226 weak German divisions were holding off 500 Allied ones which were backed by massive superiority in material and a completely dominant air power. While we must allow for patriotism, self-preservation and fear, it still remains an astonishing if unfashionable achievement.

While neither leader's character was reproduced, in other respects the whole business resembles the American Civil War: one side skilful but without an economic foundation, the other hostile and strong; both hindered by internal politics and both in search of a strategy while not being too clear where they are going. The Confederacy and Germany were only equipped to fight in a certain way and neither could think through and choose a strategy appropriate to this. The North and Russia had weight and time as allies — and needed them. History may or may not be repetitive; problems certainly are.

The Company's Objectives

We began with a dialogue with a standard Mark I Businessman and discovered that he is not really in business for the reason he thought, that in fact he did not pursue profit for its own sake.

"So you use your profit to attract capital and to finance the development of the company?"

"Yes."

"Why?"

"Why? Because that keeps the business going."

"Why?"

"It enables it to serve and keep its customers."

"Why do you want to keep your customers?"

"To survive."

This looks like bedrock. The company's survival suits everyone: the insiders keep their jobs and their dividends, they can exercise their skills, enjoy power and make money, while the outsiders — the customers (which includes all the employees) — obtain goods and services.

The purpose of the company, all can say, is to provide useful things. Its prime objective therefore is to serve its customers. It cannot do this nor satisfy the *personal* objectives of the insiders unless it survives. Thus its continuing objective is simply survival. Profit is the *essential means* to this end.

*   *   *   *

References

[1] Ed. Prof. G Barraclough, The Times Atlas of World History.

[2] Colonel Albert Seaton, The Fall of Fortress Europe.

[3] Quoted by Brigadier Peter Young, World War 1939—45.

[4] Ed. J M and M J Cohen, The Penguin Dictionary of Modern Quotations.

[5] Ed. James F. Dunnigan, The Russian Front.

[6] Colonel Albert Seaton, The Battle for Moscow.

[7] Dr Bryan Fugate, Operation Barbarossa.

[8] Alan Clark, Barbarossa.

[9] Sir Basil Liddell Hart, The Other Side of the Hill.

[10] Brigadier Peter Young, Ibid.

CHAPTER VIII

DECISION MAKING: THE BATTLE OF THE PHILIPPINE SEA

"Fierce fiery warriors fought upon the clouds,
In ranks and squadrons and right form of war."
— Shakespeare

"Dissent . . . forces the imagination [and] converts the plausible
into the right and the right into the good decision."
— P F Drucker,
Management

Project Management: Purpose and Command

A company launches a mighty project distant from its head office.
The purpose is really two-fold: to build an operating base close to
the competitor's home market while in the process undermining
the latter's whole financial base. Pursuing either objective puts the
other at risk. The men on the spot on both sides are lonely and are
loaded with responsibility. How much stress can they take? How
much risk will they run? How much *should* they run?

The project team is very skilled but still has blind spots; its
more vocal members want to destroy the competition but cannot
first identify it! The team has to make use of complementary skills
when internal politics is at work and tradition does not favour a
brash newcomer. Clearly, choice of Project Manager is critical.
Hour by hour events can make or break the entire operation, so
decision-making, at speed and in the midst of uncertainty, is of
the essence.

This example introduces fresh issues. It also features sea-air
warfare. Subjects like continuing objectives lurk in the background;
for example, do you aim to destroy the enemy fleet — when all
should accrue to the victor, or to command the sea — which may
not necessarily pre-suppose sinking the foe, but is surely all you
need? Naval aviation is briefly described. Technically, it was both

185

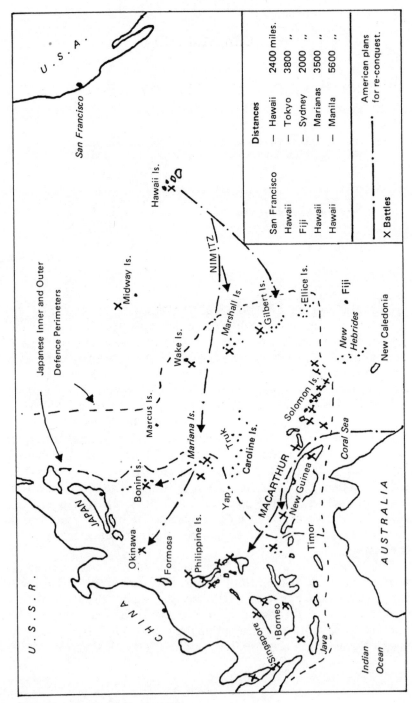

Fig. VIII. 1 The Pacific Theatre of War

ingenious and specialised. Militarily, it offered a dangerous career. Nevertheless, brave men sought it, some no doubt for duty's sake, some perhaps by chance, some probably for the simple freedom of flying:

> "Oh, I have slipped the surly bonds of earth
> And danced the skies on laughter-silvered wings."

The Pacific War

"East is east and west is west", said Kipling with his knowledge of geography. In 1941 they met again. In the thirties Japan had invaded China; mainly for economic reasons she wanted to extend her empire though this would confront America and Britain. She could not attack their homelands but perhaps could capture and fortify a rich strong base so expensive for them to retake that a reasonable peace could be negotiated.

By skill and speed she over-ran weak defences and established a front running from Burma, round the Dutch East Indies and through the central Pacific islands. Except for a corner of New Guinea and of the Solomon Islands, the defence perimeter was rapidly established *(see Fig. VIII. 1)*. Air bases were constructed and a network of islands fortified, from which land-based aircraft could assail an intruder while "the Japanese fleet was to operate as a mobile striking force which . . . could counter-attack the enemy's naval forces: the system was that of 'hedgehogs' and armoured columns transferred from land to sea".[1] This fleet would be formed round fast aircraft carriers, whose 'planes out-ranged any naval gun and so should be the leading offensive weapon. This strategy was a large, and in certain respects, well-founded conception. In December 1941, the month of Pearl Harbour, Pacific fleet strengths were as follows:

	Carriers	Battleships	Cruisers	Destroyers	Submarines
Japan	10	10	35	111	64
US and Allies	3	9	24	80	55

But Japan drew logical conclusions from wrong assumptions. The plan confronted two naval and industrial powers whose strength could only be countered by skill and luck, even when aided by bristling defences. Fuller neatly sums up:

> "Of all Japan's blunders this was the greatest: she believed

that America would be willing to barter 'losing face' for a short war, when she herself was willing to risk her existence in a long war rather than 'lose face' by a withdrawal from China."[1]

The beginning made for optimism; Britain in Malaya was weak; anyway it was busy fighting Germany while American forces were scattered over a vast ocean. Its sailors liked the contemplative life: ". . . not too much work and plenty of recreation . . . In contrast . . . The Japanese Combined Fleet was well-balanced, thoroughly trained and spoiling for a fight"[2]. Shocked by defeats, the Americans reacted by repulsing the Japanese in the Solomons and building up their strength. The outcome was an intense land-sea-air war on a vast scale. As the Japanese anticipated carriers were supreme. "You could think of a carrier as a battleship which fires piloted shells, with the advantage of being able to recover the unexpended ones"[3] But in fact the 'shells' were expendable: very high losses were accepted to sink an enemy carrier. (The US *victors* at the vital battle of Midway lost 47% of their carrier 'planes.) To give an idea of the intensity of the fighting here are the main carrier battles, which, along with others sank eighteen carriers and over 120 other warships:

Carrier Losses:		American		Japanese	
Date	Battle	Damaged	Sunk	Damaged	Sunk
May 1942	Coral Sea	1	1	1	1
June 1942	Midway	0	1	0	4
August 1942	Eastern Solomons	1	0	1	1
October 1942	Santa Cruz	1	1	2	0
June 1944	Philippine Sea	0	0	1	3
October 1944	Leyte Gulf	0	2	0	4
		3	5	4	13

The supremacy of the large carrier, a lesson ironically taught by the Japanese at Pearl Harbour to the traditional US Navy 'line' men, still left their battleships with a role. As the battle line lay on the Hawaiian seabed, they perforce had to use carriers for which the new battleships with their enormous anti-aircraft batteries — up to

180 guns — provided formidable defence. The change in technology had its social repercussions: who should now command, aviators or 'line' men? The former became in due course the majority and, "Men whose entire experience in the Navy had been in air squadrons suddenly knew more about the operations of ships and fleets than officers whose entire careers had been spent in that area"[3] A political struggle, part of which falls within our story, ensued, to be settled only at the war's end when it was laid down that an aviator admiral had to have a 'line' chief of staff and vice versa. (Such a pairing of complementary skills is a notable example of team-building.)

American Strategy

Allied communications round the Japanese perimeter were just maintained. The Australian connection and Hawaii's advance naval base status (though still 3000 miles from the 'front') were both preserved. American industrial capacity created strength and hence initiative. Bemused by modern Japanese production, we should note its novelty; US warship construction during the critical part of the Pacific War was over four times Japan's.

General Douglas MacArthur, a flamboyant and able soldier, led a rapid amphibious drive up the coast of New Guinea by a series of daring and — as they were successful — brilliant operations. Under fighter cover a town or island would be invaded, an airstrip built and the leap-frog repeated while Japanese strong points were by-passed, to 'wither on the vine'. Admiral Morison argues[2] that this 600 mile advance in thirteen weeks was a function of fine staff work, intimate inter-service team work and, above all, of the commander's superb judgement and skill. MacArthur now wanted priority given him to lunge beyond New Guinea to the Philippines, thence to Japan itself. The US Navy advocated a central Pacific drive through the Gilberts and Marshalls, on to the Marianas and the Japanese islands *(Fig. VIII. 1)*. It was finally decided to award neither priority but do both.

By the end of 1943, the US fleet was strong enough to invade the Gilberts and it was then not a great step to the Marshalls in February 1944. In March Admiral Chester W Nimitz, the Pacific C-in-C, ordered the invasion of the Marianas, by-passing Wake and Truk — to save time and cost — to seize naval and air bases on the edge of Japanese home waters. It was a bold move and a big one. It required shipping 127,000 troops 3500 miles beyond Hawaii at three months' notice to assault 30,000 fanatical and well-entrenched defenders. *Fig. VIII. 2* shows the chain of command for this enormous operation.

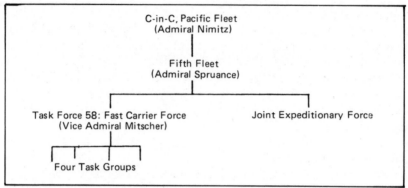

Fig. VIII. 2 Organisation for Marianas Invasion

A parallel functional organisation handled administration; all ships of the same type shared a department providing personnel, training and material. The Fast Carrier Force was self-contained with its own mobile supply train and could stay at sea for months on end.

The larger carriers each embarked up to 100 aircraft and had a crew of 3400. The principal fighter was the big strong Hellcat, with a Spitfire's speed but twice the range and fire-power. It had other virtues. The narrow flight deck usually pitched and yawed and its good "... stability and trim capabilities really made the difference in landing right square on the centreline or drifting off to the side and going into the catwalk if you were lucky or right into the drink if you were unlucky".[4] A typical US battleship, the South Dakota, had a crew of 2500 and displaced 44,000 tons. Its speed was 28 knots (five less than the carriers') and it carried 144 AA guns. The largest Japanese one (not used this time) was the Yamato class, displacing 72,000 tons, armed with nine 18″ guns to the US 16″ and having six aircraft on catapults. Both sides' ships were excellent, though the Americans' were new; only one carrier dated from peace-time and no battleship was older than five years. "This influx of ships was a result of fantastic industrial production which, in spite of little or no quality control, produced excellent ships".[3]

To meet an American thrust the Japanese were already organised for an operation called 'A-Go'. Ultimately responsible for it was the head of the Combined Fleet, Admiral Soemu Toyoda; his

commander on the spot was Vice Admiral Jisaburo Ozawa, leading
the First Mobile Fleet (FMF). Their opponents were launching
major operations at approximately three month intervals, which is
fast by industry standards. As planning was the constraint the
Americans duplicated it: leaders — Admirals Halsey and Spruance
— and staffs were alternated, and under the former the Fleet was the
3rd and its striking arm TF 38 while under Spruance it was the 5th
Fleet with TF 58. While the latter was executing the Marianas'
invasion, Halsey and his staff were planning the Philippines'
seizure. (The method was notable but did it maintain complete
efficiency, e.g. in air search ability, by 'distancing' the Admirals?)

The Fleets' Deployment

On June 6 TF 58 sortied from the Gilberts, followed by the
expeditionary force in 535 ships. In command was Admiral
Raymond Spruance; a 'line' man, he was quiet and modest, reflec-
tive by nature and fully experienced. Nearing the Marianas he

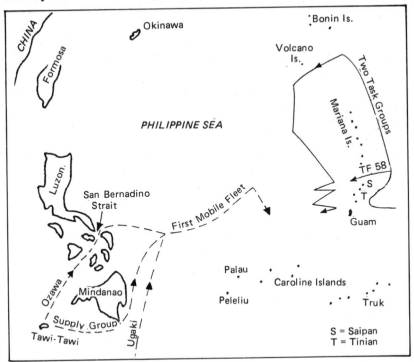

Fig. VIII. 3 Fleet Concentrations

attacked their airfields. He knew the Japanese fleet was based on Tawi-Tawi *(Fig. VIII. 3)*; it should by now have news of him. He decided he had time to cover his northern flank and on June 15 detached two Task Groups to interdict the Volcano Islands' airfields, through which 'planes could be funnelled from Japan, while marines began landing on Saipan, which with Guam were the target islands.

That same day a friendly Philippine coast watcher spotted a carrier force in the San Bernadino Strait heading east. Next day a US submarine reported a force heading north off Mindanao. Operation A-Go had been triggered. Toyoda's orders were simple: "Attack the enemy in the Marianas area and annihilate the invasion force". Ozawa was concentrating his forces — his own from Tawi-Tawi, Admiral Ugaki's — which included two battleships — from New Guinea, and a supply train. He would refuel and advance. Fleet strengths compared thus:

	Carriers	Battleships	Cruisers	Destroyers	Aircraft
American	15	7	21	69	956
Japanese	9	5	13	28	473

Ozawa, a clear thinker and a good sailor, thought relative numbers were not the whole story. His carrier 'planes' radius of action was fifty percent more than the American, and he had land-based airpower which individually was superior to carrier aircraft which suffered a weight penalty. He could use 'shuttle-bombing': standing beyond US strike range his aircraft could over-fly TF 58, attacking as they did so, land on Guam to refuel and repeat the process on the return flight. However, his aircrews were ill-trained as the experienced ones had been lost at the huge battle of Midway. Their fighter (the Zeke, son of the famous Zero) was highly manoeuvrable, given good piloting, and this was exactly what was lacking.

Spruance cleared the decks now for a major action. He postponed the Guam landing, sent the transports 200 miles east to relative safety, placed part of the fleet 25 miles east of Saipan to protect the bridgehead and ordered all TF 58 Groups to rendezvous 180 miles west of Saipan, where he could cover the landing force. It was a defensive position.

On June 18 the 99,000 men of TF 58 were in position, spread over 880 square miles of ocean *(Fig. VIII 4)*. The FMF deployment was very different. Carriers posed an insoluble problem.

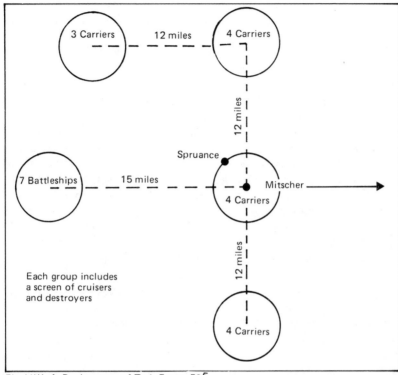

Fig. VIII. 4 Deployment of Task Force 58[5]

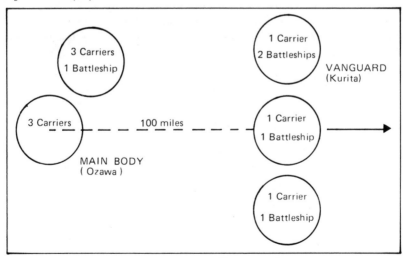

Fig. VIII. 5 Deployment of First Mobile Fleet[5]

Light armour, naked flight decks and aircraft full of fuel and bombs, all made for extreme vulnerability. Concentration aided co-operation but dispersion offered protection — a classic dilemma. The Japanese, therefore, set up a vanguard under Admiral Kurita, including four battleships and three light carriers, as a well protected scouting and decoy group *(Fig. VIII. 5)*. The main force was the same distance (100 miles) in rear as *the difference in range of the combatants' aircraft.*

For any initiative air searching was indispensable but the US Navy was much less good at it. Perhaps for administrative convenience it had down-graded the function; anyway, it felt it had fewer targets to find! Ozawa with less resources searched more: "... the scale of American air searches borders on negligence".[3] (It illustrates that simple faults can be stomached even by highly professional organisations.) Now with an accurate count of TF 58's strength he probed American intentions. From his Midway tactics Spruance seemed a cautious man who would cover Saipan closely; he therefore proposed to weaken him with land aircraft attacks, then press a fleet action. His search aircraft should pinpoint the Americans' position before they found him. Also, he held the 'lee gauge', which conferred on carriers the initiative that being to 'windward' offered sailing ships: as the prevailing wind was from the east, Spruance had to turn away to launch his aircraft into the wind while the FMF could do so while advancing.

After re-fuelling, he resumed his course on June 17. His rough position was reported by a US submarine. That evening he was still placed beyond US strike range but ready for a full-scale dawn attack. The 48,000 men in the FMF were excited and willing.

The Turkey Shoot

Each day TF 58 steamed west, while searching the seas in front of it, each night east to avoid being out-flanked during darkness. No sign of the enemy. Before dawn on the 18th the submarine's sighting report was received and a picket line of submarines set up. That afternoon Japanese scouts spotted TF 58, which had no recent fix at all on the FMF. Marc Mitscher, commanding the Task Force under Spruance's 'general direction', knew his position was known as the spotters had been seen. Would the FMF find him next morning ready to be shuttle-bombed? He felt very vulnerable. That evening he turned east as usual and two hours later received a radiofix. Ozawa had broken radio silence and

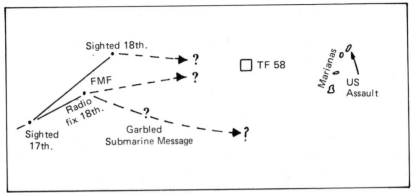

Fig. VIII. 6 The Fifth Fleet's Dilemma

appeared to be 355 miles WSW *(Fig. VIII. 6)*. Mitscher therefore proposed to reverse course, close the range during the night and attack next morning. Spruance was not sure the fix was genuine; it differed from the submarine sighting. Another (garbled) transmission suggested a closer position. The Japanese liked flanking moves: there might be a second group moving round him, to be no more easily detected than the one now apparently located. His orders only prescribed the occupation of the Marianas and protection was his prime role. He rejected Mitscher's proposal and dawn on the 19th found the Task Force ninety miles SW of Saipan. It was still ignorant of the FMF's precise position.

The morning was fine and warm with unlimited visibility; not a good day on which to attack a protected fleet. As the FMF

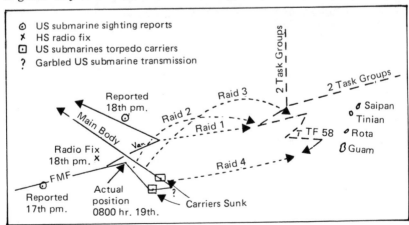

Fig. VIII. 7 Japanese Attacks on TF 58[5]

seemed still distant Spruance suggested a strike to neutralise Guam, rightly suspecting its inclusion in Ozawa's plans. This attack met a Japanese one from Guam and shot down thirty-five aircraft. The fight had not ended when American radar signalled an approaching force 150 miles to the west. Ozawa's first raid consisted of sixty-eight bombers and escorts from Admiral Kurita's Van Force *(Fig. VIII. 7)*. The aircraft were on their way when a US submarine stalked and sank one of Ozawa's carriers. The Task Force steamed west for twenty minutes, then turned into the wind and launched 450 fighters.

There followed eight hours of almost continuous action, some in air battles overhead and some distant from the fleet, over which the skies were full of shell bursts and furious attackers, while ships manoeuvred violently to avoid them. American air control was admirable. The Combat Air Patrol (CAP) mounted standing fighter cover over the fleet. The Combat Information Centre noted the CAP's fuel state, placed it for interceptions, rotated it for re-fuelling; detachments for interceptions were replaced or reinforced as necessary. The enemy could be met sixty miles out; there was defence in depth. Behind layers of fighters lay the final screens of massed gun batteries. That first attack lost sixty-five percent of its aircraft. One bomb on the South Dakota and one aircraft lost was the total of US damage.

While Ozawa's second raid was in progress a second carrier was torpedoed; ninety-eight 'planes were lost out of 130 in the raid in return for very slight damage. In the third raid forty-seven aircraft went to a false contact so only seven failed to return. A final attack lost eighty-nine percent of its eighty-two aircraft. By the evening Ozawa had lost 346 aircraft and two carriers; he had 100 'planes left. TF 58 had lost thirty aircraft. Three of its groups now steamed west, leaving one to neutralise the Mariana airfields and to refuel. What a wag called the Great Marianas Turkey Shoot was over.

The Counter-Attack

That night Mitscher launched no air searches; an aviator himself, he understood — perhaps too well — his crews' fatigue. (But there is a time for knowing when to push people beyond normal limits.) On the 20th only routine searches were mounted, when US airmen had yet to see the FMF. Actually, it was moving NW while re-fuelling, to resume the fight next day as Ozawa thought many of his aircraft were safe on Guam. Despite his losses he launched as many searches as the Americans. Not till mid-afternoon did they find him, reportedly 220 miles away. This was extreme range and returning aircraft would have to land at night, but they were armed and their engines warm. Mitscher had decided on an immediate launch when an unwelcome message came in: the FMF was really sixty miles further away than first reported. The Japanese intercepted this transmission and Ozawa called off further re-fuelling and ordered a speed of twenty-four knots homeward. Nevertheless, Mitscher let his decision stand; the carriers could close part of the range during the flight.

Forty minutes after the first sighting, ten carriers turned into the wind and launched 216 aircraft in ten minutes. While they flew NW at their most economical speed, the carriers steamed at their maximum rate after them *(Fig. VIII. 8)*. A large sea/air action ensued.

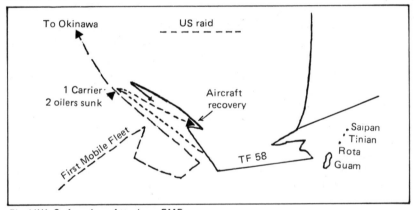

Fig. VIII. 8 American Attack on FMF

The Japanese launched all their 'planes and the AA barrage included the battleships' big guns. The American attacks were well spread and pressed home with courage: one carrier was sunk, one badly and three lightly damaged; a battleship and a cruiser were also hit, all for the loss of twenty US aircraft shot down. But the survivors now had to reach their mother ships. Cruising slowly on lean mixtures, tired crews faced a two-and-a-half hour flight in darkness, often with damaged aircraft. Many ditched in the sea as tanks ran dry. Mitscher, copying Spruance after Midway, ordered a general illumination to help recovery operations; knowing the risks he ran his aircrews were heartened while he must have found it a long two hours. They landed where they could and crashed where they could not. Many ditched alongside ships or collided with others on crowded decks. By 2250 all were down somewhere; 150 aircrew were rescued from the sea.

The Task Force was low on fuel which restricted speed. Searches revealed it was not closing the range at all; the FMF was in full retreat. Aware of pressures on the local commander, Toyoda had removed from Ozawa the authority to decide policy; it was difficult for him to recognise irretrievable defeat and his superior had to intervene. By the 22nd the Mobile Fleet, less ninety-five percent of its carrier 'planes and one-third of its carriers, was lying off Okinawa. Operation A-Go was ended.

TF 58 sailed east; within two weeks it was anchored in the Gilberts. That autumn as the 3rd Fleet it would see the repossession of the Philippines. The Marianas were prepared to accommodate 750 Boeing B.29 bombers to devastate Japan. On July 18 the Japanese Cabinet resigned.

The Marianas' operation was costly; the US took 26,000 casualties and 60,000 Japanese were killed. Their naval air force was virtually eliminated. Aircraft losses totalled 185 American to about 600 Japanese and these losses were to be repeated in the battles for the Philippines. Japan was thus fatally weakened; for it, thereafter, there remained only despairing, though violent gestures but it persisted, long after its objective had become unattainable, and holding out until the destruction of the homeland became intolerable. The hunter gets committed to the chase, persisting wishfully in his hopes. "It seems to be a human characteristic to discount evidence that does not conform to earlier ideas, especially after a particularly difficult decision has been taken."[6]

Thirteen months after Ozawa's defeat Japan surrendered.

The Post-Mortem

Though portentous, the battle left winners and losers equally concerned and, perhaps inevitably, politics intervened. "Rarely in history has so convincing a victory generated such dissatisfaction among the ranks of the victors and it seems more than mere coincidence that the ranks split almost uniformly along line officer — aviator lines."[3] Both sides could take praise and blame. Japanese air search was much superior but offset in the event by US fighter defence. Ozawa deployed and positioned his fleet with imagination. US submarines provided good, sometimes the only, intelligence and sank two of the carriers. Japanese submarines sank nothing, seventeen of them sinking in the process!

Debate centred on Spruance's decisions. Should he have let Mitscher advance on the 18th to attack next morning? His official objective was to cover the Mariana landings, themselves highly important; he was also accountable for the transports and their cargoes. But few would have described the sinking of the FMF in the process as just a happy by-product. The carrier admirals under Spruance called it an equal objective — aviators against a line man. Dickson[3] points out that they could then be expected to have mounted the searches needed to achieve it! Spruance could question the implication of the search reports: the submarine report on the 18th conflicted with the radio fix; the Japanese liked flank attacks. The simplest deduction from the *available* information was a second force aiming at the Saipan bridgehead and parrying this should, in Spruance's view, take precedence. Mitscher assumed the group left to protect the bridgehead — which included two small carriers and seven old battleships — could cope. Given a sizeable enemy and his superior reconnaissance this is debatable.

Suppose Spruance had supported Mitscher: what then? He could have attacked Ozawa's Van, the best defended group, but the Main Body would have been beyond his reach yet he within its range — which was exactly why Ozawa adopted that formation. The outcome is unpredictable but arguably much less of a turkey shoot. The groups detached to neutralise the Volcano Islands (and which destroyed over eighty Japanese aircraft) contemplated while rejoining the Task Force a flank attack on the FMF, to use its numerical superiority. Interestingly, Mitscher did not hear of the idea until after the battle, nor did Spruance debate it. Interestingly, the Japanese speculated about it and decided the US would not adopt it.

What can amateurs with hindsight make of all this? Spruance seems to have followed orders strictly; he also fought and won overwhelmingly a decisive battle. Should the destruction of the enemy's fleet have been the main objective? That attained, all is given to the victor. The suspected flank attack might have sunk the light carriers and upset, but not devastated, the bridgehead. Churchill has said, ". . . safety first may be useful in politics, but it leads nowhere in war", a perhaps debatable proposition though

Mitscher's plan was certainly a higher risk, higher pay-off option. Sinking the FMF which was irreplaceable, at the price of some American loss which was not, seems a sound exchange. With hindsight we can note that the heart of the FMF was its aviation and ninety-five percent of that *was* eliminated but this distinction may not have been clear then.

A safer option, we can now say from the safety of our own arm-chairs, would have been to follow Spruance's decisions and the resulting Turkey Shoot with thorough searches during the night of the 19th, which should have produced more and better counter-attacks. A riposte from a sound defence can be deadly, as Wellington showed, but it has to be fast. Surely it could have been, when the 5th Fleet might have had the best of both worlds? Of course the background of 1944 was influential. Spruance's responsibility was a large one, the stakes high. By nature analytical and cool (and a touch cautious) he had made sound and critical decisions in the Midway battle and he judged time to a nicety in the Philippine Sea. His orders seem to have been limited, yet the Navy expected an exciting toll of enemy carriers. This second objective was only implied — but must a senior man have everything explicit? On clear policies, no. If objectives conflict, yes. Peoples' propensity to run risks varies greatly so at least broad priorities must be specified.

For the battle of Midway Spruance's orders from Nimitz — faithfully discharged — had been clear:

> "In carrying out the task assigned . . . you will be governed by the principle of calculated risk . . . the avoidance of exposure of your force to attack by superior enemy forces without good prospect of inflicting . . . greater damage on the enemy".[2]

Perhaps, as we discussed above, there was a better technical solution to TF 58's problem — searching better and counter-attacking earlier — or perhaps Nimitz had combined a not wholly comprehensive directive with a prudent and over-thoughtful command (Spruance/Mitscher), when he might have set up one ready to run higher risks for more glittering prizes. (As so often, the outcome of team work is a force to be reckoned with — or made use of.) In either event the organisational implications are apparent — and significant.

The Chairman of Rio-Tinto Zinc Corporation (which spends hundreds of millions of pounds annually on its projects, puts the point this way:

> "The most important factor in selecting the top man is his qualities of leadership . . .
>
> Business schools tend to play down the importance of leadership in large corporations, and invariably stress management skills rather than leadership. I am sure that exactly the opposite is true in large projects, and possibly in business as a whole".[7]

To the persons most intimately affected the issues may have seemed simpler yet more urgent:

> "Nor law, nor duty bade me fight,
> Nor public men, nor cheering crowds,
> A lonely impulse of delight
> Drove to this tumult in the clouds . . ."[8]

*   *   *   *

References

[1] J F C Fuller, Decisive Battles of the Western World.

[2] S E Morison, The Two Ocean War.

[3] W D Dickson, The Battle of the Philippine Sea.

[4] Ed. A Robinson, In the Cockpit.

[5] Ed. E B Potter and Fleet Admiral Chester W Nimitz, Triumph in the Pacific.

[6] A H Cartmell, letter to the author.

[7] Sir Alistair Frame, Speech to the Engineering Project Management Forum.

[8] W B Yeats, An Irish Airman Foresees his Death.

SECTION B:

TECHNICAL CASES

"If the war didn't happen to kill you it was bound to start you thinking."

— George Orwell

"For what matters in any system is the performance of the whole; this is the result of growth and of dynamic balance, adjustment, and integration rather than of mere technical efficiency."

— Peter F Drucker

CHAPTER IX

MANAGING INNOVATION:
WARSHIP GUNNERY AND DESIGN

*"Along this tree from root to crown
Ideas flow up and vetoes down."*

— Unilever executive *

*"I pressed down the mental accelerator. The old lemon throbbed
fiercely. I got an idea."*

— P G Wodehouse

A Stomach for Novelty?

Most organisations like to think that they at least are open-minded, ever progressive and committed to encouraging creative Young Turks however junior. How often is this charming picture a laughable caricature of reality?

Two naval examples of the process of innovation remind us of aids and aspects that may not be either clever or esoteric but are still fundamental. The history of warfare is laced with great inventions; having the enemy at the gate concentrates the mind wonderfully. Obvious ones are the composite bow, the stable chariot, the breech-loading rifle, the assault gun, and there are more subtle ones: the warhorse, the stirrup, siege engines, staff organisation, radio. Mostly we know little about the inventors or the no doubt pervasive problems of development and application. We do know that innumerable inventions have been ignored or delayed. A rudimentary tank was dismissed by Lord Palmerston as "uncivilised"; the Royal Navy resisted convoy formation to combat U-boats until the eleventh hour in 1917; the British invented tank tactics but still expected to use "the well-bred horse" while Germany was creating panzer divisions.

Against this there have been notably speedy changes. The long bow became the dominant of the battlefield in one man's lifetime;

Quoted by P F Drucker, Management.

204

the Mosquito bomber went from design to front line service astonishingly quickly; 140 years previously, one of the first uses of vaccination against smallpox was the Duke of York's jabbing (not personally) the entire British army and this only four years after Jenner's experiments. Like all organisations the services have their triumphs and their failures. If to the layman the latter seem to predominate, there are sometimes reasons for this . . .

A Case Study : The US Navy's Solution

The first iron battleship was launched by Britain in 1859. Until the end of the century progress was limited to modest developments of this basic design, whose examples were numerous and sat in ports around the world but fought occasional fleet actions. Typically they mounted 9" and 12" bore guns as well as batteries of smaller ones; they displaced upwards of 16,000 tons. At the time they must have appeared very imposing.

Behind the facade were anomalies. Until 1905 all British naval ordnance was provided by the army's War Office. The battleships' fighting range was thought to be about 3000 yards, the same as the maximum range of Nelson's cannon a century earlier. The reason was that the guns were too inaccurate beyond that distance. Fleet target practice was unrealistic — and even more uninspiring: the US Navy once fired 200 rounds at a stationary target at 2800 yards to score two hits. Guns were still mostly fired in broadside; they were not fixed like Nelson's but were difficult to elevate and depress quickly so the gunners fired 'on the roll'. This meant the rate of roll, not the gun's capacity, determined the rate of fire and the gunner's judgement determined the accuracy. The result was deplorable.

Around the turn of the century a young British naval gunnery officer was serving at sea. His name was Scott, later to be Admiral Sir Percy Scott. He was a lively character, highly inventive and a free-thinker, very ready to question accepted methods. As a junior reformer his role was modest: the Royal Navy was not to be lightly deflected to new ways. Padfield[1] quotes him as saying:

> "In the end we had to do as the others were doing. We gave up instruction in gunnery, spent money on enamel paint, burnished up every bit of steel on board, and soon got the reputation of being a very smart ship".

He then started to experiment, with methods that were reveal-
ing. His first effort — the cheapest and the most effective — was
simply to encourage skill: practice results were publicised and
good gun captains rewarded. He replaced the standard sights ". . .
with telescopes, the cross hairs of which he had made with the
fine hairs of a midshipman aboard."[1] One day Scott spotted a
gunlayer who, instead of firing 'on the roll' like all his fellows,
could operate his gun's elevating mechanism quickly enough to
offset the ship's roll. Scott thereupon exercised his crews in this
technique, using a special practice target; he went on to design a
similar teaching aid for allowing for horizontal deflection. Then
loading practice, again using an aid, allowed the gun to be fired
to its limit. A comparative test showed the old technique scoring
two hits in twenty-five ship-minutes and the new fifteen hits in
one ship-minute, or 190 times as good! Pushed by *influential
sponsors* 'continuous aim firing' had by 1903 spread throughout
the Royal Navy.

While on the China Station Scott in 1901 had become friends
with a Lieutenant Sims (later, Admiral William Sims) of the US
Navy. They talked 'shop'; impressed by Scott's gunnery experiments Sims copied them with equally gratifying results and the
way was obviously open for a fantastic elevation in fleet performance. Indeed, this improvement was so vast his service would
surely recognise instantly and without cavil that this innovation
was the breakthrough of a lifetime. It only remained to tell the
Navy about it.

To call that organisation uninterested would be a great over-
statement. His report generated an enormous silence. He wrote
papers, thirteen in all, over the next two years and circulated
them widely. The response was still miniscule. What to do? He
decided to elevate his aim. He wrote to the Navy Department in
Washington. Its response, if that is not straining the meaning of
the word, was limited: first, nothing happened at all. The reports
were filed, to be found years later, some half-eaten by cock-
roaches. The next stage was almost positive: it took 'counter-
battery' form. Sims had got rougher, his impatience making for
shock tactics, and his reports rained in, with copies to other
people — men of power. Washington grew nettled under the
bombardment; it pointed out that the present equipment was
good — after all, Washington had designed it. It followed that,
if it seemed inferior, the gunners were at fault. Anyway, and here

was the clincher, "continuous aim firing was impossible".

Undeterred, Sims maintained his pressure. Washington moved to active warfare: phrases like "deliberate falsification of evidence" and "crack-brained egotist" were fired off. Sims, nothing if not consistent, took his final step and wrote to a gentleman called Theodore Roosevelt, then President of the United States. His letter, interestingly enough, was read. Even more curiously, it had an effect. Thought and discussion and controversy passed the time until Roosevelt was won over and the Bureau of Ordnance was forced to reconsider its position. In 1902 Sims was appointed Inspector of Target Practice and in due course his navy too adopted continuous aim firing.

The US Navy's Problem

It is fruitful to explore the reasons for the Navy's indomitable resistance to such an important and clearly beneficial innovation. Despite its seemingly self-evident and immense advantages, the technique for improving the *prime* weapon, fleet gunnery, languished. Why?

First, one may suppose, was the simple novelty of Sims' proposals. The human mind seems to reject newness automatically, just as the body generates physical anti-bodies against alien organisms. This confers protection. While the 19th century statesman, who opined that "any change at any time for any reason whatever is greatly to be deprecated", was rather over-stating the matter, a case can be made against untested innovation. Conservatism preserves the good as well as the bad; revolutions cause as much misery as they alleviate; rapid change often exceeds peoples' adaptability.

Second, the novelty was in this case being advocated clearly and forcibly by a remote and insignificant source. Sims was a faraway junior: why should one listen to such as him — and disturb important tradition? There are two points being made here. Because the advocate was junior one did not have to listen. Had he been Lord High Admiral one would. But one would still not necessarily be receptive unless this great man could persuade and reassure. Seniority creates an audience, not disciples. In any case the idea was Sims', not the Navy's. Just why is a prophet lacking in honour in his own country? Why does familiarity breed stolidity? Perhaps one is subconsciously saying: 'this wasn't invented by me, only by a mere colleague', implying 'that is, someone pretty like me;

if I can't — and I might have if I'd tried — no one similar to me should be able to'?

Furthermore, the old technique was Washington's. If Sims' was so much better the old must be pretty bad. Naturally people say, 'I'm imperfect but am I that bad?' Neither Washington nor others in these situations can articulate the more subtle consequences of a seemingly simple change. Sims' proposals were much more influential than they appeared. Gunfire was to be vastly more rapid and accurate but the repercussions would not stop there. This fearsome performance would drastically effect ship design, ship routines, fleet tactics. Much existing doctrine would be called into question. Much existing equipment would be made obsolete — and what would that do to Navy budgets? The sheer size and ramifications of the changes were daunting even to sympathisers, aspects a lieutenant on the China station could happily ignore.

Finally, and most disturbing of all, these massive technical changes would have social and political side-effects, not all of them comfortable ones. If so much had to be re-examined and re-cast, if gunnery could become so devastating, if even Government policy could be affected, what would all this do for the role, influence and social standing of gunnery officers and their associates and to their future numbers and promotion prospects? In ship design, in tactical planning, in routine operations and consequently in the wardroom, they would be men of stature. Was not a reaction to all this inevitable? Faced with ever-increasing repercussions and heavily committed as it was to explicit organisation, the Navy could only react with pained reluctance. One can see why.

Now consider the inventor's view-point. Sims was clearly identified with the novelty, it was not new to *him*. It was also his opportunity for recognition and promotion; after all, he was then only a junior officer standing watches on an aimless-seeming foreign cruise. Navies were then not exactly hungering for the new Consign Britain's Royal Navy:

> "The eighties and early nineties were years in which the old officers were still embedded in sails and all the thought that pertained to them. They hated engines and modern guns; the mine and torpedo were anathema to them ..."[2]

While, later, promotion was related to a ship's shooting record, for Sims the time was not propitious.

A Success Story: The Dreadnought Battleship
In 1858 the French began to introduce ships with which to challenge British naval power — steam-powered, fast, armoured, and fitted with shell-firing rifled guns instead of smooth bores firing solid shot. Larger and longer ranged guns promised prolonged stand-off action, which called for larger and better equipped ships, with heavier armour, as gun platforms. By 1900 a typical battleship had four 12″, sixteen 8″ and many smaller weapons, this mixed main armament aiming to meet all combat situations. Speed could be eighteen knots — for short periods; propulsion was by reciprocating steam engines, forced by the cramped space to rotate fast, which caused breakdowns. Engine rooms were infernos of noisy oil-spewing monsters. However, naval officers were debating ship design; one was Sims, by now well-known and, another was Scott, now the British Inspector of Target Practice. The steam turbine had just been invented and tried in large liners but not in large warships. Enter a man called Jacky Fisher.

He had joined the British Navy in 1854. Ebullient, energetic, determined, by 1897 he was C-in-C Mediterranean. His career was adorned by numerous innovations: faster ship construction, new entry and training methods, national defence policy, submarine development, lower deck conditions, oil-firing, all felt his stimulus. It was quite a record, but not without its critics:

> "Fisher had a practice of consulting young officers . . . But, regrettably, he spoke to them in a derogatory way about their superiors . . . His was not the method of leading smoothly but of driving relentlessly . . . Whether the Navy could ever have emerged from its old ways in time for the Great War without his forceful acts is difficult to estimate, but in my opinion it could not."[3]

The result was a turbulent career, sometimes ignoring orders and then confounding his seniors with successful initiatives. He too had worked to improve gunnery; he was familiar with Scott's work. He knew of the design debates and he probably knew of Sim's advocacy of the 'all-big-gun ship' which was influencing design standards. In 1904 Admiral Sir John Fisher became First Sea Lord. Now he had power. Churchill, writing after 1914, thus describes him :

> "Harsh, capricious, vindictive, gnawed by hatreds arising
> from spite, working secretly or violently as occasion might
> suggest . . . 'Ruthless, relentless and remorseless' were the
> epithets he sought always to associate with himself. 'If
> any subordinate opposes me . . . I will make his wife a
> widow, his children fatherless, and his home a dung-
> hill'. He acted up to these ferocious declarations . . . To
> be a 'Fisherite' . . . was during his first tenure of power
> an indispensable requisite for preferment. On the whole
> his vendettas and manoeuvres were inspired by public
> zeal and conduced, as I hold, markedly to the public
> advantage."[4]

Not exactly a smooth organisation man. Now he wanted a new
battleship, to outmode instantly all others with an unrivalled combination of fire-power, speed and protection. There was to be no
compromise on its main armament: a complete battery of the
largest guns would defeat a mixed-battery ship from a safe
distance. Fisher believed the technology of the time could match
his requirements. He set himself single-mindedly to secure them.
For this he was not ill-equipped. His drive and ruthlessness apart,
". . . in sheer intellect he stood head and shoulders above his naval
fellows".[4] He was an excellent organiser and must have been a
formidable 'progress chaser'. He could conceive an idea, preserve
its freshness throughout its development and manage its building.
The results were astonishing.

Fisher had already had the Chief Constructor of the Malta
Dockyard, Gard, working on a design; Gard followed him to
England. His master realised an all-big-gun ship powered by steam
turbines was not exactly uncontroversial so he set up a Committee
on Design "in which the leading naval constructors, gun designers,
and gunnery experts and scientists were to meet . . . Most of the
Committee members, however, were chosen for their known
agreement with Fisher's ideas".[5] But they were not nonentities
and four of the naval members were later to become admirals, but
unsurprisingly, Fisher's design was chosen; it was to have ten 12"
guns, steam turbines and a speed of 21 knots.

Throughout Fisher preserved strict secrecy; enemy powers were
not to be alerted and speedy building would complete the project

before the world knew what was happening. A year after he became First Sea Lord, in October 1905, the new battleship was laid down in Portsmouth Dockyard. Just 181 days later she was launched. And 366 days after being laid down she steamed on her trials — a monument to project management and industrial strength. She was named *Dreadnought*.

In recognition of the risks he was running, Fisher chose to build one ship at first, to prove the design. This she did. She burst without warning on an astonished naval world, which speedily perceived the implications of her conception. Her looks matched her power — the clean lines, the massive gun turrets — and she passed her sea trials with near-flawless ease. "She was the embodiment of confident shipbuilding harnessed to gunnery . . ."[1] In fact, innovation personified. The design had faults but subsequent versions easily rectified them. That done, Fisher proceeded to build a second revolutionary warship — a cross between a battleship and a cruiser. The concept was simple: any enemy that could fight it could not catch it, any that could catch it could not fight it. This ship was launched in 1908: the battlecruiser was a new line in capital ships.

Fisher's *Dreadnought* battleship staggered the nations. All existing capital ships were on the instant out-moded. Its fighting power was supported by its technical efficiency: it cost only 17% more[1] than obsolete designs in return for overwhelming fire-power, extra speed, improved crew conditions and clean placid engine rooms. When Britain went to war she had twenty 'Dreadnought' battleships against Germany's fourteen and seven battlecruisers against four. It altogether looked like a happy combination of foresight and determination, under-written by industrial power.

The Innovative Process

These naval cases show that improvement is a lengthy and complex process. An idea must first be conceived and born, which presupposes having a fertile inventor on hand, and then cared for by a suitable parent or foster parent; the latter may usefully be a sponsor with power. Then the invention has to be transformed into actuality — the development process. Finally, it must be put to work — building and application. So managers wanting an innovative organisation must needs be concerned with the entire procedure: generating good ideas, considering them realistically and sympathetically, realising their potential, exploiting them. These are large subjects, partly beyond the scope of our cases and my knowledge so their discussion must be selective. Let us first look at the direct lessons.

Reasons for Sims' total inability to improve quickly the US Navy's deplorable gunnery have been adduced. Now to generalise them:

- humans reject mind transplants as they do physical ones, not without reason;
- the status of the inventor influences publicity: if important he has an audience but not necessarily a willing one;
- the inventor's position influences his appeal; insiders are receptive to outsiders, which they prefer over their own kind;
- for the new to supplant the old, clearing the decks is needed, which can be done tactlessly or gently;
- the audience may correctly perceive a domino effect not foreseen by a probably blinkered inventor;
- inventors may be dazzled by the technical ingenuity of their ideas and quite miss their disturbing side-effects: that these may be "political" or "social" and not "technical" may not make them any less respectable;
- the inventor has as much reason to be biased in favour of the new as his audience has in favour of the old;
- organisations vary enormously, in time and place, in their creativeness and their receptiveness.

We shall have to remember these points when we try to define the innovative organisation. The lessons from Fisher's projects are different but complementary:

- an innovator need not be smooth and all things to all men but he does need some combination of power and persuasiveness to match his organisation's receptiveness;
- character fosters project management just as does sheer organising ability;
- development is safer and easier when taken in many small steps;
- dramatic progress may still be marginally cheap;
- a fine conception may only be preserved and reach realisa-

tion uncompromised if managed by a dominant character;
— tactical innovation may not confer strategic advantage.

Some comment or explanation is warranted. Fisher was often disliked in the Navy but he had power; he was advocating a worthy idea *and* had respectable allies; those less committed must have had a hard time — they were brutally over-ridden. If one lacks merit or appeal power is essential. "Fisher had prepared for his era of reform by securing the personal support of the King . . . and to a considerable extent that of the leading politicians and the press."[3] His personal qualities allied to British industrial capacity drove construction along. Though speed was helped by diverting equipment from other construction, it shows what can be done by clear priorities, drive, organisation and ambition.

Speed alone is rewarding. Take a project to renew a factory or a hospital, to be completed in three years. But in one year the 1944 invasion of France was planned and executed; in three years the Americans fought their whole Pacific War. By military standards we civilians seem to crawl. Maybe we do not command national resources regardless of cost but if we could erect our building in two years, not three, interest would be slashed and savings reaped early : think of the impact on the 'DCF' return!

The *Dreadnought* was a revolution but was a mixture of more or less developed components. In themselves 12″ guns were not new; a whole battery was and the effect of a broadside on the ship's structure a question. The steam turbine had not been tried in large warships. Small steps mean small risks but they may not be feasible : new aircraft do not go supersonic on the first test flight; when their test pilots become astronauts they either ride off first time on a rocket or stay at home. Anyone must dislike a project whose risk profile exceeds his organisation's insurance capacity.

One notes the modest cost of *Dreadnought's* supremacy; Scott's work cost little. So often real genius finds simple solutions. Of course technical changes are not always cheap but are they always worthwhile? Part of the problems may be fashion; yesterday's stop-valve in a material supply pipe was worked by a simple chain while today's must needs be servo-operated.

Many ideas need an extended translation into hardware. The brilliant concept may be progressed by a host of intermediaries and these, especially in the collective form called committees, will smooth and modify and compromise. Only an autocrat can keep his vision pristine.

The *Dreadnought* battleship was a tactical innovation. Strategically, its effect was not at all what Fisher wanted. By making *all* capital ships obsolete, past construction — of which Britain had the most — could not survive in the line of battle, so a late-comer in the arms race like Germany could compete. In 1914 Britain had two capital ships to every one German but its advantage in the *Dreadnought* class was only ten to seven; of course someone sometime would have forced the change but its hastening should have been a conscious decision. A different strategy was not, as far as one knows, even debated. The new is not always and instantly the good.

The Innovation Organisation

Speedily exploiting bright ideas is what every institution aims to do. Most fail. What would help them?

Most basic, inventive organisations make the business of innovation everyone's task; it is not left to the Weapons Section or the Research Laboratory, but is a corporate-wide effort. Top management makes it so; it listens for ideas and if they are 'impractical', asks 'what do we have to do to make them useful?' The ideas of the organisation are stimuli for the top, which then makes them the concern of the whole company. The top aims continually to learn; it asks juniors, 'what opportunities do you see?' Novelties are studied and the studies themselves earn reward. Ideas mean change, excitement, promotion, and change-agents are publicly encouraged. The First Commandment is, Thou shalt not kill a new idea.

These principles are sustained by organisational devices. A unit's performance is partly judged by its inventiveness; it is not fully loaded with development costs until it can bear them; good communications up and down and sideways increase fertility. Being self-confident, the competent organisation is receptive and is consciously searching inside and out for opportunities. It even asks outsiders for suggestions.

Inventors need alternative sponsors. If your own boss will not finance the exploration of your marvellous idea, then in a company like 3M you are free to ask the research department. Smallness, youth and freshness fertilise invention. An MIT study found that of seven major oil refining technical improvements all came from independent inventors and none from big companies. The University of Maryland found that of thirteen innovations in the US steel industry none originated from inside it. It is notorious that size breeds bureaucracy and constipation. The seniors may really want novelty but they have to penetrate layers of managers and specialists, all with empires to protect, to find it. Newcomers take less for granted while familiarity blanks out alternatives.

Seniors have constantly to attack these hindrances, probing, questioning, encouraging. Inventive behaviour must be seen to be privileged. Reward for valuable invention should be no less than that for management of equal value. The tradition must be for change, introduced to match peoples' adaptive abilities and to give them opportunities and a better living. This is technical leadership.*

The Young Turk also has his obligations. His colleagues may lose status or power by his changes, whose social effects they may appreciate better than he does. The old is not by definition the dud. Inventors are as biased as anyone else. A seemingly pure technical change may yet provoke a reaction. In the early sixties I advocated 'DCF investment appraisal' in my company. My senior, highly intelligent, told me: "I am totally opposed to this. It induces a citadel-like mentality whereas I prefer sallies from the fortress . . ." The rules of the game for inventors seem to be these:

- choose a company concerned throughout with novelty and improvement;
- respect the audience and try to give it advantage without hurtful side effects;
- respect the status quo: in its day it was just as novel and it deserves polite and gentle removal;
- compensating for political or social effects may exceed the technical demands;
- query both highly complex and lowly ambitious propositions;
- match the risks to the insurance capacity or sell the idea outside;
- ensure the case has real merit or, failing that, secure a power-base!

When all else fails there is a simple fall-back position: "If you

See Appendix F for other techniques for innovation.

can't live with these rules, be a bastard like Fisher but make certain that you get to the top".[6]

At the end of it all perhaps Scott teaches the best lesson. He made only one modification to his guns — the sights. He induced a competitive spirit, challenged people to hone their skills and helped them to do so. He relied heavily on training; devices that aided this were cheap yet valuable. Performance was rewarded. Nothing could have been simpler. It is salutary to think that the equipment was fairly adequate all along. When the user with insight came to take charge the proper management of people unleashed all the potential.

*   *   *   *

References

[1] Peter Padfield, The Battleship Era.

[2] E Chatfield, The Navy and Defence.

[3] R F MacKay, Fisher of Kilverstone.

[4] Sir Winston Churchill, Great Contemporaries.

[5] Captain D Macintyre, The Thunder of the Guns.

[6] A H Cartmell, Letter to the Author.

CHAPTER X

THE GENERAL STAFF SYSTEM:
THE BATTLE OF TANNENBERG

"I divide my officers into four classes: the clever, the stupid, the industrious and the lazy. Every officer possesses at least two of these qualities. Those who are clever and industrious are fitted for high staff appointments; use can be made of those who are stupid and lazy. The man who is clever and lazy is fitted for the highest command; he has the temperament and the requisite nerve to deal with all situations. But whoever is stupid and industrious is a danger and must be removed immediately."

— General Kurt von Hammerstein-Equord,
C-in-C German Army 1930—34*

"Institutionalising Excellence"

Managers imbibe certain general rules: report upward accurately, obey orders, do *not* by-pass subordinates, and many more. They may never be questioned and time hallows them. Other rules, sound ones, get forgotten or even remain untaught. Managers come in all shapes and sizes, suited to varying roles and levels, differing in courage and caution and in most other characteristics. They are required in virtue of their profession to invent exciting plans; comes the time to implement them, and the man of thought must become the man of action and make decisions and run risks and make things happen. A compendium of abilities is called for. The (British) army is by custom noted for carefully placing square soldiers into round sentry boxes, implying that industry is so much cleverer . . .

Once selected, management is concerned with the maintenance of performance over the generations (unless diverted by quarterly stockholder reports or by its own stock options). But yesteryear's high performing companies rank modestly this year: is decline then inevitable? The management profession wishes to extend its competence, codify best practice, establish and teach tested doctrines. Or does it? Is it a collection of firms and managers without any central brain and unable to demonstrate (to a

*Quoted from memory of a paper by Sir Frederick Hooper, when managing director of Schweppes Ltd. and by Viscount Montgomery in *The Memoirs of Field-Marshall Montgomery.*

statistical analyst) any superiority sustained beyond a decade
or so?

As a matter of fact, the services do have a brain for the body
politic. The device was invented in 1807 in Prussia when some
innovative soldiers were formed into an official committee concerned with the restoration of the performance of the nation's
army :

> "The Reformers' answer was unique and proved to be
> earth-shaking: They would try to *institutionalise* genius —
> or at least try to perfect a system that could perpetuate
> military excellence through the vagaries of change . . . The
> Reformers were not creating an entirely new concept, or
> even a new terminology. Rather, they were carrying exist-
> ing concepts and terms to a logical, but never-before-
> visualised, conclusion."[1]

It is altogether fitting, therefore, that one of the decisive battles
of World War I should have been fought in the forests of East
Prussia.

The Planning of World War I
In August 1914 the world went to war. Against the 'Central
Powers' — Germany and Austria-Hungary — were ranged the
'Allies' — France, Britain, Russia, Belgium and Serbia; both
groups were joined later by other allies. Some figures may convey
the scale and intensity of the conflict: *(see page opposite.)*

The total killed was about 8½ million to which must be added
about 2 million civilians. Total casualties were perhaps of the
order of 40 million, clearly running second to World War II's
price of about 70 millions, but that is progress. The proportion of
mobilised force to population shows the modern commitment to
'total war'. The relative casualties bring out three points: the
severity of the Russian losses, even though it made peace in 1917;
the Allies' preferences for costly offensives against skilled defences; and sheer German military competence when, though
outnumbered, it inflicted greater losses than it suffered.

The combatants' wholesale mobilisations coalesced into gigantic
field armies which, equipped with modern weapons, in turn
generated the monstrous casualties suffered by all armies on all
fronts. Since the American Civil War the forces had grown vastly

Table 2: The Costs of World War I			
	Mobilised Forces, mil.	Casualties mil.	Casualties % Forces Mobilised
Central Powers:			
Germany	11.3	7.2	64
Austria—Hungary	7.8	7.0	90
Turkey	2.9	1.0	34
Other	1.2	.3	25
	23.2	15.5	67
Allies:			
France	8.4	5.4	64
Great Britain	6.2	2.6	27
Russia	13.0	7.2	55
Italy	5.6	2.2	34
Serbia	1.0	.4	40
America	3.8	.3	8
Other	3.8	1.3	34
	41.8	19.4	46
Total	65.0	37.9	54

Sources: A G Enock, This War Business.

Col. T N Dupuy & R E Dupuy, The Encyclopaedia of Military History.

Ed. Prof. G Barraclough, The Times Atlas of World History.

John Terraine, White Heat.

(NB. The figures are necessarily unreliable for some countries.)

and the machine gun had easily surpassed the magazine rifle in killing power. Artillery, already significant at Chancellorsville, was now highly sophisticated. In 1914 an army's transport might still have been mostly horse-drawn but its field guns and howitzers were numerous, ably controlled, and devastating weapons; as much as two-thirds of all casualties could be caused by artillery fire.

In preparation for the holocaust the Allies had some thoughts that might just be graced with the title of 'plan': keep the enemy occupied in the west while Russia mobilised its masses, then attack extensively to impose on the Central Powers a war on two fronts. The thinking thus followed the general rules for operating successfully on 'exterior lines': use superior numbers to press the enemy everywhere so that he has neither the time nor the space within which to switch his force between sectors. (It is noteworthy that the military have codified certain strategies, whereas businessmen continue to argue, for example, whether a dominant market share in any segment is or is not vital. Hard conceptual thinking about accessible strategies seems indicated.)

German planning was much more thorough. It was carried out by its Great General Staff, which had been born in theory in 1807. In the Seven Years' War (1756—63) Prussia, led by Frederick the Great, was the most competent land power in Europe. Usually outnumbered, an array of famous battles like Rossbach and Leuthen had made its reputation. Within fifty years Napoleon was to demolish it, with brutality. The battle of Jena (1806) devastated the Prussian army and throughout the Napoleonic Wars it achieved nothing, being shown up as simply obsolete. This traumatic experience generated furious rethinking. A 'project team' called the Military Reorganisation Commission was set up: three of its members had memorable names: Scharnhorst, who became the first "Chief of the General Staff", Gneisenau who was Blücher's right-hand at Waterloo, and Clausewitz, to be famed as a military philosopher and who was also active at Waterloo. The Commission, with powerful support from above, soon reported its proposals. (British companies and trade unions are evidently not the only ones to need disasters to raise their managerial socks.)

Amongst other reforms, they recommended the creation of a 'General Staff' to direct and control, under the policy guidance of a 'War Ministry', the planning, training and standards of the army. The aim was to establish certain performance levels, to confer continuity, to maintain competence regardless of the coming and going of individuals, to "institutionalise excellence".[1] Dupuy quotes General Gerhard von Scharnhorst on the very practical objects:

> "Normally it is not possible for an army simply to dismiss incompetent generals. The very authority which their office bestows upon generals is the first reason for this. Moreover, the generals form a clique, tenaciously supporting each other, all convinced that they are the best possible representatives of the army. But we can at least give them capable assistants. Thus the General Staff officers are those who support incompetent generals, providing the talents that might otherwise be wanting among leaders and commanders."[1]

The Commission gave the General Staff responsibility for these major functions:

— planning, including recruiting and mobilisation;
— co-ordination, between army units and with other armies;
— supervision of staff performance;
— operational readiness: officer education, organisation, training, operating doctrine;

and it performed these tasks by a number of techniques, including careful staff officer selection, rotating them between line and staff jobs, setting exams to encourage professionalism, specialised training, historical study, and encouraging initiative, objectivity and the acceptance of responsibility.

These reforms restored army competence. *(See Appendix G* for a consideration of further applications of the General Staff idea.) The foreign policy of Otto von Bismarck, Prime Minister of Prussia, put it to use. In 1866 Prussia defeated the Austrians at the battle of Königgrätz. In 1870—71 France was conquered. Germany was unified under Prussian leadership and its army inherited the Prussian tradition and methods. For much of this period the Chief of the General Staff was General Helmuth von Moltke, a talented linguist and soldier. He had been ADC to the King's son and throughout his thirty-one years as CGS he had the head of state's support. Though not an intriguer, as a realistic manager he accepted good help when it was offered — and perhaps had originally cultivated it.

> "He was an extraordinary man — scholar, traveller, strategist and linguist. He was so taciturn that he was said to be 'silent in seven languages'."[2]

In 1891 there was appointed as CGS Colonel-General Graf Alfred von Schlieffen. He was to become the best known holder of the office, was most able and entirely dedicated to his work: "... his annual Christmas greetings to selected members of the Staff was to present them with a tactical problem early on Christmas Eve, expecting to get a solution by the evening of Christmas Day".[1] One is reminded of a chairman of the UK Ford Motor Company who, a bachelor, had no other occupation than work and whose staff felt they had to be seen putting in the same hours.

Under Schlieffen, the General Staff, as was its custom, planned war operations; in particular, it studied the best way to fight a coalition of France and Russia. Thinking crystallised in the '1905 Schlieffen Plan'. There had been previous ones of the same name which, after analysis in war games, required serious amendment (though hampered by war's complexities the military make considerable use of simulation techniques; maybe civilians could use them more to advantage.) Briefly, the Plan proposed putting light holding forces in the east against Russia (hopefully also menaced by an allied Austria-Hungary) and also in the south-west of Germany against the French right wing, while the rest of the army — no less than 77% of it — would be concentrated against the French left, to attack through and past Belgium and wheel round to the north of the French fortress zone to take Paris from the north and taking the French army in front and rear. Then, France crushed, the German armies would be moved rapidly east on the excellent rail system, to confront Russia. If, meantime, Prussia was attacked, the defenders could fight first whichever invading force was the nearer. The Plan was thus totally uncomprising. It would solve the problem of a two-front war by applying the principle of concentration of force using interior lines. The Allies on exterior lines could attack round the periphery but the Germans could move quicker within it. The Allies, *given time*, could attack from most directions. They must not be given the time.

Schlieffen's eastern plans were sketchy, going little beyond an aggressive defence, attacking whichever Russian force came within reach first and using the River Vistula as a final defensive line. Later, a massed German army on the Russians' northern flank and an Austrian one on the southern promised a vast encirclement — the second Cannae all generals long for.

By 1914 Schlieffen, but not his plan, was dead, whispering as he went, "... keep the right wing strong". The new CGS was the younger Moltke, nephew of the victor of Königgrätz, a humourless and cautious man. It was said he only smiled twice in his life, once on being told that a certain French fortress was impregnable, once on hearing that his mother-in-law was dead. He inherited Schlieffen's plan but not his vision: he compromised, taking thirty-two divisions from the right wing attacking the French left, in order to strengthen his left in the west and his back in the east. Dupuy says:

> "What the so-called watering down indicated, however, was the inherently cautious nature of a general, who, in Napoleon's words, 'saw too much', and who therefore would not be able to carry through the concept with the single-minded vigour and boldness that were the essential ingredients of the Schlieffen Plan ... [von Moltke's] cautious and unimaginative nature was more naturally attracted to measures which seemed to reduce or lessen the risks which Schlieffen had been perfectly willing to accept, than to seeking ways to enhance, or even to maintain, the power and momentum of Schlieffen's combination of manoeuvre and mass."[1]

The Germans duly launched their diluted Schlieffen movement. Though much weakened it nearly worked, as everyone knows. Supply difficulties. Moltke's opting out of control and French resilience just killed it. Its life and death show what a General Staff, when managed by an unsuitable character, could and could not do. But why did not this General Staff, this competence-promoting institution, evade this difficulty? The short answer is court influence. Moltke had spent (too much?) time as ADC to the future Kaiser, with whom he formed a friendship; his promotion on the Staff side was accelerated and Schlieffen, required to appoint him his heir-apparent, doubted if he had sufficient experience. The Kaiser had his way. Thus in a war the immature emperor, just like his admired grandfather, would be able to say he too had a Moltke as his CGS. So the stars were set in their courses and Germany went into the abyss.*

Our own attention should now move to the less well known east.

Prussia Invaded: Command Problems

It was the duty of the German 8th Army to protect East Prussia. This rich province — to some the jewel in the German crown — with large forests and many lakes, had large estates, some owned by Kaiser Wilhelm himself, supporting an aristocracy prominent in the army. The Army Commander was General Max von Prittwitz, a friend of the Kaiser. He had 'under command' ten divisions plus some garrison troops, in all some 200,000 men. He was then sixty-six, an intelligent but a hard superior, with less talent than corpulence and without quite enough nerve for his job. The organisation around him was simple and clear:

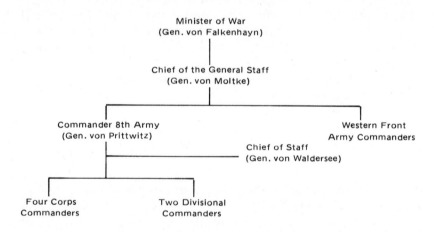

Thus the Kaiser virtually lost his own war — a classic example of the argument for the division of power. I knew a company whose Chairman, not himself also President or Chief Executive, refused to have one under him. The result was that there was no one charged with implementing the Board's policy and making sure everything that needed to be done was done. His reason was his fear of a concentration of executive power in one Board member (there were other executive directors). Maybe the Germans would have agreed with him! Given shareholders' ignorance and inactivity and the uncertain independence of non-executive directors, at the least it would seem imprudent to have one person as Chairman and Chief Executive.

For Russia wars were often both embarrassing tests of competence and notable chances for courage. This one was to show again . . . "ancient truths of Russian administration . . . centralisation brought inefficiency, decentralisation brought anarchy."[3] In overall charge was the Grand Duke Nicholas, uncle of the Tsar, an able, determined and austere character of whom the court was jealous. His power was limited by factions. The War Minister was corrupt, the military staff incompetent, munitions short, training poor and the outlook lacking a sense of urgency. However, the country responded most generously and gallantly to urgent French calls for help and army mobilisation was rapid, even if its application might be more dramatic than effective: "It is perhaps a hard saying to suggest that casual and unbusinesslike persons are very ready with chivalrous gestures, just because they attach so little value to their own plans".[4] (Empty gestures do not nowadays seem confined to the "unbusinesslike"; the uncommitted, full of false promise, seem to be an increasing business menace.)

Being the nearest target East Prussia was to be invaded immediately. The commander on this front was a court appointee, Jilinsky, aged sixty, an experienced but unpopular incompetent. The organisation looked straightforward:

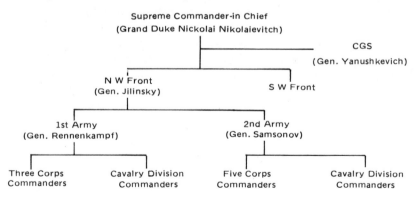

Jilinsky was no leader. He was loath to leave his HQ; he never visited his army commanders nor did he send his staff officers instead. His plan *(Fig. X. 1)* was for Rennenkampf's 1st Army with twelve divisions to invade from the east while Samsonov's 2nd Army with ten divisions advanced from the south. A hand-

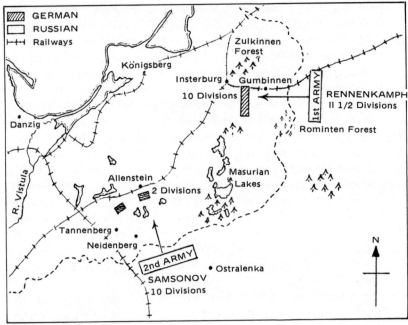

Fig.X. 1 A Plan for Prussia

some lively cavalryman, Rennenkampf was sixty, with a reputation for energy, courage and ability. Samsonov was fifty-five, a kindly but unimaginative gentleman, popular with his troops and thought to be quite competent. The two were long-standing personal enemies, having fought with fists in public during the Russo—Japanese War. Together they now had a 70% superiority in infantry and 170% in cavalry but were weak in artillery; they numbered 450,000 men. Some officers had no maps; supply lines were crude and training skimped. Sensibly, the plan was simple — always a military virtue — and in theory sound: the 1st Army would advance to draw the Germans onto itself while the 2nd Army advanced behind them, to cut off their retreat. Practical considerations and personal factors, some unpredictable, would make it all rather optimistic. Furthermore, the terrain favoured the defence; forests, swamps and lakes restricted movement — "a labyrinth of defiles" Hilaire Belloc called it — and called for generals who knew their local topography. And, on the Russian side, for co-operative generals: Jilinsky's selection of known enemies to execute his plan is not the finest example of team-building

As the 1st Army seemed likely to move first, von Prittwitz concentrated eight divisions on its front, with two only screening the 2nd Army, a text-book Schlieffen move. So far it was what the Russians thought they wanted. The combatants collided at Gumbinnen and the Germans, many of them East Prussians so understandably forceful, attacked frontally by mistake, were worsted and retreated. Rennenkampf, short of shell and supplies, pressed on with modest energy. Samsonov thought the Germans had taken a severe defeat and proceeded from his base at Ostralenka across the frontier. Communication between the two generals was kept minimal by their mutual dislike but the Germans knew fairly accurately what both armies were now doing. And now, upset by his repulse in the east and increasingly worried by the menace from the south, von Prittwitz listened to his fears. He spoke on the telephone to Army HQ in Germany and described his view of the situation to von Moltke, saying the outlook was bleak; the 8th Army would have to evacuate East Prussia entirely and retreat behind the Vistula, and even that line might not for long be tenable.

Von Moltke was appalled. He was already gripped by a rising concern at the faltering advance in the west; he hated the thought of a defeat in the east, much less the complete abandonment of a precious Prussia, the Teutonic heartland, to the invading Slav. The Kaiser's Prussian friends vehemently shared this outlook and were agitating via the 'Supreme War Lord' for Prittwitz's reinforcement at the very moment that the west needed every corps it could keep. At this crisis the 'system' went to work. Von Moltke was CGS; he knew personally the staff officers of the 8th Army in Prussia and now he telephoned them to get their views and make his own assessment of their position. (This by-passing of Prittwitz, as we would call it, was not really such to the CGS; as a soldier he would expect 'staff' relationships to reinforce 'line' ones. In any case, it could well be argued that the end here justified the means — and maybe in other circumstances too.)

The Staff for their part had already taken stock and decided that the day was by no means inevitably lost : a bold manoeuvre could play on Russian weaknesses. Privately, they were aiming to convert their commander to this view. Foremost in this discussion was a Colonel Max Hoffmann, head of the staff operations branch. Then forty-five, Hoffmann was fat, lazy and clever, with sybaritic tastes; he was also efficient and extremely able. Before the war he had been sent by Schlieffen to Russia to gain experience while being attached to their staff. In all respects it proved to be a most rewarding and far-sighted piece of 'management development'. It was in this way that he learned that Rennenkampf were enemies and that Russian communications were abysmal. He concluded that one army might be stalled while concentrating quickly and heavily against the other, using the efficient rail system. Which army? Clearly the one threatening the Vistula, the one advancing towards German communications — Samsonov's. Thus was born the 'Tannenberg manoeuvre'. The staff prepared a plan.

Von Moltke was comforted by his enquiring behind the Army Commander's back — which, however indiscrete managerial tradition might label it, was to prove invaluable to him — and decided the 8th Army needed, but lacked, firm leadership. He thereupon sacked von Prittwitz and Waldersee, his chief of staff. As successors he selected Major General Erich Ludendorff, who had just distinguished himself by capturing Liège almost single-handed, as the new Chief of Staff and, as a rather nominal superior as C-in-C 8th Army, the bulky form of General Paul von Hindenburg — recalled on the instant from retirement. A famous partnership was born, to play an increasing role in the Central Powers' war. (This is to us yet another example of a complementary pair working to great effect in unison. This one was set up deliberately. Others, such as Lee and Jackson or Marlborough and Eugene, arose by accident. Given their demonstrable value, rather more deliberation seems indicated.)

The Battle of Tannenberg

What von Moltke did not know — because no one, not even the man himself had told him — was that the present Army Commander had meanwhile been persuaded by his staff to adopt their plan. This was rather late. Ludendorff and Hindenburg were on a special train to take up their new command and their arrival in East Prussia was the first intimation of his supersession. Without complaint he went on his way. (Companies have been known to discharge the redundant just as brutally.)

Hindenburg was then sixty-seven, of massive frame, rather unimaginative and wholly imperturbable — in fact, a shrewd and quite unintellectual old warhorse. He was also immensely experienced — he had seen action at Königgrätz against Austria and at Sedan against France and well knew the Prussian terrain. Ludendorff was a mere forty-nine, with cropped hair, an abrupt manner and severe in aspect:

> "Harsh and overbearing in temper . . . [his] power of work and mastery over detail can rarely have been equalled in history. He was the finest product in all its excellencies and defects of a staff whose technical training was unrivalled."[4]

Very bright and studious, he was a sort of German Montgomery. To get his foot in the command door, he had cabled his prospective corps commanders, telling them to act independently (of von Prittwitz?) until he arrived. He had in mind some concentration against 2nd Army. The new team was met on arrival, just three days after the affair at Gumbinnen, by Colonel Hoffmann, who explained the orders already given. An immediate and precise plan was formed: in effect Ludendorff, supported by Hindenburg, confirmed Hoffmann's ideas. All now rested on the execution.

It was not going to be a comfortable few days. Rennenkampf was advancing, though slowly, and Samsonov was well across the frontier. Ludendorff decided to switch three divisions from the east front facing 1st Army to the south front to threaten the flank of 2nd Army *(Fig. X. 2)*. Next day it became apparent that Rennenkampf was not damaging the screen confronting him and Ludendorff enlarged the scheme: a further three divisions were to be transferred from the east to the south, leaving two infantry divisions and one cavalry division holding off Rennenkampf. Actually, the distant Jilinsky thought the Germans were doing what von Prittwitz had contemplated and retiring behind the Vistula so he instructed Rennenkampf to invest the fortress of Königsberg, which dangerously dispersed Russian force, while lashing Samsonov with repeated telegrams: he was to move across the German rear. Thus did the Russians grasp the noose for their collective neck.

At that moment Samsonov's unciphered radio orders to his corps commanders were intercepted. Some Germans thought them a 'plant'; Hoffmann, knowing his man, thought they correctly matched some captured documents. (Ability to read the enemy's intentions is invaluable and many have tried it; Montgomery had a photograph of Rommel in his mobile HQ

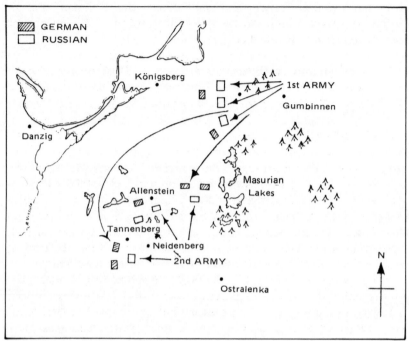

Fig.X. 2 The Tannenberg Manoeuvre

so perhaps the Chairman of GM should have one of Toyota's President in his office.) The intercept and Rennenkampf's sloth decided Ludendorff; leaving a mere two cavalry brigades to cover his rear, all the remainder were moved to surround Samsonov.

The comfort provided by the intercepts was limited. The Germans knew Rennenkampf's advance was not being pressed — then. They knew only too well the cavalry screen was paper-thin: Rennenkampf did not — yet. Indeed, his cavalry patrols reached as far as Allenstein. Ludendorff's memoirs record his fears that the two German corps attacking Samsonov's right flank were highly exposed to a Rennenkampf only a few marches away. He goes on to describe the burden making war places on a general and his nerves:

> "It is a case of wrestling with powerful, interwoven physical and psychological forces. It means working with men of varying force of character ... The only quality that is known and constant is the will of the leader."[5]

And not always that. At times this leader was near to calling off the whole operation. No doubt the placid Hindenburg, who did little more than provide guidance and support throughout the battle, helped to calm him but the whole plan depended on Russian slowness. If that altered disaster would be transferred from the Russians to the Germans. As Fuller says, ". . . it was a plan of supreme daring and good judgement"[6] — like Lee's at Chancellorsville. They had resolutely to watch and pray in the north while battling mightily in the south.

For the next four days the German troops gathered round and set their grip on Samsonov's. He had allowed his corps to diverge, some veering west. Ludendorff attacked the right wing and the Russians counter-attacked. At the height of these actions Samsonov wired Jilinsky: "I am now proceeding to the staff of XV Corps . . . to take control of the Corps offensive. I shall be temporarily without communication with you". He had moved out of control of his army. (He showed spirit but neglected his command role. Hindenburg and Ludendorff always visited their corps commanders at important moments but ensured that contact with their HQ was maintained; they could thus exercise their leadership and control functions simultaneously. Of course this worked because HQ could interpret and issue orders and was not just a post office; the business equivalent must therefore have at least a Personal Assistant, if not a chief of staff, back at HQ if it is to enjoy the same facility.)

As the Germans de-trained they went straight into action. Some of the attacks ordered by Ludendorff were ill-chosen and twice a corps commander, von François, ignored orders and both occasions proved him right. Starved of troops, he set up a mere string of outposts east of Neidenberg to bar Samsonov's retreat; fortunately for the Germans the Russians were tired, dispersed and ill-led, wandering like stray sheep, not lightly caged lions. Heavy attacks rained in from all sides and the toll of killed and captured mounted. By August 31 — "the day of harvesting" Hindenburg called it — the 2nd Army had ceased to exist. Samsonov committed suicide in the forest. 60,000 prisoners and 180 guns were taken, and 70,000 Russians were killed and wounded. It was complete and decisive victory for German arms.

The battle had taken place near a small town called Tannenberg. In 1410 it had been the site of a ferocious struggle between Teuton and Slav: a combined Polish and Lithuanian force routed the Knights of the Teutonic Order. It pleased their successors, at Hoffmann's suggestion, to recall the name when the roles were reversed.

Two months later von Moltke was retired on the well-deserved grounds of ill-health. In the west he had lost the decisive battle, the Marne, and to support the east he had withdrawn two corps to be railed back over the Rhine — soon enough to weaken the vital right wing in France and late enough to miss the Tannenberg action.

It was a depressing exercise in futility: loss of nerve and an instinct for compromise were inflamed by political pressures. Thus, having appointed a person of inappropriate character as CGS, the Germans compounded the error by allowing him to be imposed on by extraneous and ill-considered influences.

It is very probable that, had the modified Schlieffen Plan conquered France, Britain would have been confined to its island and Russia exposed to the Central Powers' full strength. Had the Germans lost at Tannenberg, they must have responded by switching many more troops to the east, and this before the west congealed into trench warfare. What might the Allies then have achieved? As it was, the war dragged on for four terrible years. Everyone knows the western story. In the east a series of enormous battles with much territory lost and won to both sides ended in 1917 with Russia's suing for peace.

Von François's disobedience (or "initiative" as it is called when successful) had been sanctioned by events, perhaps its saving grace. Falls sums up his role thus: his commander, Ludendorff,

> ". . . was quick as lightning, with an extraordinary gift for summing up a situation. But Tannenberg was planned by Hoffmann and mainly won by Hermann von François, whom Ludendorff's jealousy prevented from ever-rising beyond the command of a corps . . ."[7]

(Clearly there is a right and a wrong time to disobey orders. The disobedient must ensure their actions prove correct and their organisations have to distinguish between initiative and the rules essential for survival and which *must* be obeyed.)

Rennenkampf now fell back but Hindenburg brought him to battle in February 1916 in the battle of the Masurian Lakes and heavily defeated him; he deserted what was left of his army, fleeing eighty miles east to Kovno. This and his supine behaviour while his colleague Samsonov was in a meat-grinder fostered the theory that, being of German origin, he was a traitor. Jilinsky was dismissed. Ludendorff ended the war as No. 2 in the German Army with Hindenburg No. 1. Hoffmann became Chief of Staff for the whole eastern front.

The October Revolution in 1917 capped three years of heroic struggles which cost Russia, Germany and the Austro-Hungarian Empire around 14 million casualties — a very reasonable contribution to the Great War's blood-letting.

Epilogue

Two final comments, one from a history of the German General Staff:

> "It is idle to speculate whether Hoffmann or Ludendorff was the more responsible for the resultant triumph at Tannenberg . . . In fact, if one person has to receive credit, it would be Schlieffen, because he was the one who had trained all his General Staff officers to seek and boldly exploit such opportunities. Most judiciously, however, the credit should go not to an individual, but to the German General Staff system . . ."[1]

And one comment from a selective account of the battle of Tannenberg: after the war Hoffmann used to show interested visitors over the house which had been 8th Army HQ:

> "Taking them into one room he would tell them, 'This is the room in which General Hindenburg slept before the Battle of Tannenberg'. And into another, he would say, 'And this is the room in which General Hindenburg slept after the Battle of Tannenberg'. And into a third, 'And this is the room in which General Hindenburg slept during the Battle of Tannenberg'. Rarely can a general have slept so greatly to his country's and his own benefit."[2]

*   *   *   *

References

[1] Col. T N Dupuy, A Genius for War.

[2] Brig. Peter Young, The Victors.

[3] Dr Norman Stone, The Eastern Front 1914—1917.

[4] C R M F Cruttwell, A History of the Great War.

[5] General Erich Ludendorff, Memoirs.

[6] Major-Gen. J F C Fuller, The Decisive Battles of the Western World.

[7] Ed. Capt. Cyril Falls, Great Military Battles.

Some Contemporary Events

1904—5	Russo—Japanese War.
1909	M Bleriot flew the Channel.
1910	Japan annexed Korea.
1911	Italy in control of Libya.
1912—13	Balkan wars.
1914	Panama Canal opened.
1914—18	World War I.
1919	First transatlantic flight.
1920	First meeting of the League of nations.
1922	Greek army forced out of Turkey.
1923	The French occupy the Ruhr; runaway inflation in Germany; General Motors Corporation set up.

CHAPTER XI

COMMAND AND CONTROL: MACEDON TO MONTGOMERY

"From Plato to NATO, the history of command in war consists essentially of an endless quest for certainty."

— Martin van Creveld

Managing Time and Pace

In managing business, as for soldiering, there is never enough time or knowledge. How, then, can one command with inspiration and control with precision? The time to propel the organisation at even a humdrum rate of progress seems scarce while real speed, itself very profitable, takes far more managerial time to generate. The commercial world thus resembles Red Queen country where Lewis Carroll's Alice had to run twice as fast to move at all. Adequate information is equally elusive — and securing it itself a time-user. There seems to be a Heisenberg uncertainty principle here: you can have time or knowledge but not both. The more senior the decision-maker the more critical his work (usually) and the more information he needs — and the more remote he is from it. On its way to him it (what there is of it) is massaged and filtered . . .

These conundra propel the manager into stereotyped responses: his time problem he 'solves' by working longer hours, by pruning inessentials (i.e. delaying the important in favour of the urgent), by neglecting his personal affairs and by worrying; though his concern for information appears less pressing because 'ignorance is bliss', he still seeks to satisfy it by more detailed reports, access to raw data, real-time systems, and by quantifying what can (or cannot) be quantified. If he then gets indigestion he may in despair opt out: (my gut-reaction tells me . . .) Underlying this is a constant aspiration: if only I could be certain, then I might be in control.

The military have and have always had identical problems in principle and even more discomforting in degree. Much of their information, said Clausewitz writing in the 1820s, ". . . is contradictory, a still greater part is false, and by far the greatest part is uncertain". Using it gives equal frustration: "As Moltke* once wrote, 'in war with its enormous friction even the mediocre is quite an achievement' "[1] The subject is called by soldiers 'Command, Control, Communication' (C^3 for short), though the first two are ends in themselves and the third only the means for exercising them. Vast experience of the difficulties involved has called forth some constructive responses. A little history helps by setting them in context.

The Military Control Experience

Consider first the direction of an ancient army. The general, himself commanding his right wing, sits on his horse, surrounded by a few aides and guards. His battle line is perhaps two or more miles long; being on one side he can see little of it and not much more of the enemy's. He has arranged his troops beforehand in large clusters (as in the Macedonian phalanx) to simplify any needful communicating, each commanded by trusted relations or colleagues to reduce the need for communicating. He well knows that any orders sent later will be either ill-chosen or mislaid en route or late or misconstrued or ignored — or simply inaudible in the din of fighting. (An Alexander, exceptionally well equipped with foresight and colleagues and trained men, could mitigate these difficulties, as we shall see.)

About all he can do is arrange his army moderately cleverly beforehand and push it into contact with the enemy. Thereafter control must be limited and tenuous, so he can either manage part of his force passably or all of it badly. (Most generals opted for the former, hence their position on the prestigious right wing.) The larger the army the worse the problem. It took 3000 years of military history to ameliorate significantly the difficulties of keeping a sizeable army supplied, while finding the enemy, grasping the tactical situation, and making sensible moves when the generals lacked staffs, maps, telescopes, roads, railways,

---

*Chief of the Prussian General Staff 1857—1888: see Chapter X. The quotation is from Martin van Creveld's seminal work Command in War, published in 1985 by Harvard University Press, from which this chapter has drawn heavily.

watches, radios — all now so commonplace as to be unnoticed.

The great Napoleon inaugurated a revolution by creating for himself a large competent (and private) staff but even his genius with their support could not control armies much bigger than 100,000 men. In the Waterloo campaign we saw him disastrously lose control of his 124,000 and even Wellington with half this force misplaced (or forgot?) one whole valuable corps. Napoleon's command structure was a flat organisation with a large span of control, giving a quick response to orders (though in actual transmission they travelled on average at 5½ mph[1]) but increasing army size defeated the system and, later, more destructive weapons compounded the problem. By the end of the nineteenth century quick-firing breech-loading rifles, which could be rearmed quickly by a man lying prone behind cover, had destroyed the fairly controllable parade ground volley firing and the empty battlefield had arrived:

> "Entire armies turned into clouds of uncontrollable skirmishers, especially when on the attack. The situation was not to be fundamentally altered until the arrival of the portable radio in World War II."[1]

(A parallel is the big company seeking innovation and entrepreneurial behaviour by forming 'venture groups' which can only operate with less control from Head Office.) The invention of the telegraph allowed states to increase control. Kings could intervene (i.e. interfere) and tell the generals what to do, who thus had to fight on two fronts. (Managers can be similarly placed.) In Prussia's case the powerful General Staff aimed to control but was realistic about the feasibility. Its development of the Napoleonic staff system worked on different lines. Moltke made simple plans, manoeuvring the army in large self-contained units, so that they could sustain themselves while waiting for help after blundering into trouble (which they did); there was thus the opposite of fine-tuning of resources for (unpredictable) missions.

Information channels were supplemented by an informal network. The Prussian General Staff was stable; staff officers had slow but steady promotion, mainly on seniority, and everyone knew everyone else. Red tape and over-specialisation were eschewed. Staff officers would supplement official reports with private correspondence and would ride around to see the action and to transmit information. "With their livelihood and advancement quite secure . . . junior commanders in particular had no mortal fear of committing mistakes . . ."[1]

Van Creveld warns against any glib generalising on sound staff organisation, by comparing Napoleonic and Prussian systems:

	Napoleonic	Prussian
Official organisation	Private	Military
Span of control	Large	Small
Central reserve	Large	None
Methods	Improvisation, ad hoc	Methodical, practiced
Atmosphere	Hyper-active	Calm
Orders	Hasty	Cool, short

(Prussia's technical approach seems paralleled by Frederick W Taylor's study of work.) "One was based on command from the front, the other on management from the rear. Nevertheless . . . both systems were among the most successful of all time . . ."[1]

In World War I the control problem was set in new dimensions. The mobilised forces were enormous while moving them by railway was easy (the Railway Department was the most important part of any General Staff) and the available fire-power was stunning. It remained to control this monster. The aircraft had arrived — but was silent until it returned to base, cars could speed messages — but roads were cratered; telephones relied on vulnerable wiring; radios were slow and jammable. HQ could be out of touch for days . . .

To start with the Germans were as ill-prepared as their opponents, with no reinforcement of conventional and fallible communication channels by organised message-carrying and information-gathering nor was authority delegated to compensate for the centre's incapacity to command. But they learned. Their signal service in 1914 numbered 6000 men, in 1918 190,000;[1] which illustrates both the solution and the problem. They were to learn how to 'control' — in their fashion — their dispersed uncommunicative troops, by either eschewing what cannot be centrally managed or dispensing with top control. But the British wanted to direct their great Somme battle in 1916 and, given inexperienced troops, made a rigid simple detailed plan defining hopefully attainable objectives which were not to be exceeded. All moves were standardised; independence was discouraged;

battalion commanders and above were ordered to stay behind —
to keep in touch with their superiors. Thus Haig, the C-in-C,
tried to make his offensive an industrial operation — planned,
predictable, precise. As no conventional communication was
possible beyond the front line and no back-up was ready the
higher command could only wait for the information that never
came. There were promising breaks into the defences but exploitation was forbidden; it seemed uncontrollable — and was by conventional means. As van Creveld says, ". . . centralisation is a
highly contagious disease".[1]

In contrast the Germans were already treating ". . . confusion
as the normal state of the battlefield"[1] and one general was
defining minimum longer-term objectives for his troops' attack:
the Army, he said, fixes ". . . certain lines, which should be
reached by the force as a whole, and if possible simultaneously.
*Any progress beyond the lines will be thankfully welcomed by
the Army and made use of.*"[1] (Speaking as an ex-private: for
once a human message . . .) A later order forbade commanders
". . . to delay counter-attacks while permission of the next higher
headquarters is requested".[1] For his massive 1918 offensive
against the British General Ludendorff carried decentralisation
further. The training directive emphasised local decisions, speed,
commanders to be up front; special arrangements for signalling
and spotting movement, to supplement troops' own reports, were
created. Staff officers were to tour the front for information, in
the process checking on local initiative. (Interestingly, Ludendorff,
standing theory on its head, preferred to attack ". . . where a
tactical breakthrough was possible, not where a strategic one
was desirable".[1] This readiness to exploit success opportunisti-
cally inhibited pre-planning and exacerbated the control problem.)
All this was well done — and needed. The enormous attack went
in. The outcome was that HQ and Ludendorff were not much
better informed than the Somme attackers but sensational
advances were made . . .

World War II found communications speeded enormously by
portable radios. They needed to be when increased complexity
vastly increased information flaws. Here is one example, but
embracing a complete 'command and control' situation.

A Middle East Command Problem
In search of a land perfectly suited to fighting, troops were

gathered in the Western Desert. Between the Nile and Tunisia
sprawled 1500 miles of dusty emptiness, baking hot by day and
roofed with cold starlight at night, starved of civilians, its terrain
mostly negotiable by men and machines, one flank covered by the
wine-dark sea, the other open to the Sahara. At one end of this
corridor one could in 1942 hop, via Sicily, into German-controlled
Europe; at the other only the Suez Canal separated the Axis' grasp
from Arab oil and Caucasia. Both sides therefore sought to control
this strip of featureless desolation.

The pendulum motion of the resulting front is well known.
By 1942 the British 8th Army manned a defence line thirty miles
west of the Tobruk fortress; May saw the hard-driving opportunist,
General Erwin Rommel, break that line, capture Tobruk and
sweep into Egypt. After a headlong retreat the 8th Army — now
commanded by General Claude Auchinleck who was also C-in-C
Middle East — turned at bay near El Alamein, a mere sixty miles
from Cairo, where an impassable sand-sea protected the southern
flank. There the line held — with difficulty; Auchinleck fought
the Germans to a standstill. He was, and looked, a fighter, a
soldier of the highest integrity, undemonstrative and reserved,
but human. Conscious of his army's defeats he magnanimously
proposed to London that it consider having a fresh mind take over.
Meanwhile, he refused to be pushed by an impatient Churchill
into a premature offensive. He artlessly believed facts could speak
for themselves: after all, the Middle East had just been saved.
Reassuring communication with a London remote from the
military scene but close to politicians' pressures was left undone.

In August the Germans attacked in southern Russia; this pre-
saged a gigantic pincer to menace the Caucasian oilfields, then to
join up with an attack by Rommel through Suez to sever the
Persian supply route to Russia, seize Arab oil wells and force all
Far East supplies to circumnavigate Africa. At this interesting
moment the British War Cabinet, much influenced by Churchill,
sent Auchinleck to India in a nominally sideways move, replacing
him as C-in-C with General Sir Harold Alexander and as 8th Army
Commander with General Bernard Montgomery. It was quite a
familiar 'reorganisation', beloved by worried managements, but
with here a measure of justification, in the army command's
performance, over-laying political expediency and a personal
incompatibility.

Montgomery found a brave but bewildered army, experienced

yet inexpert, outnumbering yet out-fought by the Afrika Korps and lacking in inspiration, confidence and stability. Allocating much of the British effort to this theatre of war had achieved only the maintenance of a beleaguered presence. Much was therefore expected of the new Army Commander who had to learn all about the area, to defeat any enemy attacks, to study foe and friend — leaders, morale, resources, organisation, tactics, skills — to evaluate these factors, to improve any on his side that were deficient and to design and execute an offensive and pursuit to eject the Axis totally and for good from the Western Desert. If all that took more than a few months he would be deemed a failure.

He flew into Cairo on August 12 and saw Alexander. Next day, one that he and the 8th Army were long to remember, he went down into the desert and assumed command. In the event he and his army implemented this time-table:

Day   0 : Montgomery assumes command
D +   25 : Rommel repulsed in the 2nd Battle of Alam Halfa
D +   71 : Montgomery attacks : Battle of Alamein
D +   92 : 8th Army advances 350 miles to capture Tobruk
D +   163 : 8th Army advances a further 800 miles to occupy
              Tripoli

A productive twenty-three weeks. How was this done?

The new Army Commander was a lonely figure, unsympathetic, ruthless, of limited high command experience, and distinctly naive. He was also ambitious, an expert soldier, with a calculated flair for public relations, an able tactician, highly realistic about his troops' abilities and vastly talented at motivating them. He could see the wood well apart from the trees and his religion removed any doubts he might have had about his own judgement. He was in active command throughout the war, during which he maintained and refined certain habits. He lived simply but comfortably in caravans equipped for command and for rest. He slept well (or claimed to), turning in early before a battle while his staff worried and worked through the night, and each day he would try to visit his corps commanders, however much time it took, meeting them well forward to minimise the distraction. At the end of the day he dealt with administrative matters: technical reviews, personal correspondence, 'personnel' subjects like promotions and gallantry awards. He closely interested himself in appointments down to battalion level, i.e. four ranks below his own.

His control was close. "When he had issued an instruction to a subordinate . . . he would always try to make a call one further down the line . . . to see how the instruction was being implemented."[2] Montgomery took much trouble to be quickly and reliably informed. His staff had a special wireless network fed by reporting centres and roving observors. He had a small group of officers who visited front line units daily. General Sir Francis de Guingand, his Chief of Staff, thus describes it:

> "[Montgomery] selected these young men most carefully, and they were exceptional officers. They had drive and courage, and developed considerable judgement and a sense of responsibility. They would go anywhere and find out everything. To hear them giving their report to [Montgomery] after dinner each evening was something not to be forgotten. One got a clear and vivid picture of the battle. One could sense the state of commanders, and morale of their men . . ."[3]

By the time they reached Tunisia morale was very high.

A Command Takeover

On the evening of his arrival in the desert Montgomery had addressed all the HQ staff. De Guingand recollects the message:

> "He was going to create a new atmosphere . . . the bad old days were over, and nothing but good was in store for us . . . The mandate . . . given by the Prime Minister . . . was to destroy the Axis forces in North Africa . . . If anyone didn't think we could do this, then he must go, for there were to be no doubters . . . Any further retreat or withdrawal was quite out of the question . . . The Prime Minister was going to see that we had a sufficiency of reinforcements and material . . . He would start immediately with the planning of a great offensive."[3]

The effect was instantaneous. "We all felt," says de Guingand, "that a cool and refreshing breeze had come to relieve the oppressive and stagnant atmosphere."[3]   The feeling at once radiated throughout the army — one man generating an electrifying force. The man in question went on to describe his management system:

> "He said that he always worked the Chief of Staff system, and that he issued *all* orders through him. His Chief of Staff had considerable power and responsibility, and he could issue orders in his name — within of course the framework of his policy."[3]

Montgomery spent several days visiting units, meeting people, telling them his ideas, assessing abilities. The HQ he inherited was uncomfortable; when Churchill visited it, he was given breakfast "... in a cage full of flies and high military personages". It was moved to the seaside and next to the RAF's, with whom it had anyway to collaborate closely. In the mess good food was served on white tablecloths and for himself Montgomery wanted the best batman in the Middle East. Though mentally austere he did not believe in 'strength through misery'.

Warned by 'Ultra' wireless intercepts of a coming German attack, he planned a cautious defence. He sent for two new corps commanders, men of his own choosing, to replace those sacked — fairly abruptly — and his organisation was simple:

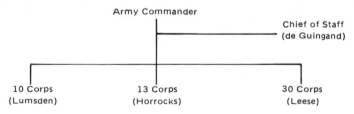

Like a good tactician Montgomery had a network of friendly contacts: with his boss, Alexander, who gave him great latitude and support; with Churchill, who liked his leadership and his 'PR'; with the War Secretary for political aid; with the Chief of the Imperial General Staff. Useful allies. But behind the PR there was substance: "He toured endlessly through his command, his bleak eyes seizing on the idle, the slack and the imcompetent, his metallic voice questioning, ordering, denouncing and dismissing. He was like Florence Nightingale putting a hospital in order."[4] Like his predecessor, he was pressed by London to attack early.

He retorted that the Cabinet could have either an early probable failure or a later guaranteed success; which did it want? Truculence and self-confidence won.

While himself with time to measure up his senior officers, to plan the next battle *and* the next but one, to see and be seen by his troops — 230,000 of them — his staff had to turn his plans into operational instructions. These included: battle plans for each corps; deception schemes and feints; troop training; battle rehearsals; forming a port reconditioning team and shipping programs; building supply dumps; hiding troop concentrations; assessment of Libyan terrain. Halfway through this little program Montgomery reviewed what one may call his Critical Areas — those command factors at any level which the manager at that level must personally make work to fulfil his contribution. At the Army Commander level we can discern three — leadership, equipment, training — and Montgomery found the last wanting. He would therefore form a less ambitious plan: the Axis infantry would be attacked first, forcing its armour into either immediate and expensive counter-attacks or into later and unsupported defence. Even so, much training was needed, to be disturbed only by the need to fight the defensive battle of Alam Halfa. Sixteen days later the 8th Army launched its own attack and broke the enemy front. The Alamein battle is too well known for any description but the scale and severity of the combat are noteworthy:

	8th ARMY		AXIS	
	No. Engaged	Casualties	No. Engaged	Casualties
TROOPS	220,000	13,500	108,000	55,000
TANKS	1,440	500	540	450
AIRCRAFT	530	97	350	84

The assault on a strongly fortified line lasted twelve days and finally broke it completely though Rommel succeeded in extricating part of his force while executing a superb fighting retreat. In cautious pursuit Montgomery followed, covering 700 miles in fifteen days. When the 8th Army in triumph entered the Libyan capital, Tripoli, Rommel had halted 180 miles beyond, on the Tunisian frontier, occupying a strongly fortified line of pre-war origin at Mareth, from which he was not to be easily prised. The whole army with its supplies and impedimenta gathered up itself for another set-piece assault. To keep the staff fully occupied it was now the military government of a large province and had to look after the civilian population. The 8th Army had to be fed and watered and its munitions mustered. In the three weeks preceding the next battle 41,000 tons of supplies were trucked from Tripoli to the Mareth Line.

Command Work and Staff Problems
Just two months after entering Tripoli an attack was planned. 30 Corps, primarily an infantry force, would drive a corridor through the defences and then 10 Corps, primarily armoured, would pass through it *(see Fig. XI. 1)*. To outflank the Line and divert German attention the New Zealand Corps would be formed under General Sir Bernard Freyberg (who had won his VC in World War I to crown a record of dazzling gallantry) to make a wide sweep south through Wilders Gap to come up on the weaker German flank. (Wilder was the officer sent by Montgomery to reconnoitre the Line three months previously, i.e. when still a month away from Tripoli!)

Preparation followed the now established routine: the staff did all the detailed work while Montgomery studied the ground, chatted up his troops and briefed personally all officers down to lieutenant-colonel level. The battle began on time. On March 19 the NZ Corps, 27,000 men and 200 tanks, marched out of Wilder's Gap, while 30 Corps assaulted the Line but after two days had merely a precarious lodgement, costly and uncertain to exploit. On the 23rd Montgomery met his corps commanders and decided to withdraw 30 Corps while strongly reinforcing the flank attack. 10 Corps, plus the 1st Armoured Division, was to follow Freyberg and with him break through a gap in the hills called the 'Plum' into the German rear. To underwrite this move the 4th Indian Division was to force the Hallouf Pass flanking the Mareth position.

The Hallouf move was to start immediately; the 'Plum' attack was timed for the 26th, three days hence. "We had, of course," says de Guingand, "anticipated a move such as this, and an outline staff plan had been prepared . . ."[3] (I like the "of course".) He lists *some* of the work involved: ". . . traffic control and move-ment tables were the first priority . . . All our tank transporters had to be got up to move the tanks of the 1st Armoured Division,

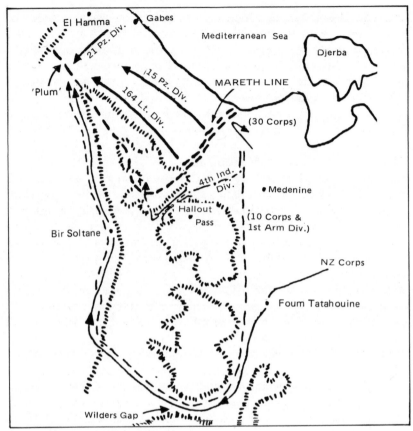

Fig.XI. 1 Turning the Mareth Line

and a complete change in the maintenance centre of gravity had
to be laid on. Special AA protection for the various road bottle-
necks had to be arranged for."[3]   Intensive air support — hitherto
not an Allied speciality — was agreed with Air Vice-Marshal
Broadhurst, in command of the Desert Air Force. "The 24th and
25th were spent in a maze of planning . . . we prepared detailed
maps showing the exact location of enemy guns, transport and
defences . . . there was all the detail in connection with landmarks,
timings and coloured smoke signals."[3]

The enemy reacted with his customary professionalism. The NZ
Corps had been spotted and reinforcements switched to the
'Plum' gap; its assault was planned for 4 pm. so that the sun shone
in the German eyes. That morning a sandstorm grounded all RAF
aircraft but it shielded the land attackers. During the afternoon

the skies luckily cleared and relentless air attacks fell on everything that moved. By evening a hole was drilled and through it a
five mile tank penetration made; in two days of further fighting
the outnumbered Germans were seen off, while the Indians had
forced the Hallouf Pass. El Hamma and Gabes were taken, though
the bulk of the Mareth defenders eluded capture though not
severe losses; the momentum built up enabled the next defence
line — a gully a few miles north of El Hamma — to be 'bounced'
a week later and with relatively few casualties. The whole operation exemplified Montgomery's adaptability. He forewent surprise
but had novel air support; this "...worked very effectively —
although frowned on by [Broadhurst's] distant RAF superiors
as a breach of Air Staff doctrine".[5] De Guingand comments:
"I happen to know that there was considerable anxiety shown
by those in high RAF places ... Great efforts were made to write
down the story, and to infer that the support was normal ..."[3]

Montgomery's Methods

With Montgomery the man obscures the lessons. He claimed his
battles went as planned; neither Alamein nor Mareth did and
flexibility seized success. Perhaps he preferred a reputation for
predictability to adaptability. His deriding of predecessors, his
vanity, his disloyalty (to his later boss, Eisenhower), discourage
one from learning from a skilled craftsman. Of course he sometimes had help and we have all met Dame Fortune. No doubt
she was anathema to Montgomery, though she was in attendance
at Mareth and elsewhere too. She might have smiled more on one
less cautious: "A bold general can be lucky, but no general can
be lucky unless he is bold."[6] Some have disliked Montgomery's
publicity-seeking and arrogance; they did not hurt his leadership.
"If the trumpet give out an uncertain sound who shall prepare
himself for battle?" It is difficult to lead if you are unknown.

While establishing himself incredibly quickly as the 'saviour
with a sword' for a large heterogeneous force not without experience and cynicism, Montgomery diagnosed its needs and his
own priorities. To these Critical Areas he had to direct his time,
his resources, his appraisals, his information system. He liked
tidy organisation though he was not always embraced by it. We
saw the RAF's attitude on air support at El Hamma. De Guingand
had to get his personal transport plane from America. He comments generally:

> "I don't want to be critical of the air support . . . To get
> new ideas accepted, however, did sometimes require a
> great deal of lobbying . . . Many of us were very struck by
> the different attitude . . . adopted by the US Air Force.
> But then this is understandable, for their Air Force was
> part of the Army and the Army Commander would just
> give orders."[3]

An organisation with its own quite separate direction, tradition,
uniforms and technology, is likely to have its own objectives. It
shows the limitations of a functional organisation and the non-
senses even able people can occasionally commit if left to themselves.

After Mareth the Germans retreated into Tunisia where the
8th Army joined with other Allied forces to help take 250,000
prisoners. Montgomery was prominent in the invasion of Sicily
and Italy. All know the story of D-Day and the liberation of
France. German resistance evaporated. The Allies, notably General
George S Patton's 3rd Army, rushed over the Seine, through Paris,
into Belgium, the War was won . . . well, nearly.

Though conducted with caution and a large material advantage,
for the general in the black beret it was still a record of consistent
success and exemplifies a consistent management style:

—   the organisation to suit the commander's methods, to
    which his staff must accommodate themselves;
—   meticulous preparation, including the nurturing of morale
    and attitudes, backed by relevant training based on a
    realistic view of needs;
—   tight control of operations by being physically close, in
    touch with subordinates and using personal information
    channels;
—   radiating confidence while being quietly flexible, pressing
    a chosen line with utter but not too obstinate deter-
    mination;
—   handling promotions, appointments and rewards personally
    to maintain control and morale;
—   thoroughgoing use of a professional staff to handle all
    detail, to delegate severely but without abdication.

To the civilian this last seems the most novel — and noteworthy.

As a device to free the top person for his unique contribution, to buttress any weak points he may have, to improve communications and co-operation, it demands attention *(see Appendix H)*. All these methods, as one would expect, reflect the man: careful, precise, monopolising praise, rationalising errors, a determined and narrow professional animal. Their effectiveness, as we may cynically expect after looking at the battle of Waterloo, where all three commanders all world famous made serious mistakes *(see Chapter V)*, was inconstant; but it is interesting that a flaw in his strict pattern of success could be demonstrated by one so moved by predictability and inner certainty.

More Market, Less Gardening

It was September 1944 and the Rhine, the final German defence, might be crossed in one mighty bound to end the war forthwith. A concentrated force could debouch into the north German plain with dazzling prospects. For this a narrow corridor had to be drilled through the (hopefully) sparse defenders; over the Rhine and the rivers paralleling it and the deed would be done. Airborne troops in Operation Market would seize the bridges and 30 Corps (part of 2nd Army) would force a path, in Operation Garden, through to them. We all know the outcome of this unusually bold plan.

Montgomery later wrote, when in generalising mood: "Operational command in the battle must be direct and personal, by means of visits to subordinate HQ where orders are given verbally".[7] To my brother-in-law, Lieutenant-Colonel (later Major-General) John Frost, then rather busy clinging with his battalion to the bridge at Arnhem, precept and practice seemed to differ:

> ". . . there does seem to have been a lack of drive all the way through the British chain of command . . . XXX Corps Commander was not once visited by . . . the 2nd Army Commander during the whole nine days of battle . . . XIII Corps Commander on the right flank [of XXX Corps] was not even told about the operation until the day before it was due . . ."[8]

Other commentators have similar messages. Furthermore, airborne plans had been faulty and reports of enemy strength brushed aside; help from the Dutch resistance was neglected. The casualty figures sum up the story:

FORCE	STRENGTH	CASUALTIES
Airborne troops and air crew	3 divisions	11,800
Relief force (2nd Army)	9 divisions	5,400

Here if ever, one would have thought, was a high-risk, high pay-off operation that called for the 'hands on' management that Montgomery liked to advocate. It is intriguing that it was a special occasion, rich in potential personal reward, that found the Field Marshal (as he then was) wanting. Why the poor direction, the lack of a sense of urgency? In part it was due to failures of inter-unit and inter-national co-operation, in part to haste, in part perhaps to a euphoric reaction after great and successful endeavours. Fatigue and chance, in the form of inclement weather and the accidental presence of the high-powered German Field Marshal Model near the dropping zone, were also factors. It reminds one to allow for the contingent and the personal elements, even in an ordinarily consistent leader. Another message is clear: beware comfortable optimism and relaxation. At least one Allied general, leading in highly personal fashion the competent US 3rd Army, was in this respect wholly guiltless:

> "Patton had a keener sense than anyone else on the Allied side of the key importance of persistent pace in pursuit. He was ready to exploit in any direction . . . There was much point in his subsequent comment: 'One does not plan and then try to make circumstances fit those plans. One tries to make plans fit the circumstances' . . ."[5]

Patton did, however, share with Montgomery a high talent for organisation. He trusted his staff, had daily informal meetings with aides, monitored subordinates' radio networks and had his staff officers tour the front. He was thus well equipped with what van Creveld calls a 'directed telescope', to illuminate at will a critical area of his command; his HQ was markedly less burdened with communications and ". . . no other Allied commander at his level had so much free time at his disposal".[1] We know how he used it. Was his success in part due to his sophisticated control system, which underwrote his dynamic personal qualities?

Undistributed Authority

We have seen how the ability to control the action has varied with the technology of the time. The portable radio in World War II, for example, removed the World War I problem.

It would be satisfying to record that modern communications and computing power have rendered all this history irrelevant. It puts our era in perspective to find that nothing basic has changed. With its fearsome technology and specialisation, the modern army is many times as complex an organism as World War II's and the information needed to control it is therefore a large multiple of the past's; van Creveld argues that a 1965 army, for example, needed twenty times the control information as a 1945 one. Political sensitivities and role of the media work against delegation, further increasing the information demanded by the centre to make the extra decisions. Computing *appears* to make all this mass of data transmissable and assimilable, so tempting senior people irresistibly. Centralisation appears simultaneously necessary, feasible and satisfying. Consider the example of Vietnam, as described by van Creveld. There 'signals support' for the US forces occupied 23,000 men full-time, the Defence Secretary in Washington specified air targets in person; in 1967 US Intelligence there was printing *half a ton of reports daily*.[1] In desperation only senior officers were allowed to order stationery, thus solving one problem with more centralisation. The flood of information caused indigestion: the outcome was "... a situation in which messages could not be read but had to be counted instead".[1]

Planning became bogged down. While the Germans captured Crete in 1941 by airborne assault after three weeks' planning, the US Army now took rather longer. US Intelligence in 1970 identified American prisoners of war being held in a jungle camp; two months later they were quietly moved; the camp was raided successfully four months later — and found vacant. It seems that, pushed by politicised decision-making and the cost of making mistakes, the current trend for 'distributed computing' is meeting a reverse traffic in authority. What to do?

There seems to be some, if rather vague, guides through the jungle. A command system is a function of time, place, seniority level and technology. It must work for and not against the institution's interests, sieve out what is relevant, simplify the organisation so it can manage with less information, divide tasks to suit delegation. What suits the making of plans may not suit their execution. To have self-contained units reduces vertical and lateral communications. The extra procedures needed to secure reliability create formality and rigidity; informal communication networks can counter these trends, aided by pushing information down and by actively chasing it from above. We have seen how the military did this. Regretfully, the more the certainty at the top the less at the bottom: while waiting for decisions the latter is in danger. Time spent on clarifying what is critical and controllable at the top is a valuable investment.

Decentralisation and delegation are risky but for industry, as for the military, may be inescapable if done selectively. The German Wehrmacht in World War II had 3% of its troops on the staff, in 1975 14%. The exponential increase in the cost of C^3 conducted by conventional means simply displaces combat power. "The quest for certainty, in other words, will logically end when there is nothing left to be certain about."[1]

*   *   *   *

References

[1] Dr Martin van Creveld, Command in War.

[2] R Lewin, Montgomery as Military Commander.

[3] Major-General Sir Francis de Guingand, Operation Victory.*

[4] Corelli Barnett, The Desert Generals.

[5] Sir Basil Liddell Hart, History of the Second World War.

[6] Field Marshal Lord Wavell, 1939 Lees Knowles Lecture.

[7] Field Marshal Viscount Montgomery of Alamein, Memoirs.

[8] Major-General J D Frost, A Drop too Many.

Reprinted by permission of Hodder and Stoughton Limited.

CHAPTER XII

LEADERSHIP: A CONTRAST IN STYLES

"Only one man in a thousand is a leader of men —
the other 999 follow women."

— Groucho Marx

Part I. Charismatic Leadership:
The Career of Alexander the Great

The Manager as Leader

Managers work through people. Everyone agrees that performance is a direct function of the commitment, cohesion, sense of purpose and enthusiasm of these people. But how much training to evoke these responses is given? Leadership is talked about; is this really more than lip service? The quality is rated a by-product, a matter of chance. 'Leaders are born, not made', so we will let them emerge as they will.

The military tell us that there are general guides, useful to memorise, that help performance, and we have seen how applying or failing to apply these 'principles of war' helped or hindered. They mostly guide external action, not internal management: the inspiration of the organisation to effect concerted and heroic action — or more plainly, "the art of getting others to want to do something you are convinced should be done"[1] — is to be learned in other ways.

Leadership may not be unanimously defined but the men under Hannibal, Marlborough, Nelson, Wellington, Napoleon, Lee, Grant, Montgomery and Patton knew very well its influence and what it meant to them. These people seemed to embody or enjoy certain qualities: craftmanship, capacity for detail, empathy, an ability to carry responsibility, a sense of purpose — and, not least good fortune and a modicum of ruthlessness. Equally, all differed in values, rank, authority and charisma. Clearly the leader role can be played in varied ways. "All styles are good," said Voltaire, "except the tiresome sort". Here, two examples are looked at, differing vastly in style.

Alexander, saluted by his world as its king, was born to privilege and rank and gifted with high talent. Nevertheless, his apprenticeship was taxing. The gifts of the gods were to be improved upon. We shall see what he was and what he did: one variety of commander, the sort that dazzles people. In World War II one Allied force fought the Germans throughout — Britain's Bomber Command. Lacking equipment and skill, its casualty rate was frightening, yet continuing action was demanded of it. Its new chief, taking over in mid-stream, could not have differed more from the Macedonian king, yet he filled very well the need of its people for a common objective, for teamwork, and for individual treatment.

These requirements can be met in various ways: leadership takes many forms. The point is, some form of it *must* come from somewhere. Every company director must see the supply matches the demand.

Apprenticeship in Macedon

Alexander the Great was born in 356 BC, when Rome was a modest state in central Italy and northern Europe was peopled by simple tribes who have left no written history; to the east the powerful Persian Empire stretched from the Aegean Sea to India; Greece was an array of lively city-states weakened by mutual strife. On its northern fringe lay Macedon *(see Fig. XII. 1)*, the mountainous area beyond modern Salonika, and a dynamic country already becoming a nationalist power, armed and expansionist. Its king, Philip II, was its prime mover, a man of ambition, energy, guile and strength. He married a strong-minded, emotional woman from nearby Epirus, of royal blood and fiery temperament; her name was Olympias. Their first child was Alexander.

Throughout his youth his father was regularly going off to war; he subjugated the whole of Greece for which the final battle was at Chaeronea where Alexander, then eighteen, commanded the Macedonian cavalry and led the decisive charge. (Heirs apparent were expected to develop fast in the Ancient World and boys could find themselves loaded with all the responsibilities

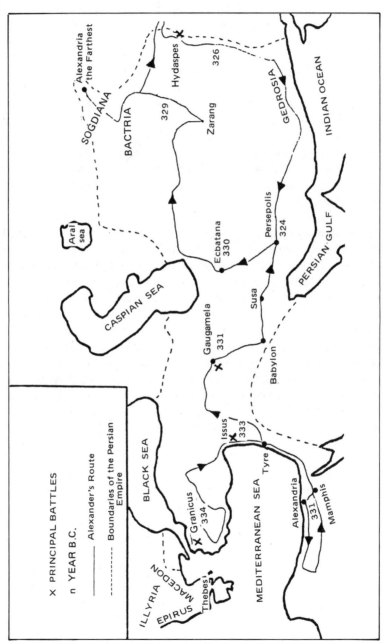

Fig.XII. 1 A Short Walk in the Persian Empire

they could handle; this 'management development' appears to have been productive.) This particular boy was below medium height and of very athletic form, a runner of Olympic standard (the first Games was held in 776 BC), most handsome of face and with fair hair. Proud and highly emotional, he was yet practical, with an aptitude for politics and a genius for war. Fearless and with a magnetic personality, men liked to follow him. He had intelligence and vision and was driven to excel, perhaps to surpass the father he could not love.

> "Alexander's need for self-assurance was equal to his genius and strength of will. If he ever consciously resolved to be greatest among men, it was probably in his school-days."[2]

(Some firms now look to promote 'lean hungry' men, a motivation similar in principle to Alexander's; while not all the leaders we have looked at have been so driven, all must somewhere in themselves find a demand for excellence.) To this drive Alexander was to add practical skills; he was brought up to be a master of arms and a ruler. The great Aristotle was his tutor (a notable instance of a father seeking the best possible tuition for his heir), from whom he learned Greek science, history and culture — in fact a broadly-based education — and probably a hatred of Persia. This was an overbearing neighbour, an early Soviet Russia, which had twice invaded Greece, to be twice — with difficulty — repulsed.

Only three years after Chaeronea Philip was assassinated — an occupational hazard for Macedonian kings — and Alexander, not without some political manoeuvring, succeeded him; he was then twenty-one. First of all, the young but well trained king secured — by his personality, his reputation and his patronage — the backing of the aristocracy, the army and the people. He was then free to look to more distant horizons. Philip had been contemplating an attack on Persia, by crossing the Hellespont (now the Dardanelles Straits) to liberate the Greek colonies in Asia Minor from Persian rule. His son's destiny fell out naturally for him.

He had first to secure his birthright. The Greeks and his northern neighbours both rebelled at once. He forced a quick but temporary settlement on the Greeks, then turned like lightning on the north. While his back was turned Persia tried to subvert his Greek rule, bribing Thebes, a city-state, to attack its

Macedonian garrison. On a rumour that Alexander had died in Illyria (Albania) the Thebans readily complied. He reacted on the instant and while they were engaged on the Persians' work the Thebans heard a new story: Alexander was fifteen miles away; unfortunately for them this one proved to be true. Thebes was levelled and its population killed or sold into slavery. All the other Greek cities promptly submitted. Alexander's base was now secure; so was his status, having shown at the outset his right to his position — important as it was an inherited one. The young king was ready to make "war as no man in the world had made it before . . ."[3]

His father had created the army, transforming the components — horsemen, personal guards, spearmen — into sharp and specialised instruments. The main arm was the cavalry, of which the Royal Guard was called the Companions, armed with spears; the stirrup had not been invented and the horses were small so their impact in a charge was modest. They manoeuvred round a base formed by the heavy infantry set up in phalanx *(see Chapter I);* this was drilled to move in close order except over rough ground. A well-trained one advancing with heavy tread, shouting war cries, skirmishers protecting its flanks, spears bristling, must have been a fearsome sight. (Equally, once set in motion, it must have been a beast to control.) Alexander took over Philip's creation unchanged, simply leading it with inspiration. (Quite unlike the father, the son was not an innovator though his varied battle tactics show a creative mind.) He eschewed brutal punishments and instead of making speeches he greeted men by name, singling out those noted for courage. He was generous with praise and with awards for bravery. He had an instinctive understanding of his soldiers' feelings and, being emotional, a strong personal bond with them. (The whole army was to file past his sick-bed when he was dying, to say farewell.)

The army of 30,000 foot and 5,000 horse crossed into Asia in 335 BC; reinforcements followed later, reliably if not regularly, no matter what the distance. Alexander's personal staff included surveyors, sappers, architects, an official historian and physicians — the latter most useful: swords, and scythes on chariot wheels, produced hideous wounds. (Ancient battles lasted only a few hours so the rate of slaughter was high. The losing side lost disproportionately heavily because, once formation was broken, infantry could be easily cut down by horsemen, so relentless pursuit was particularly rewarding.)

The Destruction of King Darius

The Persian Empire had arisen from the forcible unification of
several competing states two hundred years earlier by Cyrus
the Great, the first of a line called the Achaemenids — mostly
talented men of whom the last but not the greatest was Darius III,
who now sat on the 'peacock throne' and pondered the matter
of Alexander. His dominion was vast *(Fig. XII. 1)* but had a
competent civil service to administer it; the Great King delegated
authority to provincial governors called satraps, all being linked by
a rapid courier service using the fine road system.

The Persians' information system made them well aware of
Alexander's movements and they immediately confronted him; a
battle was fought on the river Granicus just south of the Hellespont,
which Alexander won. This opened Asia Minor to him. He visited
the Greek cities, projecting himself as their liberator. He appointed
locals, some Persian, as governors but reserved military authority
for Macedonians, thus for safety using a functional organisation to
divide power and reserving the ultimate sanction to himself. While
it was his nature to be a reconciler — though he could be totally
uncompromising when it suited him — only such a policy could
control the huge Persian Empire economically: "A merely fallen
enemy may rise again", says Schiller, "but the reconciled one is
truly vanquished". (This principle could usefully apply to company acquisitions, especially opposed take-overs.) Alexander could
sympathise with and soothe proud Persian sensibilities.

The army proceeded through the Taurus mountains into present-
day Syria; again the Persians sought to halt Alexander and on the
river Issus were again defeated. Darius now wrote to his enemy,
to ask for an alliance, to which Alexander's reply was forthright:

> "Come to me and ask . . . But for the future, whenever
> you send to me, send to me as the King of Asia, and do
> not address to me your wishes as to an equal . . . and if
> you dispute my right to the Kingdom, stay and fight
> another battle for it . . ."[4]

The appetite grows with what it feeds on. Hitherto, Alexander's
ambitions embraced control of Asia Minor; now he was to be
head of an empire; the giant was feeling his powers. Strategically,

he had room for manoeuvre but on land only; seizing an advance port would deprive the strong Persian fleet of a base and also ease his supply line. Having thus secured his flank and his communications, he could win control of Egypt with its wealth and grain — both much needed in Greece — and of the whole eastern Mediterranean. His Greek base would be enriched and secured from counter-attack and his rear protected. The time for Darius would then be at hand. (These were immensely taxing objectives and, to have seemed realistic to his followers, must have been based on deep trust. "A man's reach must exceed his grasp", said the poet Browning. It must have looked so to the Macedonians.)

Alexander proceeded with his plan. He laid siege to Tyre, a very strong fortress port in Lebanon. After seven months of incessant and imaginative struggle against skilled defenders, the city was stormed. Meanwhile an embassy had arrived from Darius to offer truly a king's ransom for his previously captured family (10,000 talents — perhaps £800 million in today's money) and in addition all his land west of the Euphrates. Alexander's senior general, Parmenion, said: "If I were Alexander I would accept these terms", to which Alexander replied, "If I were Parmenion so would I". He quickly marched into Egypt while Darius was forming a new army and founded the first of the seventeen Alexandrias he was to plant as colonies throughout Asia. Darius continued with his task and soon felt ready for a confrontation on a flat plain east of Mosul, near a village called Gaugamela. It was to name one of the decisive battles of history.*

It was now the autumn of 331 BC. The Persian host was drawn up in line of battle. It was enormous; accounts differ widely on numbers but a modern estimate[5] gives 56,000 infantry and 35,000 cavalry to the Greeks' 39,000 and 7,000 respectively. It overlapped them, threatening an encirclement. In front of it the ground had been levelled to give Darius' chariots full play. His great cavalry strength meant he was geared for offensive action. The core of the Greek army was its heavy infantry in phalanx and the Companion Cavalry. Alexander set up flank guards, particularly on the right wing. In full armour he was (no doubt consciously) conspicuous to his men; he took post with the Companions, in charge of the (senior) right half while Parmenion commanded the left. We can imagine the scene: the huge plain, the crisp morning air not yet dusty from feet and hooves, the massed ranks perhaps two miles long, the 18 foot spears of the

Also called Arbela.

phalanx raised, the cavalry riding bare-back. Over against them the enemy: dark bearded men, innumerable horses, elephants, 4-horse chariots.

By interrogating prisoners Alexander, schooled to meticulous preparation, had already learned Darius' order of battle; he had personally reconnoitered the battlefield; he had briefed his generals on the importance of the coming battle and had demanded complete silence during the opening phase to permit orders to be heard. In the light of his appreciation he had made his battle plan. This was to adopt a defensive formation while advancing, unusually in oblique order, and inclining to his right across the Persian front, to force its left wing to counter him. His left, being 'refused', would invite the Persian right wing to advance. These moves should uncover the army's front which, if exactly identified, constituted an opportunity; if penetrated, the whole front could be disrupted.

> "Alexander's aim was to defeat an attack of double-envelopment by an attack of penetration, and to achieve it his tactical order was based on the idea embodied in Napoleon's maxim: 'The whole art of war consists in a well-reasoned and extremely circumspect defensive followed by rapid and audacious attack'."[4]

(Quite incidentally, one wonders if this subtle strategy is given conscious consideration by businessmen.)

The Greeks' advance triggered a desperately exciting battle. They were traversing off the levelled ground so the Persian left was ordered to arrest them *(Fig. XII. 2)*. Because he was on the spot, Alexander could feed the resulting fight with just enough reinforcements to preserve his flank guard while holding to his advance. Darius sent his chariots to unbalance the phalanx but these were met by light troops with a hail of javelins; passing through gaps made for them, the survivors were taken care of by the second line.

The Persian right attacked Parmenion's cavalry and the Greek rear. While thousands of horsemen were absorbed in melées, the Persian front had cumbrously to side-step to match Alexander's oblique approach. A gap beckoned. Alexander, leading from the front and placed to identify for himself the critical moment, directed the phalanx at it *(Fig. XII. 3)*, while forming the

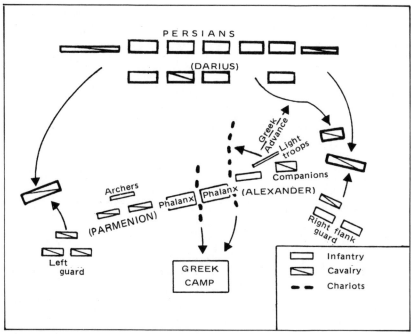

Fig.XII. 2 Darius' Attack at Gaugamela

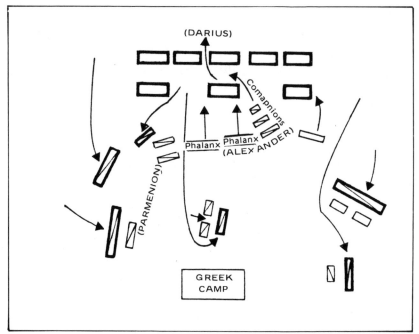

Fig.XII. 3 Alexander's Attack at Gaugamela

Companion Cavalry into a wedge formation; this he then personally led in a fierce charge into Darius' centre. The King's nerve
promptly broke; he fled in his chariot and the Persian centre
thereupon dissolved. Pursuit had started when a very hard pressed
Parmenion sent for help. Found (by luck or by design?) by some
no doubt anxious staff officer, Alexander broke off his cavalry
battle to take the Persian right in rear. A general rout ensued
and the pursuit was pressed relentlessly throughout the day.

Leaving behind a Persian army two-thirds killed or captured,
Alexander pursued the fugitive Darius, and occupied the key
cities of Babylon and Persepolis:

> "Is it not passing brave to be a king,
> And ride in triumph through Persepolis?"

Certainly it was a personal triumph. Careful material preparation,
ensuring the army's morale, a flexible plan beautifully adapted to
circumstances, the bold exercise of command, the maintenance of
command over the decisive actions, all underwritten by courage,
determination and judgement, made for a richly deserved and
massive victory. Now the empire was his. At Ecbatana he heard
Darius was ahead of him; after a 400 mile dash, ever speedy and
never a procrastinator, he caught up, to find his enemy dead,
meanly killed by a follower. The Macedonian war lord could now
call himself the Great King.

Occupation of an Empire

The march east continued, through barren desert and bleak mountains, remote, hostile, lonely, but four years and 5000 miles from
home found the army's devotion to its cherished leader quite
undiminished. As he went, Alexander settled some of his troops
as colonists, appointed governors, coerced numerous recalcitrant
tribes, quelled rebellions. He respected Persian religion, appointed
Persians to senior posts, adopted their customs. The policy was
rare then, and later. His Macedonian generals found it incomprehensible: rights of conquest seemed self-evident. Then arose a
highly personal problem.

Alexander had left the now elderly Parmenion, life-long colleague and senior general of his father and himself, at Ecbatana
to guard the Persian royal treasure (worth perhaps £14 billion
today) and the army's vital lines of communication. When a

thousand miles out from that city the cavalry commander, one Philotas and *Parmenion's son*, was implicated in a plot to kill his king. A cordon was thrown round the camp to seal it and then the plotters were tried by public assembly, judged guilty and executed. This still left the most painful problem. Macedonians believed in the blood feud; a family could avenge a member's murder; practical custom sanctioned the killing of the member's close relatives to stifle the feud at birth. In any case, could the army risk leaving a suspect with military force on its life-line; "Till now the young conqueror had known only the rewards of power . . . For the first time he learned power's terrible necessities. He knew them when he saw them; yet it is possible he kept a last option open . . ."[2]

Before any signal could reach Parmenion armed agents were sent on racing camels to Ecbatana. There, it is suggested, they gave him a forged letter ostensibly from Philotas; when its contents seemed to please him he was instantly killed. Did the letter secretly signal a successful plot, by signs extracted from Philotas under torture, to which Parmenion should not have reacted if he were innocent? Perhaps. Whether it was murder or not, the army went on its way. The remoter provinces, with their proud tribes mouthing defiance from hill-top forts, needed two years of guerilla and mountain warfare to subdue — a sufficient test of a general's versatility.

Thence the army traversed the Hindu Kush range into India — via a 12,000 foot pass, a feat excelling Hannibal's more famous alpine crossing — to be confronted by the local king, Porus, in a very strong position behind the river Hydaspes (now the Jhelum). By complex strategems Alexander forced a crossing and defeated Porus in a severe battle. He then wanted to anchor his eastern frontier on the Ganges, the edge of the known world, but his troops at last refused to go further from home and Alexander settled for the line of the Indus. They turned south. In 2000 ships, somehow requisitioned or constructed on the river, he sent part of his force back to Persia by sea, but the fighting was not yet done.

The nearby Mallian tribe resisted him and their fortress had to be stormed. Relying on speed to pre-empt the defence, Alexander ordered an instant escalade of the citadel's walls and himself mounted the first ladder with three companions. The weight of others following broke the ladder and their leader, now a target for missiles, leaped down into the courtyard, the other three following; the little band defended itself until rescued but Alexander took an arrow in the lung. He was desperately hurt *but* the fort was taken. (And his superb constitution overcame what was then normally a fatal wound.) More or less recovered, he then led the remainder of his army across the Gedrosian desert, a nightmare of a journey, to arrive — after ten years and a 17,000 mile march — in Babylon.

Fame Everlasting?

The problems of peace now lay ahead and all around him. The future would deal with these in its own way. Behind lay almost limitless achievement. He had led a far from homogeneous army to the ends of the earth and it had followed with rare complaint; the troops would themselves achieve victories, praise, loot, women, land to settle on. If they did not share their general's purpose, at least he and they shared common interests. They had made an heroic march together. They were looked after as well as conditions permitted — which was not always much. Not least, this army was given cohesion and enthusiastic determination by the charisma and empathy (as we would now say) of its dazzling commander, ably supported by his generals. Alexander's capacities extended from the moral sphere to the most practical:

> "In only one of his Asiatic campaigns did Alexander lose touch with his home base, and then only for twenty-four hours before the battle of Issus; only once is it recorded that his supply system broke down, and that was during his march across Gedrosia. This is sufficient proof of the superb staff work of his headquarters."[4]

In Babylon he at once addressed innumerable administrative matters, removing faithless or avaricious governors, and was beginning to create the cohesion and control that might have held his empire together when he contracted a fever — or was poisoned. Within a fortnight, at the age of thirty-three, having conquered most of the known world, he was dead, mourned by his army and saluted by his contemporaries. His body was mummified, and buried in Alexandria in Egypt.

He left a legacy of incalculable promise and tragic fragility. He had made no provision for the succession and his generals, who had been totally over-shadowed by their leader, fought over the division of his empire. For decades the successor-states quarrelled and warred, to lose their political unity though Hellenic culture was diffused throughout western Asia. Men's horizons were widened. "He had left his mark upon Asia . . . and even today there can be found traces . . . of the legends that gathered in hosts about that terrible name".[3] What if he had lived his proper span? It can be entertainingly speculated, quoting Arnold Toynbee,[6] that the whole Mediterranean world would have been incorporated in Alexander's empire, whose Buddhist religion would have been imported from India, whose ally would have been a shackled Rome, and whose remote descendant, Alexander LXXXVI, would have ruled the current world!

Born to rule and adorned with royal prestige, Alexander had still to develop his talents for leadership before he could so impress all who knew him and a chronicler of the times could say: "By universal consent it was recognised that the genius of the King surpassed human measure" — an epitaph satisfactory surely even to the man himself. Perhaps in the end we can make him sum up for us: "It is a lovely thing, he said, "to live with courage, and die leaving an everlasing fame".[2]

Part II Leadership by System: 'Bomber Harris'

The Care and Feeding of Bomber Command

The Alexandrine example leaves one somewhat breathless. It is easy to move on to the common view that leaders must by definition be dazzling or lovable public figures, or at least have magnetic personalities. Thus equipped by nature, they can — by showing off their prestige, by conducting public ceremonies and by regularly touring the 'front line' — enthuse their people to great and concerted efforts. We have witnessed several of this sort already; Alexander was simply one more, albeit very exceptional. Now consider a rather different type of animal.

Air Chief Marshal Sir Arthur Harris inherited the job of Commander-in-Chief, RAF Bomber Command in February, 1942. It was a moment when that devoted and courageous force had inflicted very modest damage upon the enemy *(see Appendix I* for some statistics) at the price of severe and increasing casualties. Bomber Command lost over 10,000 aircraft during World War II,

79% during Harris' tenure of command. Dead and prisoners
numbered 67,000, the injured 22,000, and this collection of men
probably the cream of the country's enterprising young manhood.
For much of the time the "chop rate" was about 5%; thus if you
were the average airman you disappeared after twenty operations.
Yet an "operational tour" was thirty! Just one in five airmen
could expect statistically to survive them. In one raid alone — on
Nuremberg — over 100 aircraft were lost, a rate of 13%. If ever a
situation called for leadership this was it.

What happened? A dumpy figure, parochial, seemingly remote,
hard driving and very single-minded, the new chief rapidly made
his personality felt throughout his command. All who served
under him, as Martin Middlebrook remarks, knew his name, gave
him their loyalty and acquired a lasting self-esteem. "All this was
achieved in remarkable fashion because he rarely left his headquarters and not one person in a hundred in Bomber Command
ever saw him."[7] What was the fashion? Harris led by cocooning
Bomber Command personnel in a thorough-going system that was
felt by them to be well directed, meticulous and mostly as secure
for them as was reasonably possible. "I never saw Harris", says
Wing Commander Ian Debenham, for much of this period a
Halifax bomber captain, "and I heard of him infrequently; instead
I saw the Group Commander. I felt looked after by the 'system'
for several practical reasons.

"First, it seemed most concerned about needless losses; for
example, an 'op' would be scrubbed if the weather looked
ominous and the aim was always to flood the enemy radar with
closely grouped aircraft. This impression was reinforced by our
equipment, as modern and good as possible. Harris also provided
'top cover' for us from worries about the press or visiting VIP's.
(A simple example of this shielding was the CO who said to us
pilots, 'For heaven's sake tell me when you've been low-flying,
then I can tick you off: that way you won't be court-martialled —
you can't be punished twice for the same offence.')

"We had aircrew losses, of course, but these were replaced
within individual units, whose staff and basic cadre of experienced
airmen could often guide and support and carry the fledglings
until they could return from an 'op' safely. Remember, too,
the background. It was part of the Harris 'system' that the press
was used to tell the country and us that the bombing offensive
was an important part of the war effort and we were shown air

recce photos of bomb damage in Germany to show how we were succeeding. (Also, the campaign made strategic sense. Germany was being got at in virtually the only way we could at the time and this both paved the way for the Second Front and allowed it to be delayed until its success was far more likely.)

"Our role as aircrew was not only known to be useful, it was also very clear: well trained, anxious to get going, we arrived on a squadron, went — as a normal part of RAF routine — to the briefing and our aircraft, to fly off with a bombload to be dropped in the right place and to get back safely. On the question of getting back, I hold the personal view that the greater proportion of aircraft losses was due to 'finger trouble' — the pilot's choosing the wrong switch or forgetting the right one, or bad navigation, leading one to be jacked up on the searchlights over Antwerp when one had no business to be within miles of it . . ."[8]

It seems the emphasis on system and on the simple principle of doing what was expected of one was highly appropriate when, as Debenham knew, mistakes were not difficult to make. With complicated equipment it is drill, habit and system that make for accuracy in the heat and fright of battle. And this equipment became increasingly complicated as the 'system' generated innovation, prodded by Harris himself: for example, the technique, initially thought most dangerous, of saturating the defences by a dense concentration of aircraft in time and space, or the means for quicker target indentification, or better navigational aids.

The 'system' was demanding of high and sustained performance — a challenge to a professional force. One example can show the attitudes of leader and led, the latter here being the commander of the newly formed Pathfinder Force, whose job it was to identify targets for the main bomber force:

> "It was in August 1942, that the squadrons of the Path-finder Force assembled. Typical of the attitude of Bert Harris . . . was the order which he issued to me that the squadrons were to operate the day they arrived, without missing a single night, and that no period would be allowed for preparation or for training. This was quite unreasonable, but the spirit behind it was so thoroughly 'press-on' that I made no attempt to argue. In accordance with the general principle of never wasting war effort or of ceasing to strike the enemy, I entirely agreed, and we were there-

fore prepared to operate the night the squadrons assembled."[9]

Finally, the 'system' was conclusive, making firm unambiguous decisions. To dramatise the bomber offensive to friend and foe, Harris wanted to mount a thousand bomber raid on Germany, when such a number was unprecedented, navigation at night suspect, saturating the defences wholly unproved and the risks of aerial collisions frightening. Furthermore, mustering such a force would commit his whole front-line strength, all his reserves and much of his aircrew training capacity to one risky operation. With great difficulty enough aircraft and aircrew were found. Now Harris had to have a target, a full moon and the right weather. A staff officer, Group Captain Saward, describes the scene at command HQ.

> "... the C-in-C entered the Operations Room at ten minutes past nine for his planning conference ... There was that characteristic hunch about his shoulders as he walked slowly but deliberately to his desk ... Not a muscle moved and no sign of an expression stirred his face whilst the [weather] forecast for the next twenty-four hours was outlined to him ... It was not a forecast which held much promise for good operational conditions: in fact, it rather bordered on the side of being unsuitable. I held my breath, for this was probably the last possible night for the great operation, unless it were undertaken another month hence ... If it were postponed ... it might never take place at all. I am sure I was not the only one present who held his breath.
> The C-in-C moved at last ... He lit [a] cigarette ... He continued to stare at the [weather] charts and then slowly his forefinger moved across the continent of Europe and came to rest on a town in Germany. The pressure on his finger bent back the end joint and drove the blood from the top of his finger nail, leaving a half circle of white. He turned ... his face still expressionless.
> 'The 1,000 Plan tonight.'
> His finger was pressing on Cologne."[10]

*   *   *   *

Finale

Not many people are as decisive, determined, ruthless and single-minded as Harris but a lot fewer are as royal, fearless, visionary and dazzling characters as Alexander. There is surely comfort here. Many managers can fairly aim to create the environment of competence and care, and the atmosphere of purposefulness and usefulness, that Bomber Command enjoyed. A well-known trainer of leadership to military and civilian people, John Adair, identifies its three components* as:

— establishing a common aim for the organisation;
— encouraging teamwork;
— looking after individual needs.

In their very different ways Alexander the Great and Air Chief Marshal Harris exemplify this view and nothing we have studied disputes it. The 'principles of war' cover the first two points. But that is not enough. The leader may be gruff or charming, distant or intimate, modest or out-going, but his organisation must give me the feeling that *my* concerns are *its* concerns. The final principle we need to remember, therefore, is — individual care.

*   *   *   *

Most of us have our failures. Success in war, as we have seen, does not come easily; nor does it in business. The military and the civilian worlds overlap because they in part share a common framework — management. Each can help the other to perform this better. The military have simply been at it rather longer.

*   *   *   *

*These components deserve looking at in more detail. See Appendix J.

References

1 Vance Packard, The Hidden Persuaders.

2 Mary Renault, The Nature of Alexander.

3 Ed. W N Weech, History of the World.

4 J F C Fuller, The Generalship of Alexander the Great.

5 John Warry, Warfare in the Classical World.

6 Phil Barker, Alexander the Great's Campaigns.

7 Martin Middlebrook, The Battle of Hamburg.

8 A I S Debenham, Letter to the Author.

9 D C T Bennett, quoted by Gavin Lyall, The War in the Air.

10 Dudley Saward, quoted by Gavin Lyall, Ibid.

APPENDIX A

AN HISTORICAL SKETCH

"The past is a foreign country; they do things differently there."
— L P Hartley

On reflection school-taught history now seems patchy and parochial. Britain appeared to leap into existence in AD 1066, except for a brief flash-back 1000 years to the Roman invasion. Not too much of importance seemed to happen beyond the English Channel. A bare sketch of previous western history may at least indicate gaps schooling may have left and also provide a time perspective.

The Ancient World
The earliest civilisations arose in Mesopotamia and the Nile valley *(see Fig. A. 1)* around 4000 BC. Both areas were fertile and both nurtured sophisticated states — populous, skilled and creative. Egypt evolved into a static theocracy; its pharaohs and priests organising a wealthy society, building pyramids and a bureaucracy, which lasted through the millennia until the Roman occupation a few years before Christ's birth. Its last monarch, Cleopatra, was defeated with her lover, Antony, by the Romans at the naval battle of Actium in 31 BC.

The Tigris-Euphrates valley produced the Sumerian civilisation, later combined with nearby Akkad. Around 1800 BC, when the Hebrews' claimed ancestor, Abraham, was journeying to Palestine, the Babylonian Empire supplanted them while a new state,

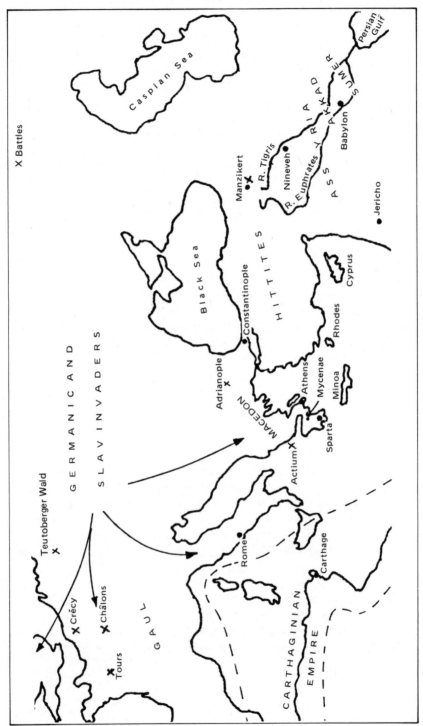

Fig. A. 1 The Ancient World

Assyria, was growing just to the north. When the biblical David was uniting Israel and Judah around 1150 BC, "the Assyrians came down like a wolf on the fold" to build a mighty empire. Their energy and unpleasantness were inexhaustible: they impaled prisoners on stakes or cut off their feet, hands and heads — in that order. Being skilled at war their empire extended from the Persian Gulf to the Mediterranean but an alliance of their neighbours finally defeated them and sacked their capital, Nineveh, in 612 BC, only in turn to be absorbed by Cyrus the Great into the Persian Empire, which stretched from the Aegean Sea to India.

While the Jewish kingdom was developing, Achaean tribesmen were moving south into Greece. It was their cities like Mycenae which made war on Troy. By 600 BC Greece had coalesced into an array of city-states — flourishing, clever but parochial. They clashed with their overbearing neighbour, Persia, which attacked them, only to be defeated at the decisive battle of Marathon:

> "The mountains look on Marathon
> And Marathon looks on the sea . . ."

Ten years later there was a repeat performance when the Persians, marshalled in very great strength, tried again. This time 300 Spartans, aided by 3500 allies, delayed the invaders for three vital days at the pass of Thermopylae:

> "Go, tell the Spartans, thou that passest by,
> That here, obedient to their laws, we lie."

Battles at Salamis and Plataea (near Athens) repulsed the invasion totally. The Greeks could then devote themselves to what they were best at: culture and internecine war. The leading powers, Athens and Sparta, carried on the Peloponnesian War for twenty-seven years. While thus occupied, a new power was growing just to the north; under King Philip Macedon was expanding and in 338 BC he secured Greek hegemony. His son, Alexander, we saw extending that rule throughout the Persian Empire.

Unnoticed by any of these states, a near contemporary was growing to manhood in distant Italy. Rome was devouring its neighbours and by 44 BC it controlled the whole Mediterranean littoral, including — after a century's life or death struggle — the

Carthaginian empire, plus Macedon, Gaul and much of Asia Minor. Only Parthia, Persia's successor-state, in the east and the German tribes in the north, remained independent and obstreperous neighbours. The Rome Empire was at its greatest extent in the emperor Hadrian's reign, around 120 AD. Germany, unlike the rest of western Europe, was never colonised and perhaps that has differentiated it ever since. In AD 9 three Roman legions were annihilated in the Teutoburger Wald. (I heard a German at a party sing a commemoration of this 2000 year old battle — what a folk memory.)

The pressure of Asiatic migrations and invaders steadily increased over the next 300 years and maintaining the Empire's frontiers became increasingly burdensome to a decadent unstable state. Its centre of gravity shifted to the wealthier east and the emperor Constantine set up a new capital, Constantinople, in 330 AD at a strategic and easily defended point between Europe and Asia. The west had to look after itself. The protective legions in Britain were withdrawn to defend Italy and the island was submerged under Saxon invaders, despite the best efforts of local war lords like Arthur. In 410 Alaric the Goth sacked Rome. In the east a Roman emperor and 40,000 legionaries were killed by a Gothic army at the battle of Adrianople in 378. The mailed horseman had arrived, to rule the battlefields for a 1000 years. The barbarians settled the land. In turn they were assailed by the fiercer Huns, who poured out of Asia to create appalling devastation throughout western Europe and who were — with difficulty — defeated at the battle of Châlons in 451. (Attila's camp is still visible there.)

Transition to the Modern World
The Dark Ages folded over the Roman Empire in the west. The Empire in the east became Byzantium, rich and famous and which lasted for a further 1000 years, until a hitherto obscure tribe called the Ottoman Turks captured Constantinople after a monumental seige in 1453. An Asiatic people, they had first entered the marches of the empire 400 years previously, destroying a Byzantine army in the decisive battle of Manzikert in 1071. Thus, while Joan of Arc was ejecting the English from France, the Turks were obliterating the remnants of Roman culture and power in the east.

In the west, colonising and farming and fighting each other, were the Goths, the Vandals, the Franks and many other tribes; something of the civilisation they over-ran rubbed off on them and in addition they had their own vigour and enterprise. Many kingdoms covered the land; the Franks set one up in France. Its main threat came now from the south. Mahomet had died in Mecca in 632 AD; his religion and Arab energy formed an explosive mixture and his followers erupted out of the Arabian peninsula and within an astonishingly short time over-ran north Africa, then Spain, before invading France. They were just defeated by the Frankish king, Charles Martel, at the battle of Tours in 732. The following time-chart may help to put some of these events in perspective.

	Fig. A. 2 Time Chart for the West
B C 1200 1000 800 600 400 200 0 200 400 600 800 1000 1200 1400 1600 1800 2000 A D	Ramses II defeats Hittites at B. of Kadesh. Seige of Troy Solomon king of Israel Rome founded Carthage founded. Cyrus the Great forms Persian Empire Buddha born. Persia invades Greece. Alexander overthrows Persian Empire Peloponnesian War. Rome destroys Carthage. Birth of Christ. Pompey conquers Syria. Roman Empire at greatest extent Hadrian builds his wall. Huns invade Western Europe B. of Adrianople. Rome sacked B. of Châlons. Mahomet born. Arabs defeated at Tours Moslems invade Spain. Viking raids Normans invade England. Turks invade Anatolia. The Crusades. Mongol invasion. 100 Years War. Black Death. Rule of Aztecs. Turks take Constantinople. Armada defeated. Spaniards conquer Incas. Thirty Years War. Great Northern War. Wolfe takes Quebec. Waterloo. World Wars. American Civil War.

Under Charlemagne the Franks ruled much of western Europe. His successors broke the nascent political unity and no secular institution could restore it, thus leaving with individual states the freedom to make war from which Europe has suffered to this day. Western Christendom was a collection of ethnic or political groups — France, England, the German states, Poland, and many others — who were throughout the Middle Ages (say 900 to 1500) coalescing into modern states empowered with national sovereignty and motivated by aggrandisement.

At first the infant Europe was menaced from outside. After repelling the Moslems it was harried mercilessly by the Vikings, who sailed into the Mediterranean and also besieged Paris. They were traders as well as fighters and took their long-boats to Russia and by river to Byzantium; they traded in slaves extensively (hence the name Slav). Europe then counter-attacked Islam by the Crusades, which absorbed some of its knights' superabundant energy and greed. Thereafter, it was free to enjoy its internal quarrels and to pursue its rulers' ambitions in local fights and inter-state wars. These adventures spread misery widely: harrying the enemy's lands was customary so the peasants often starved, provided they had survived the preliminary rape and pillage. Later, religion reinforced the ferocity: the sword was doing God's work.

Came a change for the better. The 18th century kings made virtually private wars with small professional armies. These mercenaries were not over-violent as they had no cause to kill for and they could be disciplined; being expensive they were not killed needlessly. War was never before, or again, so moderate. Social upheaval and progress changed all that. Democracy and revolution came to power. The pride and vehemence of nation-states, exemplified by French revolutionary fervour injected into Napoleon's mass armies, progressively increased the scale and the length of wars. Voters can be quite easily induced to fight for pride or freedom or democracy or some other abstraction but their passions, once aroused, take long to cool. Limited war for moderate aims has been transformed into 'total war' which pursues intolerable conditions like 'unconditional surrender', a self-defeating occupation under-written by the ever-increasing impersonality of modern weapons.

It seems ironic that, unwittingly, democracy and technology should have combined to induce a reversion to barbarism.

*   *   *   *

APPENDIX B

FREDERICK THE GREAT'S PRINCIPLES OF WAR

"You rogues, do you want to live for ever?"

— Frederick the Great, to his Guards when
they hesitated at the Battle of Kolin, 1757

In Chapter I was listed the widely accepted 'principles of war'
but by no means all would agree with them. Here is but one
alternative.

King Frederick II of Prussia was born in 1713. His father,
Frederick William, had been a man of huge energy and tiny
manners, who built a considerable army by conscription and
impressment and trained it with brutal discipline. His hobby
was a regiment of giant grenadiers, recruited by kidnapping:

> "No abnormally tall man was safe . . . and any girl who
> in inches matched his grenadiers was seized in order to
> mate with them."[1]

His son's upbringing was strict and in some respects abomin-
able; his father spat in his food to discourage him from over-
eating. Despite his education, he was a broad-minded and cultured
king and as an ally of Britain during the Seven Years' War he
was a great general, audacious and aggressive, was usually outnumbered and won eight out of his ten major battles. He was
a great believer in mobility and, as an 18th century army manoeuvred as a drill, the basic methods had to reflect this. Frederick
enunciated four principles:[2]

1   Discipline: "The men must fear their officers more than the enemy".
2   Subsistence: make sure of your own supplies, attack the enemy's lines of communication.
3   Offensive action: "War is only decided by battles."
4   Practicability and rationalism: from study and experience decide what works well and is really needed.

The list is short, simple and reasonably comprehensive. Frederick was a very practical soldier. Being head of state and commander-in-chief his power was absolute; all decisions were centralised where any conflicts of interest could be immediately resolved. Despite his penchant for the offensive he enjoyed and found useful philosophising about warfare and abstracting general guides from his experience. It is appropriate that a century after his birth, the Prussian general staff was formed as an able and professional institution.

*   *   *   *

References

[1] J F C Fuller, Decisive Battles of the Western World.

[2] D Chandler, The Art of Warfare on Land.

APPENDIX C

HANNIBAL'S ALPINE ROUTE

". . . I don't care much if I never see another mountain in my life."
— Charles Lamb, Letter to Wordsworth

The first traverse of the great Alpine barrier by a complete organised army has never ceased to intrigue people, perhaps because its route *is* uncertain so romancer and detective can be married. It does not matter overmuch for my purpose which was the actual Carthaginian track but for sheer narrative convenience I have baldly assumed it was the Montgenèvre Pass, which connects Briançon in France with Turin in Italy and whose summit is at 6100 feet (1850 meters). *

It is very likely that Hannibal took one of the then well-known routes and to avoid the consul Scipio — a more inland one, though some argue he was misled by his guides into using a little-known and hazardous track. The ancient chroniclers refer to his passing the "Island" and a feature that fits this description, more or less, is the triangle of land bounded by the River Rhône, the River Isère and the mountains. The main passes thus indicated are the Little St Bernard, the Mont Cenis, the Montgenèvre and the Col de Larche but many lesser ones have also been advocated by investigators. Some scholarly detectives have argued for the Great St Bernard which — connecting Martigny with Aosta — looks to the amateur too circuitous. However, most potent was the report that elephant bones had recently been found on it. I visited the monastery that reclines on its summit and asked a

*See Peter Connolly's "Greece and Rome at War" (Macdonald Publishing Company) for a detailed argument for this choice.

good monk if such important relics had been found, receiving the bland reply : "No, no elephant bones have been found on this pass because no elephants have passed this way"!

What really matters is that Hannibal found a pass without much difficulty but it was then narrow, bleak, menaced by un-friendly tribesmen, a snowy wasteland. Except for the dangerous natives, the Montgenèvre still is.

*   *   *   *

APPENDIX D

SELECTION OF LEADERS

*"Mediocrity knows nothing higher than itself,
but talent instantly recognises genius."*

— Sir Arthur Conan Doyle

No doubt many of us selectors are mediocre!

In Chapter II the influence of individuals on events was obvious. Romans found themselves in, or forced their way into, powerful positions by varied means: party politics, family influence, popular acclaim, experience, performance record, visibility and/or chance, combined to select what one might predict from such a process — a majority of passably satisfactory generals and a few much better or worse. Judging from the successful Roman expansion, the combination of a very sound military organisation and system and generals of mostly quite modest competence is a fine example of the maxim that one should not organise so as to depend on a supply of geniuses.

A period of Barcid predominance gave Carthage a collection of rather talented generals. Both it and Rome delegated (by business standards) much authority; given the then state of communications they had little choice, though the Roman Senate controlled initiatives where it could — sometimes aided involuntarily by the dual consular command system. No doubt without meaning to, the freedom and opportunity offered by Rome to the young Scipio Africanus in his detached Spanish (and first) command made for a fine bit of 'management development', as it did to the Duke of Wellington 2000 years later *(see Chapter V)*. In each case family power to some extent covered their backs and encouraged them to take risks — and neither would have been selected at all without such nepotism.

There is, of course, the extreme opposite: selection by seemingly independent choice and judgement and without any external pressure. Here, according to that most entertaining novelist, C S Forester, is a naval example. Admiral William Cornwallis, C-in-C of Britain's Channel Fleet *(see Chapter IV)* is talking to the well-known but then rather junior character, Horatio Hornblower:

> " 'Don't you remember what is the last privilege granted a retiring Commander-in-Chief?'
> 'No, sir.'
> 'I'm allowed three promotions. Midshipman to Lieutenant. Lieutenant to Commander. Commander to Captain.'
> 'Yes, sir.'
> 'It's a good system,' went on Cornwallis. 'At the end of his career a Commander-in-Chief can make those promotions without fear or favour. He has nothing more to expect in this world, and so he can lay up store for the next, by making his selections solely for the good of the service.' "[1]

Whatever the selection method, its success is measured by, not present, but future performance. The process is by definition the mitigation of uncertainty — by extrapolating from apparent present to predicted future effectiveness — and history demonstrates its frequent fallibility:

"Good generals come in all shapes and sizes. Some reach high rank as the result of long training, and carefully thought out selection procedures. Others are wafted upward by the changes and chances of the period in which they live . . . What qualities would you look for if it fell to your lot to sit on a selection board charged with the promotion of general officers? Had you been one of Barras'* colleagues would you have sent the young Bonaparte to Italy in 1796? Had Abraham Lincoln sought your advice would you have spoken up for Meade, or Reynolds, or who? Would you have advised Winston S Churchill to send Montgomery to try conclusions with Rommel? Even with hindsight it is hard to say whether good decisions were made in these three cases."[2]

Leaders can be and are 'de-selected' as well as chosen. That

---

* *The most powerful member of the oligarchy then ruling revolutionary France.*

this implies a faulty selection process does not appear to affect the rigour of the usual procedure. It appears to be a coarse one in the West: you are in or out — though modesty about selection accuracy and extended tolerance about unsatisfactory performance might suggest a corporate responsibility to try to anticipate problems or, at worst, to consider also downward moves as in Japan. Even so, industry still lags. In World War II 1095 German generals died or 'disappeared', of which 110 were suicides.[3]

Given the difficulties of choosing well, all possible aids must needs be adduced. Judging how well someone has actually done in varied situations is obviously a principal guide, but only if jobs are organised to distinguish between individual and team results, between control and luck, between self-determination and external forces. Like the philosophers, we are concerned to detect any divergence between appearance and reality. The examples in this book show the ideal may not be the practical, that the view of a person's characteristics from below may totally differ from that from above.

One counter to this is to consult the team: to each member you (privately) say, "You are of course one candidate; omitting yourself for the time being, who would you think the best choice?" Much can be learned from this simple procedure. In one instance the least obvious candidate was chosen — time showed correctly.

Of course, if you ever become depressed with your selection record (however unlikely that may be) you can recall Max Beerbohm's comforter: "Only mediocrity can be trusted to be always at its best".

* * * *

References

[1] C S Forester, Hornblower and the Hotspur.

[2] Brigadier Peter Young, The Victors.

[3] Colonel Albert Seaton, The German Army 1933—45.

APPENDIX E

THE STRATEGY OF BRITAIN'S NAVAL BLOCKADE

*"The principles of war ... can be condensed into a single word —
'concentration' ... the concentration of strength against weakness
depends on the disperson of your opponent's strength, which in
turn is produced by a distribution of your own that gives the
appearance, and partial effect of dispersion ... True concentration
is the fruit of calculated dispersion."*

Sir Basil Liddell Hart [1]

In Chapter IV, the blockading of French and Spanish ports seemed
to occupy much of the British navy's time: say it was 95% dispersed on blockade duty and 5% concentrated for decisive battle.
Intricate thinking directed the oscillations between these two
states, which constituted the mainspring for the Trafalgar campaign's manoeuvres.

The Navy's continuing objective then was command of the
sea. Its specific aims were to preserve Britain from invasion, to
protect its vast sea-borne commerce and to support continental
landing operations. These objects could be mutually exclusive
but the first had priority because invasion could be instantly
lethal. Thus the Navy's role was focussed to the country's needs
by having well thought through objectives. (It will be noted that
defeat of the enemy fleet was not an objective, not being an end
in itself. It might, however, be a means to that end in certain
circumstances.)

To carry out this role the Navy could be either in a concentrated mass (off the Isle of Ushant), so that no enemy fleet to
convoy Napoleon's invasion barges could enter the Channel
without a severe battle, or it could be in a series of linked fleets
girdling the enemy's coasts on blockade duty. The first stance
would be a purely defensive one: it would leave British commerce

284

vulnerable and British army sallies against the continent infeasible. Being self-confident, the strategy chosen by the Admiralty was the offensive one, to seek decisive battles against a (concentrated) enemy fleet and to push through army convoys, all without sacrificing the priority attached to protecting the British Isles because the fleets' moves could be rearranged into a defensive concentration at the Channel entrance at will and according to prior rules.

At the outbreak of war in 1793 the British had 113 ships of the line to the French 76. Therefore, any British dispersal could incur a local inferiority in numbers if the enemy were skilfully opportunist. That he was not wholly supine is shown by his capture of perhaps around 11,000 merchant ships between then and 1815. The degree of British dispersal and the decision rules governing its termination in favour of a defensive concentration were thus of critical importance to the country's survival and priceless guides to the (lonely) admirals on detachment duty.

The enemy initially preferred dispersal, to facilitate sporadic action against merchantmen. The Navy, therefore, could only retain an offensive stance by a corresponding dispersal. No blockade would be perfect; if it were broken, or the would-be blockading squadron driven off station, it was to fall back on Ushant, to reinforce the Western Squadron normally positioned there, and to defeat any concentration of the enemy. This would not only protect Britain but also instantly secure the overall objective — maritime supremacy. If this decisive action failed to materialise, the offensive was to be resumed as soon as was feasible, thus restoring convoy protection and the free movement of commerce. It was hoped the prior British dispersal would tempt the enemy to concentrate for his own decisive action — invasion; then the Navy's movements and its tactical superiority could be brought to bear.

This strategy — a very demanding but wholly effective one — explains certain decisions. The British ship deployment had to conform to the initial French dispersal. It did indeed entice Napoleon to concentrate for a decision, though in practice for his naval destruction. After he had broken the blockade, the British fleets fell back on Ushant: that August day saw 36 battleships massed and ready there. Cornwallis held this concentration for less than 24 hours, before dividing this fleet in order to resume the offensive mode. Nor was he putting himself at great risk: his individual 'divisions' were in as close touch with each other as Napoleon's. When Nelson sailed off to the West Indies — after providing some protection for the army convoy — it was to protect the rich sugar islands, not primarily to destroy Villeneuve's fleet. [2] When the French concentrated, he concentrated. Eventually Napoleon found his squadrons neither concentrated for a favourable decision nor dispersed conveniently for sporadic action against convoys and commerce.

The whole scheme appears an admirable example of the view that "the essence of a manager's task is to think"[3] : the Admiralty designed a clear strategy, appropriate to a complex situation, and executed it by steeping the practitioners in its principles.

*   *   *   *

References

[1] Sir Basil Liddell Hart, The Strategy of Indirect Approach.

[2] Sir Julian Corbett, Some Principles of Maritime Strategy.

[3] Robert Heller, The Business of Winning.

APPENDIX F

IN SEARCH OF INNOVATION

"Whenever anything is being accomplished, it is being done, I have learned, by a monomaniac with a mission."

— Peter F Drucker [1]

Chapter IX mentioned some techniques for countering the numerous inhibitors of invention and improvement. Peters and Waterman, in their rightly acclaimed book "In Search of Excellence", mention others and, furthermore, comment on the total setting for innovation: what sort of company can best stimulate it? Here are some of the ideas they stress and also some generated by reading their book.

3M has already been mentioned. As well as having alternative sponsors for inventions, it organises their investigation and nourishment in venture teams whose members are full-time, volunteers and semi-permanent; if they fail, they can return to the level of job they left. A 3M product champion has the chance "... to manage that product as though it were his or her own business ... " [1] With a new idea the onus is on disproving its goodness, not on its defence. In Bell & Howell an invention may not be dismissed as rubbish; instead, the onus is on asking, 'Why might it work?' Then, very usefully, 'How can it be tested cheaply?'

Peters and Waterman primarily discuss here product ideas. But their methods can be extended. If a doughty champion for a product is critical, why not also for people? Future talent must needs first be identified, sponsored and encouraged. A conventional organisation may be as resistant to new people as to any other form of novelty. Japanese companies have guides or mentors for the young. These, like managers, have an educative role; the expert teacher's ability to interest, enthuse and clarify is similarly potent for a manager.

Peters and Waterman laud smallness. But there are customarily incentives to build empires, visibly influencing equally the clerk, the junior manager, the staff adviser, the chief executive. This should be modified. The person who can work himself out of a job is, in my experience, a useful citizen. Organisational contraction deserves reward; why not special praise, extra authority, even a payment or credit for resources released? This for lower ranks; the chief executive may need additional curbs or goads to contain or guide his will to power.

We look at companies and their people from the top down, not from front to back. It is the rifleman who kills the enemy, not the general. It is the company's production and sales people who directly meet the customers' needs; it is fruitful to think of the rest of us as supportive. Nevertheless, for innovation there is a general responsibility: as Peter Ustinov says, "Revolutions have never succeeded unless the establishment does three-quarters of the work."[2]

*   *   *   *

References

[1] Quoted by Thomas J Peters and Robert H Waterman Jr, In Search of Excellence.

[2] Quoted by J M and M J Cohen, The Penguin Dictionary of Modern Quotations.

APPENDIX G

A CIVILIAN VIEW OF THE MILITARY GENERAL STAFF SYSTEM

"The military invention that will last longest in business is the distinction between line and staff."

— Robert Heller

Chapter X sketched the birth of the General Staff concept. What is a civilian to make of it?

The system embraces two practical schemes. One is having a 'chief of staff' to help handle a commander's work, to prevent an overload *(see Chapter XI)*. The other is concerned with breeding sound doctrine and practice and passing it on to each generation. An army makes its General Staff a repository of theory, and attempts to keep it uncorrupted yet modern. The Prussian example *(in Chapter X)* was copied in the fullness of time by all the armies in Europe and America. Britain's navy was a late-comer:

> "Authoritative doctrines of war emerge from a consensus of professional opinion. Such a consensus is embodied in a General Staff, and there was no naval General Staff until 1912 ... the Navy consisted of a collection of admirals and ships. The corporate central brain was lacking."[1]

It appears still to be lacking in the worlds of government and business.

Of course the system is not infallible. All the armies that lost their wars since adopting the Prussian scheme make the point!

It did not preserve the French army from defeat in 1940 and had actually contributed to its enormous casualties in 1914—15 (2 million) when the all-out attack, backed by the superb national *élan*, was the gospel too widely preached. The supreme problem of revitalising a management, whose doctrine or people or practice is obsolete, has not been solved by the military. Perhaps nature's model for rejuvenation is the only reliable one: divide activities or functions among many performers and have a constant supply of potential replacements — a fresh crop — breeding profusely and thrusting up to push the established ones aside when they have become the weaker. Free enterprise business copies this — few of the top twenty companies listed twenty years ago would now appear -- to maintain, more or less, the vigour of a country's industry. Informal 'company politics' rather than official 'succession planning' works to the same effect within any one company.

Given a staff that is practised and professional — even if sometimes regrettably out of date — it is natural for its head to assist the line commander to handle his administration, to detail his plans, to act for him (within a defined remit) in his absence, in fact to place a smoothly running machine at his disposal. The method, at least for the military, seems to have incalculable benefit. Despite the size and complexities of modern war machines the general has the time for two uniquely command activities: designing strategy and looking after his army's morale. Each has to be done by the commander in person and each demands time. As a character Field Marshal Montgomery may well have deserved Churchill's quip, "In defeat unbeatable, in victory unbearable", but as a professional soldier his thorough-going use of the system in North Africa (as seen in *Chapter XI)* is a practical illustration of its value.

In the German Army units of corps size and up had a Chief of Staff and on major matters the corps commander *had* to consider his recommendations before making his decisions; in fact, the Chief of Staff had both the right and the duty to give his opinion. It was only after 1938 and then by Hitler's influence that ". . . the Chief of Staff could no longer record his dissenting opinion and forward it to the next superior headquarters."[2] To a political philosopher a system of checks and balances is commonplace; business on the other hand tends to isolate the individual's discretion and hence to have control biased towards a 'feed-back' basis. The German organisation was nothing if not thorough-going: its staff officers were prepared to think ahead and accept responsibility, which ". . . was one of the reasons for German tactical flexibility in the early days of the war."[2] This combination of timely control with a stimulus to exercise initiative is noteworthy.

Both the General Staff system and the role of a Chief of Staff as the supportive administrator reflect an organisation's general attitude and this is not to be altered easily if it is to use these instruments. Churchill argues this, from the same Royal Navy experience. Writing of his becoming First Lord of the Admiralty in 1911, when the war clouds were already climbing the sky, he says:

> "I never ceased to labour at the formation of a true General Staff for the Navy . . . The dead weight of professional opinion was adverse. They had got on well enough without it before. They did not want a special class of officer professing to be more brainy than the rest. Seatime should be the main qualification, and next to that technical aptitudes . . . I found that there was no moment in the career and training of a naval officer, when he was obliged to read a single book about naval war, or pass even the most rudimentary examination in naval history. The Royal Navy had made no important contribution to Naval literature. The standard work on Sea Power was written by an American Admiral*. The best accounts of British sea fighting and naval strategy were compiled by an English civilian.** 'The Silent Service' was not mute because it was absorbed in thought and study, but because it was weighted down by its daily routine and its ever-complicating and diversifying technique. We had competent administrators, brilliant experts of every description . . . but at the outset of the conflict we had more captains of ships than captains of war."[3]

One can think of contemporary institutions of which much the same can be said.

Any civilian application of the concept must take account of the level of managerial homogeneity. There is a measure of common ground helpful to most managers which is covered by business schools, the Administrative Staff College at Henley, and

---

* *Actually a captain, A T Mahan (quoted in Chapter IV.)*
** *Sir Julian Corbett (also quoted in Chapter IV.)*

university and polytechnic management departments. Within one industry or company further detailed application is sometimes taught. A company may or may not consciously educate its recruits in its doctrine, methods, attitudes and values. Those that do not seem to be ignoring military and civilian experience. Perhaps they should listen to Franklin D Roosevelt: "A man who has never gone to school may steal from a freight car, but if he has a university eduction he may steal the whole railroad."

*   *   *   *

References

[1] John Terraine, The Western Front 1914—18.

[2] Colonel Albert Seaton, The German Army 1933—45.

[3] Sir Winston Churchill, The World Crisis.

APPENDIX H

THE CHIEF OF STAFF CONCEPT AND
THE SPAN OF CONTROL

*"I have always believed it is important to maintain the
distinction between policy and administration."*

— Alfred P Sloan Jr

*"I was not going to play every position myself, administer to the
wounded, and bring on the lemon at half time, but would be a
deep-lying centre half, concentrating on defence, distributing the
ball and moving upfield only for set-piece occasions."*

— Sir Harold Wilson

In Chapter XI we saw a soldier's thorough application of the
chief of staff idea. A civilian adaptation looks feasible and beneficial. Many managers pitchforked into command of the 8th Army
in 1942 would first have spent time in 'Head Office' being
briefed, then with their predecessor for a proper handover, before
organising an office and a personal staff, going on to meet the
management team, reading reports, writing plans, attending
meetings. Freedom to spend half of every day touring the factory,
meeting and assessing all senior staff, examining marketing opportunities and customers, looking in on canteens, addressing mass
meetings of workers, while selecting a strategy and approving
a complete plan of action and executing it, all within twelve
weeks, would have looked miraculous. That was how the Army
Commander, not a uniquely placed one, spent his time. The
army organisation and its staff system and Montgomery's wholesale use of it was the mechanism.

Though business needs a similar device it has not to my knowledge worked on it. Look at the size of staff departments. There
is feast or famine: they appear luxuries or unavoidable nuisances,
except for Accounting and 'PR' Departments which expand as
sales drop. (My theory to explain the PR fashion is that when we
are doing well we want to trumpet our superiority and when we

293

are not we want a front man to justify the sacking of employees previously described as invaluable members of the team.) The services do not change their organisation when moving from attack to defence; why do industrial companies?

The chief of staff role was developed over many years by far-seeing commanders. It typically runs all staff functions. Lacking the business world's defensive attitude (admittedly less prevalent in America than in Britain), top staff officers manage effectively planning, intelligence, administration, logistics, movement and personnel functions. The chief of staff runs this HQ team and ensures that the Army Commander has the vital services put at his disposal as a smoothly running machine, so that he can concentrate on the battle. (It can be noted in passing that the military never vest authority in a committee unless politics intervene: e.g. a "Joint Chiefs of Staff Committee" at the inter-service or at the national level.) While Montgomery was blessed in his choice of de Guingand, who brilliantly combined competence, industry and a happy harmony with his colleagues, the chief of staff role still looks very useful without such a paragon occupying it. We have sketched its scope but de Guingand stresses two guides: the chief of staff ". . . ensures that the Armies recognise that the Army Group HQ exists to serve them . . . There must be complete mutual confidence and trust between the Commander-in-Chief and his Chief of Staff . . . no subject should be banned . . . Unpleasant facts must never be hidden from the Chief, although there are the right and wrong times to present them . . ."[1] Sound advice.

Incidentally, de Guingand deplores excessive (and tempting) reliance on successful commanders. Here are individuals, we say, of proved competence: fairness to them and to the business shouts for their selection. But this can overload these few — whoever rejected a job by saying 'I'm tired'? — and retard developing others. Though obvious, the mistake is easily made. I know of two large companies, both with tiny top executive groups — three or four key people. Their overload is patently clear, with a personal wear and tear while their companies miss opportunities. I suspect we fail to assess work-loads when allocating responsibilities: the person can delegate more, can't he? We forget we expect him to know as much detail as before. And he doesn't argue; whoever asked for his responsibilities to be reduced?

De Guingand points out that a command is more than an

individual; when moving him some key men can go too; a competent team is not to be lightly broken up. (De Guingand stayed with Montgomery through moves to four theatres of war.) In industry senior people may take their secretaries with them; lacking the military staff system they cannot take a management support team too. Given a chief of staff, they could be as well equipped as Montgomery.

What of the business counterpart? While not a panacea for all workload problems, one can think of effective applications. I knew a small company whose managing director worked excessive hours without producing results; he was good at the commercial and marketing aspects but a poor delegator and an indifferent staff manager. A Chief of Staff would have placed a smoothly running office at his disposal, with which to execute his (admirable) marketing plan.

In practice the role is to be varied to suit the company and the people concerned. The least venturesome staff organisation looks like this:

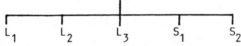

There are three line subordinates and two staff ones. The latter can manage administrative and staff functions for the Manager and help, support and advise their line colleagues. It is not clear from the diagram whether they can speak for the Manager. They could do so, especially if they worked for a Chief of Staff as the Manager's right-hand man (but not his deputy). This could be presented to indicate some authority:

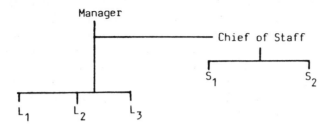

The military system *could* be copied completely. For a senior manager to concentrate on the critical areas of his business and on the work he alone can do, he has to be freed from distractions while being sure that other work is done as well as if he had managed it himself. Unlike a deputy, a chief of staff can do just that.

There should be, of course, some limit to the numbers of $L_1, L_2, L_3 \ldots$ But what? Here is a British air force view:

> "With three squadrons on the station the CO had as many as eleven officers under his immediate control . . . Senior RAF officers handle such concerns efficiently, thus denying the oft-repeated statements of leading business men that the span of control for one man should be a maximum of six. The captain of a large battleship has the same wide span of control and can fight his ship just as well. Either the theory of the limited span of control . . . is false, or the business men who make such statements would do well to learn from the Navy and the RAF."[2]

I think the different view-points given here are reconciled by the fact that five of the eleven subordinates were either the administrative responsibility of or received their technical guidance from the staff officers of the next senior HQ. Nevertheless, a point has been made. The benefits of some limit, however high, are very attractive.

> "The growth of the Ministry of Munitions had far outstripped its organisation . . . All the main and numberless minor decisions still centred upon the Minister himself . . . I found a staff of 12,000 officials organised in no less than fifty principal departments each claiming direct access to the Chief, and requiring a swift flow of decisions upon most intricate and inter-related problems. I set to work at once to divide and distribute this dangerous concentration of power. Under a new system the fifty departments of the Ministry were grouped into ten large units each in charge of a head who was directly responsible to the Minister . . . The relief was instantaneous. I was no longer oppressed by heaps of bulky files . . . Instead of struggling through the jungle on foot I rode comfortably on an elephant whose trunk could pick up a pin or uproot a tree with equal ease, and from whose back a wide scene lay open."[3]

Every manager needs access to a zoo.

       *   *   *   *

References

[1] Major-General Sir Francis de Guingand, Operation Victory.

[2] Dr T T Paterson, Morale in War and Work.

[3] Sir Winston Churchill, The World Crisis.

APPENDIX I

STRATEGIC BOMBING: COSTS AND PROFITS

"I had not thought death had undone so many."
                                    — T S Eliot

RAF Bomber Command aircraft losses were mentioned in Chapter XII. Over the whole war they amounted to 2.7 aircraft lost per 100 sorties despatched.[1] Total Command strength peaked at about 1600 bombers, mostly four-engined heavies. Production to build up this striking force and replace losses (10,122 aircraft) was a major economic operation. The British Army Minister noted in 1944:

> "We have reached the extraordinary situation in which the labour devoted to the production of heavy bombers alone is believed to be equal to that allotted to the production of the whole equipment of the army."

The peak strength of the US Army Air Force in Europe was 5600 bombers (8th and 15th Air Forces). Losses were 8314 aircraft, or 1.7 per 100 sorties[2]. (When comparing this loss with the RAF's, it needs to be remembered that RAF missions were typically longer and with a heavier bomb load; US aircraft often returned to base safely but with dead crew members on board.) 6378 crews[2] were lost, at ten men per crew a total of 63,780 — a heavier loss than Bomber Command's.

Bomber Command's morale is the more striking when it is

noted that to some its methods were imperfect.

The bombers' high losses were stomached by its higher command without great qualms — not that it had much choice. The penalties for opting out were severe: such airmen were labelled LMF — lack of moral fibre, modern equivalent of the white feather. Cases were astonishingly few but the discipline was not always selective:

> "There was one case of a bomb-aimer ... who ... fell through the forward hatch of his aircraft. It was only after several minutes that the crew realised he was still desperately hanging on underneath. They finally got a rope round him and dragged him in. When he got on the ground he flatly refused to fly again. The poor man was pronounced LMF"[4]

Aggression was deemed all, with less thought given to bomber defence than to enlarging attacks. Belly turrets to protect the vulnerable undersides were rare. It was not the British but the Americans who developed the long-range fighter, thus revolutionising their bombers' protection.

German production during the campaign was as follows:

	1940	1941	1942	1943	1944
AIRCRAFT	10,200	11,000	14,200	25,200	39,600
ARMOURED VEHICLES	2,100	5,100	9,400	19,900	28,900

Of course these outputs are the resultants of the bombing on the one hand and increased mobilisation and efficiency on the other. It should be noted that 83% of the Allied bomb tonnage was dropped after 1 January 1944. The table excludes the vital areas of transport capacity and oil production; in May 1944 the latter was running at the annual rate of 7.94 million tons and in March 1945 at 0.96 million. This calls into question navigation or target selection.

German aircraft losses are difficult to compute with any accuracy. It is said[3] that 593,000 civilians and 3.37 million dwellings were destroyed in Germany. The injured numbered around 800,000[2].

The moral issues and the questions on the optimum allocation of scarce Allied resources raised by the strategic bombing offensive cannot be dealt with here. It may be noted, however, that the the other side of Harris's robust leadership was to make these matters considerably more difficult to settle at the time than would have been the case with a less single-minded character. His pressing for massive weaponry and for its use solely in the way he wanted, caused a sound strategy to be hard to formulate and almost (at times) as hard to implement. This may usually be the inescapable price of effective leadership. After all, a principle reason for a leader's 'selection' by the led is his perceived ability to obtain for them *at the least* a fair proportion of the corporate resources.

*   *   *   *

References

[1] Max Hastings, Bomber Command.

[2] Roger Freeman, The US Strategic Bomber.

[3] German Federal Statistical Office, quoted by Max Hastings, Ibid.

[4] Flight Lieut. W Thompson, Lancaster to Berlin.

APPENDIX J

A DO-IT-YOURSELF LEADERSHIP KIT ?

"The little affair of operational command is something that anybody can do."

— Adolf Hitler

In Chapter XII two leadership styles were contrasted and the Adair analysis was very briefly mentioned. It is worth taking it a little further.

Ian Debenham, whom we have already met as a flight commander doing a tour of operations in Harris's regime and is now a management consultant and trainer, has his personal approach. Based on his own experience and on his study of a highly successful RAF commander, Sir Basil Embry*, Debenham has distilled the following conditions that make for high morale in a unit:

"1. **An aim or purpose.** This aim needs to be clearly understood and accepted by all. It needs to be seen as desirable for members (and probably of value to society). There needs to be a reasonable chance of the unit's attaining this aim. A leader understands this aim, interprets it and shows the way to it; intelligently overcoming or showing how to overcome any set-back or blockage; he makes use of the ideas of people involved.

2. **Suitable means/equipment** to achieve this aim. If this is not available, the leader must show the way to getting it or get it. Personal check at the operating level by the leader reinforces the message.

---

*See "Mission Completed" by Air Chief Marshal Sir Basil Embry, CCB, KBE, DSO (3 bars), DFC, AFC.

3. **Training** in the use of the means/equipment to the highest pitch of proficiency. Planning this by the leader after understanding the problems involved reinforces the effect.

4. **Adequate movement** (success) towards or adequate achievement of the group aim. This achievement needs to be observable by the group and recognition by the leader is important. It will have a 'cost' — casualties in war, effort, danger, discomfort, in peace. The leader must know what it is and, if high, be able to convince the group that the effect and risk are worthwhile. (Here the group may have to accept his judgement purely on their acceptance of him as a leader.)

5. **'Fair reward'** to all members of the group for their part in the activity. Members need to feel one of the group (by participation) aided by recognition by the leader. Risks also must be fairly apportioned in relation to the reward. This fairness needs to be felt by members of the group — the concept of equity.

6. **Opportunity for 'creative' action** by group members. Members need to feel that they belong and are contributing usefully towards the group's achievement and its aim."[1]

Harris scores top marks under all criteria, Alexander similarly except for providing his army with a generally accepted common purpose. One doubts if members of the phalanx were consulted about overthrowing King Darius. However, they could no doubt see that personal objectives — loot, land, a living wage — could be forthcoming, so peoples' aims must be complementary, they need not be indentical.

Other leaders we have looked at mostly score highly but with qualifications. The ones with a personal magnetism or with inspirational power — like Lee and Hitler — could make the level of "acceptable cost" very high : individual sacrifice and hardship was the lot of their troops. Others — like Patton and Montgomery — could by some mental electricity create an eager atmosphere incredibly quickly, well before the other factors like having enough equipment could come into play. Hitler, anyway in his later career, would have scored poorly. The German army in 1944 — 5 lacked equipment, fuel, numbers and training; the measure of its achievement was negative — a defensive role marked by (gallant) defeats; the cost in terms of casualties, discomfort, a poisoned atmosphere, family worries and enemy threats, was hideous. Nevertheless, as we saw in Chapter VII, fighting power was maintained to an extraordinary degree, almost to the last bitter second.

More specifically, Debenham's last two criteria overlap. People want to sense fairness, and also personal satisfaction through participation in the group and helping it. These are basic human needs. It seems we need recast Debenham only slightly to accommodate these comments. Thus: A unit expects its manager in his leadership role — which is a precise part of his job — to provide or obtain for it —

(1) **A sense of purpose,** from either a worthy corporate mission or from feeling this furthers individual aims.

(2) **The means to achieve it,** through obtaining at least its fair share of accessible resources, plus the skills to use it.

(3) **A continuing feeling of achievement,** by measured progress towards the goal.

(4) **Individual care,** a broad concern for individual welfare, set as high as the corporate weal allows.

(5) **Individual reward,** fairly apportioned, relative to contribution and personal 'cost'.

(6) **A feeling of self-determination,** by participating in the unit's decisions where these are of personal interest.

(7) **A sense of belonging,** from encouraging teamwork.

(8) **Personal inspiration,** to evoke abnormal effort and capacity.

The feelings of fair reward, belonging, self-determination and of individual contribution may not all be equally fulfilled; it is their totality that must exceed the "costs" by some acceptable measure.

What Debenham's approach has done, when looking at our examples, is to show that high scores under all headings while desirable, are not essential. Most of us, though confined to quite prosaic ways, should be able to do tolerably well. Let us check all this against a rather simple civilian case.[2]

The Lincoln Electric Company was established in the US in 1896 and within four decades was "the largest lowest-cost producer of electric welding equipment" anywhere. Sales per employee in 1942 were 3.5 times those for an average large US electrical company, despite its prices being lower. Wages, including a large bonus element, varied between 1.5 and three times the average! Absenteeism was 1.5 — 2.0% compared with 5.4% in twenty-five comparable plants. While average wages increased from $1600 per year in 1932 to 5400 in 1942, the dividend paid per share went from $20 to $63. Productivity, measured by sales per employee, increased five times in the same decade.

These results stemmed from a tough straightforward sincere management. When John F Lincoln became president, he set out an explicit philosophy: aim always for cheaper and better products to give increasing reward to workers and shareholders. There was no union. He relied, he said, on employees' "selfishness" (more accurately, enlightened self-interest) to motivate them to work fast and increasingly productively. The bonus system was not amended or 'cooked' to curtail unforeseen or massive bonus inflation. If a worker invented a new method or tool, he could either increase his bonus or 'sell' the idea to the Suggestion Board, to obtain public credit and a share of the saving. Inspection was deemed part of the production process and quality naturally emanated from "self-policing". Like the suggestion scheme, a joint consultation system was formalised (in 1914!): an Advisory Board of elected employees met fortnightly with the President, each being paid $100 per year for his services. It could and did by-pass normal channels and its communication lines were freely used; it speeded consultation, influenced non-members and disclosed emerging managerial talent. The emphasis throughout the plant was on personal development and teamwork.

Management, Lincoln believed, had to be acceptable — "fair, able and intelligent". Employee selection was very careful (and no doubt guided to those motivated by money). Foremen were young, a source of managers. They had their own special meetings with the General Plant Superintendent and had to be well-informed on the company to be able to inform the workers.

Though ready to consult and to listen, Lincoln was formal and dominant. He had a very plain office. Capital projects had to have a pay-back period no greater than five years. The company was expected to rely on new ideas instead of new machines. The aim was customer service. "Profit cannot be the goal. Profit must be a by-product." He was invariably very frank and open; many thought him a hard man and sometimes plain wrong but always honest.

Debenham's elements of leadership are readily perceivable here. In some ways Lincoln had advantages: his company was young, fashioned in his own image, growing fast in its formative years, and above all small in numbers (it was around 1100 strong for much of its life). Nevertheless, he achieved much — but not by exercising a rare talent or a rarer personality. The message is still the same. We too can lead.

And here, for the record, is an example of the antithesis. The speaker is an Army Commander just before the 1918 German offensive in France, addressing informally some of his troops on its importance: "I expect you to hold your positions to the last man and to the last round of ammunition and if you have to die there then I expect you to do that."[3]

There is another angle on this. A fine leader may yet be ill-suited to a particular type of organisation. He may have all the charisma and dash but is that always appropriate? "Night bombing", says Debenham, "was a bloody drag from start to finish". Could Alexander's panache have conducted it any better than Harris's stolid approach? Civil aviation, while hopefully not a bloody drag, similarly demands discipline, meticulous work and steadiness. The business must define the leadership, which makes it still more interesting — and difficult to select.

The criteria for the leadership type should fit the 'critical areas' of the organisation at the operational level (not the top level) — we are defining here the leadership role, not the overall managerial one). A fighter squadron and an advertising agency need someone dashing, a nuclear submarine and a production scheduling department need a calm thinker, the British Army of the Rhine and a health care company need a head with flair and vision. In short, the top must match what is underneath: as Winston Churchill said, "If you are the summit of a volcano the least you can do is smoke".[4]

*   *   *   *

References

[1] A I S Debenham, Letter to the author.

[2] Prof. J D Glover and Prof. R M Hower, The Administrator:
   Cases in Human Relations in Business.

[3] Martin Middlebrook, The Kaiser's Battle.

[4] Sir Winston Churchill, Great Contemporaries.

INDEX

This is a selective index, mostly covering managerial and military entries.